Cook Something

Macmillan • USA

Cook Something

Simple Recipes and Sound Advice to Bring
Good Food into Your Fabulous Lifestyle

by Mitchell Davis

Macmillan · USA

MACMILLAN
A Simon & Schuster Macmillan Company
1633 Broadway
New York, NY 10019-6785

MACMILLAN is a registered trademark of Macmillan, Inc.

Library of Congress Cataloging-in-Publication Data
Davis, Mitchell.
    Cook something : simple recipes and sound advice to bring good food into your fabulous
    lifestyle / by Mitchell Davis.
        p.   cm.
    Includes index.
        ISBN: 0-02-861255-8 (alk. paper)
        1. Cookery.   I. Title.
TX651.D38 1997
641.5--dc21   97-3158
                                                 CIP

Manufactured in the United States of America
10 9 8 7 6 5 4 3 2 1

Book Design: Julia Byrne and Edwin Kuo, Inkspot Design, Inc.

Photographer key—

TK   = Tom Kirkman

TBS   = T. Brittain Stone

EK   = Edwin Kuo

EKim = Edmond Kim

JB   = Julia S. Byrne

AB   = Alix Brown

HC   = Howard Coe

Photography credits
(clockwise from top left corner)—

Page i: TBS, TBS, TK, TBS, TBS; page ii: AB, EK, TK, TK; page vi: TK, TK, TK, TBS, JB, TK, center TK; page viii: AB, EK, EK, EK, TBS, JB; page x: TK, TBS, AB, TBS, EK; page 3: EK, EKim, AB, TK, TK; page 4: TK, TK, TK, TK, TBS; page 8: TK, TK, AB, TK, TK, TK, center TK; page 10: TK, TK, TBS, TK, TK, TK; page 14: EK, AB, TBS, EKim, TK, TK, TK, center TK; page 18: TK, EKim, EK, TBS, TK, TBS; page 22: TK, JB, TBS, EK, TK, TK, EKim, center TK; page 26: TBS, TK, TK, TBS, TBS, TK; page 28: TK, TBS, HC, TBS, TK, TBS, HC; page 30: TK, TK, TK, EK, TBS, EK; page 32: HC, TBS, AB, TBS, HC; page 34: JB, TBS, TK, EK, TK, EK, center TK; page 38: TK, TK, TBS, TBS, JB; page 44: AB, AB, EK, JB, TBS, TK, TK; page 50: EK, TK, TBS, TBS, TBS, HC; page 52: TK, TBS, TK, EK, EKim; page 54: TK, TBS, TBS, TBS, TBS, TBS, TK, TBS; page 66: TBS, TK, TK, TK; page 70: TBS, TBS, HC, HC, HC, TBS, TBS; page 74: all TK; page 80: TBS, TBS, EK, EK, JB, center TK; page 86: TBS, TBS, TBS, TBS, TBS; page 90: TBS, TK, TK, TK, EK, EK; page 102: EK, EK, TK, TK, TK, EK;

page 110: TK, TK, TK, TBS, TK; page 118: EK, TK, TK, EK, AB, EK; page 126: TBS, TBS, TK, EK, TBS, TBS, center left TBS, center right TK; page 130: EKim, TK, TK, HC, TK; page 136: TK, TBS, EK, TBS, TK; page 142: TBS, TBS, TBS, HC, HC; page 146: TK, TK, TK, TK, EKim, EKim; page 156: TK, JB, TK, AB, TK, TK; page 168: TK, TK, TK, TK, TK, EK; page 170: EK, TK, TK, TK, TK, TK, TK; page 174: TBS, HC, AB, TBS, HC, TBS, center TBS; page 184: all TK; page 186: all TK; page 190: TK, AB, TK, AB, TK, EK, center TK; page 192: TBS TBS, HC, TBS, HC, TBS; page 194: TBS ,TK, TBS, HC, HC, center HC; page 198: AB, AB, TK, TK, TK, TK, center top TK, center bottom TK; page 202: EK, TBS, EK, JB, TBS, TBS, center TBS; page 208: JB, TBS, TBS, TBS, TK, TBS; page 210: AB, TK, AB, TK, AB, AB, AB, TK; page 218: EK, EK, TBS, EK, HC, EK, EK, HC, EK, HC, center top TBS, center middle BS, center bottom TK; page 222: JB, TK, TK, TK, TK, EKim, center EKim; page 232: TBS, EK, TBS, TBS; page 238: TK, AB, TK, TK, TK; page 242: all TK.

This book is dedicated to my mother,
who taught me how to love with her food.

Contents

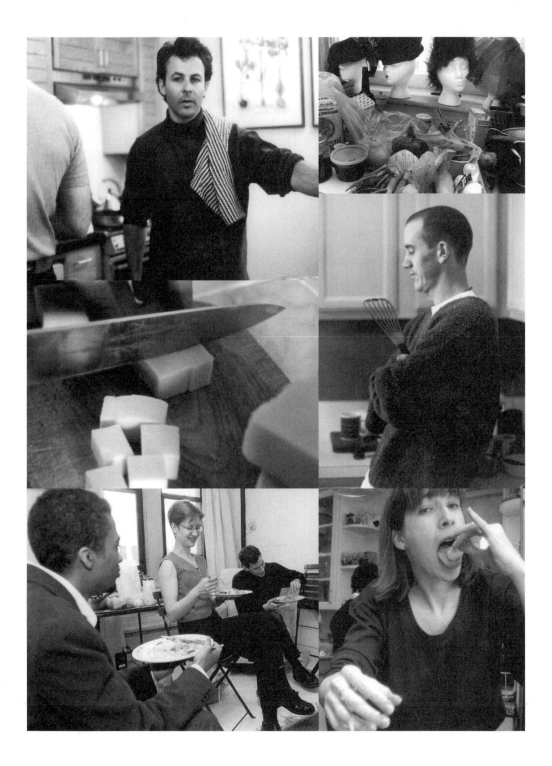

Acknowledgments

Cooking is a social activity. It's about giving and sharing and having fun. There's only so much one person can eat, but there's a whole lot one person can cook.

Myriad people have contributed to this book in myriad ways. Designers took photographs, vegetarians tested roasts. It was total, fabulous mayhem. I've tried to mention everyone at least once, but if I've forgotten anyone, I promise to write many more books so I can thank you in the future.

My friend David Roth put me in touch with John Meils at Macmillan, who wanted to do a cookbook targeted to a young audience. John left and Justin Schwartz took over. Then Justin left and Amy Gordon took over. And Amy brought this baby across the finish line. I'm grateful for her perseverance and her help. It wasn't easy.

Gwen Hyman, Adam Rapoport, Judy Blumenberg, and Izabela Wojcik helped me brainstorm recipe and title ideas for the proposal. Evelynne Patterson, one of my cooking inspirations, graciously let me use her apartment to host a potluck party for 150 guests. They all brought dishes and recipes and had a blast (there are too many to list here, but I thank them all). Many of their recipes are included in the book. Thanks to Monica Grandy who tended bar.

Amy Davis and Jen Gentile helped test recipes on the West Coast, where Jon Moritsugu and Jason Rail helped taste them. Matt Barolo came to the recipe-testing rescue on the East Coast, where tasters included Arlyn Blake, Julia Byrne (who also worked on the design of the book), Andrew Carmellini, Libby Darrow, Paschal Fowlkes, Yvette Fromer, Ed Guttman, Diane Harris Brown, Tom Kirkman (who's also the principal photographer), Edwin Kuo (who worked with Julia on the design), Lauren and Peter McGrath, Shelley Menaged, Yvon Moller, Marion Nestle, Felice Ramella, and Carrie Weiner, not to mention messengers, delivery people, and friends of friends.

Then, just when we thought we were done, we decided to host five more parties to photograph people cooking, eating, and just plain having a good time. Heartfelt thanks to my photo-shoot hosts who let me destroy their apartments: Karla Vermeulen and Michael Frank, Matt Barolo and Erik Mercer, Felicia Stingone, and Yvette Fromer and Phil Hirschkorn. Thanks also go to our team of tireless photographers led by Tom, but with a serious contribution by T. Brittain Stone, and help from Alix Brown, Howard Coe, Ed Kim, Edwin, and Julia.

And then, of course, thanks go to the guinea pigs, I mean models, who rolled up their sleeves, got in the kitchen, and actually cooked something for the pictures. In addition to the people I've already mentioned for having done various things, the models included Cynthia Agustin, Elizabeth Blau, Brian Byrd, Daniel Citron, Bret Cook, Shelley Crier, David and Erica Friedman, Lara Greco, Alison Halper, Jimmy Harris, Liz Kuan, David Maltby, Oded Marcovici, Joe Meisel, Elizabeth Ngonzi, Felice Ramella, Julia Schulhoff, Sabene Selassie, Jane Shufer, Bill Stingone, Mary Anne Sullivan, Lonni Tanner, Amy Tarshis, Naomi Urabe, and Todd Williams.

Of course, none of this would have ever been possible without the support and encouragement of my family: my mother, Sondra Davis, who is still a great cook and who thankfully didn't stop me from sneaking down to the kitchen early in the morning when I was five to bake cookies that I would then hide in the drawers of my captain's bed; my sister Leslie, who has been both therapist and spiritual adviser on the difficult path to cookbook completion; my sister Carrie, who also just finished the manuscript for her first cookbook, and who kept calling to make sure I was working on schedule (which I wasn't); and my brother Sheldon, with whom I have always enjoyed cooking, eating, and talking about food. They will forever inspire me to cook something.

Introduction

You're living the life. You've got a pretty good job that's put you on the fast track to a fashionable career. You're either sharing a cool apartment in a soon-to-be-trendy neighborhood, or you've got a lifetime's worth of junk crammed into a small studio. It doesn't matter, it's your own space and it makes you happy not to have to make the bed when you don't feel like it.

Once in a while on a weeknight—never a weekend—you surf the Web, looking for an interesting chat room or a cool Web site. You limit yourself to one night of television per week. You watch *Friends*, and if you're not meeting anyone for drinks later, you stick around to see *Seinfeld*. You probably drink Dewar's. When you're not eating late-night dinners at trendy new restaurants—places where the noise level is so high you have to shout at the waiter, who is unselfconsciously wearing a black vinyl apron—you eat a lot of take-out Chinese.

I like chow fun and eggplant in garlic sauce as much as the next person, but now that the rest of your life is going so well, isn't it time you learned to cook something?

Anyone can cook. All right, maybe not everyone can make elaborate multicourse meals with exotic ingredients and complicated techniques. But anyone who can read—and if you've made it this far, that includes you—should be able to take a couple of good recipes into the kitchen and come

out with a meal that even the great French chef Escoffier would have been pleased to eat.

I know this firsthand. So many of my friends don't know how to cook because their parents didn't cook or they didn't pay any attention when they did. Or they think it takes too much time or too much fuss or too much money or too much equipment to make anything decent. But over the years I have helped get a lot of my friends into the kitchen. In my opinion, the most important thing for a novice cook, or even an experienced one, for that matter, is a good recipe. Good recipes have enough detail so that the cook doesn't have to wing anything on his or her own, but they are also flexible enough to accommodate substitutions, omissions, and even mistakes.

Once you take a good recipe into the kitchen to cook something, anything, you'll see that cooking isn't that difficult. It may even pique your interest so much that you'll want to attempt more elaborate dishes and techniques. Of course, it's also possible you'll never cook another thing again. But I doubt it.

This book is a collection of more than 200 good recipes and variations. They run the gamut, from soups and stews to desserts and dips. There are Chinese, Eastern European, English, French, Italian, Korean, Japanese, Jewish, Mediterranean, Mexican, Middle Eastern, South American, Spanish, and good ole Yankee recipes. There are

some recipes that take a scant five minutes to prepare, and others that take more than five hours. But all of them are simple, almost foolproof recipes that anyone who can read will be able to use. I know this to be true because I had many of my friends, who claim not to be able to cook, test the recipes for me. Just about everyone I know now makes the Cheese Thing (page 87). My friend Matt couldn't believe he made an apple pie!

How To Use This Book

As you may have already guessed, this is not your typical cookbook. For instance, the recipes are arranged alphabetically. Although this may not help you find recipes like Aunt Josephine's Chocolate Cake, which is located under "A," sometimes I think just the structure of the average cookbook can be intimidating to the would-be cook. Authors seem to be suggesting that there's no point to cooking anything unless you are going to make a handful of hors d'oeuvres, a soup, an appetizer, a main course, a selection of side dishes, and a dessert. That sounds a lot like the elaborate multicourse meal we've already decided you probably won't ever make. I hope that the random organization of the recipes in this book will encourage you to flip through and pick something to cook, whenever you feel the urge.

There's another reason for the randomness. I feel strongly that fewer people eat by category these days.

Soups have become main dishes, side dishes have become vegetarian entreés, pizza slices are eaten cold for breakfast. We're in a time of culinary anarchy. I'd encourage you not to get hung up about when to eat what dish. Experiment with new variations and combinations. Serve smaller portions of entreés for appetizers. Serve two side dishes for dinner. Eat whatever you want for breakfast. It's all just food.

If you know what you want to make, in "The Recipe Guide" section you'll find the recipes broken down into several different categories to help you find your way to the meal of your dreams. For example, categories point to recipes with certain main ingredients (you have some cooked chicken lying around), time constraints (you've only got thirty minutes before you have to meet a friend at the movies), eating preferences (you want something that's low fat and vegetarian), or cravings (you're in the mood for some comfort food).

Say you've had a rough day and all you want to eat is something warm, filling, and gooey. You've got about an hour before you will be ready to eat dinner, and after cross-referencing comfort food with things that take about an hour to prepare in "The Recipe Guide," you've made your way to the Cheese Thing (page 87).

Your culinary exploration has only just begun. Each recipe is packed with information to help you succeed. First there's the headnote, which contains background about the recipe, advice about unfamiliar ingredients, and other useful information. The "Required Reading" list refers you to all of the techniques in "The Basics" section of the book that you should be familiar with in order to make your way through the method.

The ingredients list begins with the recipe yield. I like to eat a lot so you might find the portion-size to be pretty large. That shouldn't be a problem because most of the dishes in this book are also good as leftovers for lunch or dinner the next day. Ingredients are presented in the order in which they will be used, with preparation and possible substitutions clearly indicated.

Under the "Kitchen Stuff" heading, you'll find a list of equipment that will be called for in the method. Although the most basic equipment—knives, a cutting board, a fork, a plate—are not mentioned in every recipe, most everything else is. If you don't have something, don't worry. Make do with what's available to you. Be creative.

At the end of each recipe I've included something I've called "Links." This listing refers you to other recipes in the book that either go with the dish you are making, share some of the same ingredients or techniques, or that I just think you might want to try at another time.

If you choose to approach this cookbook more like a regular book, by reading it from beginning to end, what you'll have is a basic cooking course. In the beginning chapters, "Essentials," "The Basics," and "Do's and Don'ts," you'll find all the culinary background you need to be able to make almost any recipe, whether you are an accomplished cook or you have never made anything more complicated than Pop-Tarts. Read them. Find a recipe that you think sounds good and give it a whirl.

The most important thing to remember is that cooking should be fun. I know this sounds trite, but it's the truth. Unlike in our parents' day, when cooking was often a chore and the idea was to hide all evidence of having done it, cooking has become a popular hobby, a creative pastime. There are gourmet clubs and weekend culinary retreats. A whole industry of food-related travel has evolved.

Overall interest in food has piqued. Mail order makes it easy to get hard-to-find ingredients and equipment, even in the most remote locales. We've got a successful 24-hour Television Food Network, a handful of lush new food magazines, and an ever-increasing range of cookbooks, covering topics as far flung as chips and dip and the classic dishes of the Ligurian coastal towns.

I have a theory that the more people cook, the better food will be all around. Once people see how easy it is to prepare tasty, healthful, and delicious food, they will no longer tolerate the watered-down slop offered by the characterless chains. They will rise up against tasteless take-out and over-processed convenience foods. This is an exciting time. Don't let it pass you by. Don't just sit there, cook something.

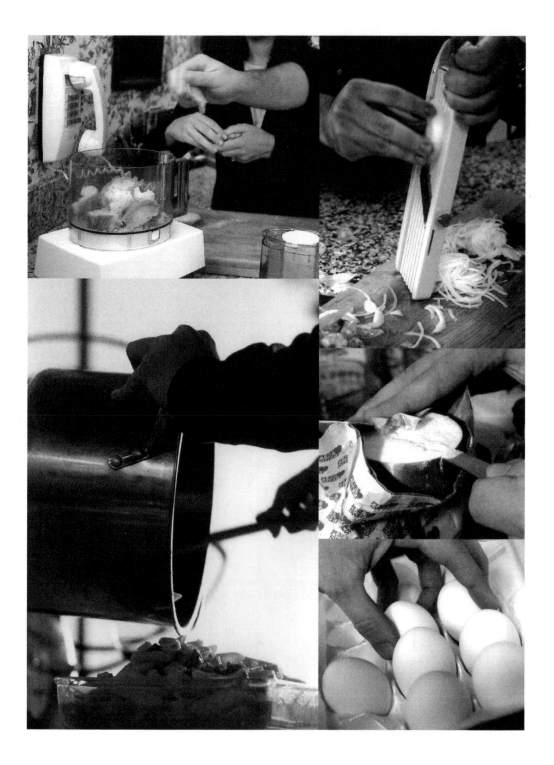

Essentials

What do you need to have on hand to be able to cook? Well, the answer is nothing, really. If you are only going to make one meal in your life, there's no need to stock up on staples. Just buy what you need and chuck whatever's left over when you're done. But if you are going to be cooking the occasional dish, or making your lunch to take to work, or baking cookies sometimes late at night, then there are a few ingredients and pieces of equipment you should always have at your disposal. Although many ingredients do keep for a long time, nothing stays fresh forever. Even spices, baking products, and other ingredients with a long shelf life have to be replaced every couple of years, whether you use them or not. Here's some advice for when you find yourself staring helplessly down a long aisle at the grocery store. You don't have to go crazy buying everything in sight. Think realistically about what you are going to do, and choose the best you can afford.

Ingredients

When talking about ingredients, there are two types of essentials: staples you need to have on hand so that you will be able to prepare the most basic recipes (salt, pepper, flour, sugar, butter, etc.), and luxuries you need in order to whip up something from nothing when you have a sudden craving or when guests just happen to drop in and stay for dinner (Dijon mustard, capers, garlic).

My great-grandmother Eva used to say, "You put in good, you get out good." Here is a list of ingredients that I always have on hand, and that you will need for some of the recipes in this book. When I have specified a certain type of ingredient (unsalted butter, as opposed to salted butter, and unbleached all-purpose flour, as opposed to bleached all-purpose flour), this is the one you should use. Obviously, you don't need to go out and buy all of this stuff tomorrow. But if you want to have a well-stocked kitchen, using this guide as a shopping list will put you on your way.

In the Cupboard

- All-purpose flour (unbleached)
- Anchovies (fillets or paste)
- Baking powder
- Baking soda (in addition to the one you keep in the fridge to absorb odors)
- Black peppercorns (always use freshly ground)
- Bread crumbs (unflavored)
- Brown sugar (I use light and dark interchangeably)
- Cake flour (if you intend to be making a lot of pie crust)
- Canned chickpeas (hummus is one of the fastest things to whip up when you're hungry)
- Canned Italian-style plum tomatoes
- Capers (nonpareils are the smallest and the best)
- Chocolate chips
- Cocoa powder
- Coconut milk
- Confectioner's sugar, aka powdered sugar or 10x sugar (a dusting of powdered sugar hides a multitude of sins)
- Cornmeal (yellow is good for baking and for polenta)
- Dijon mustard (I don't know what I'd do without it)
- Fine-quality semisweet chocolate (good to eat and to bake with)
- Grainy mustard (for an occasional switch from Dijon)
- Granulated white sugar
- Hot sauce (as fiery as you can stand)
- Kosher salt (I use it exclusively because it has a better flavor than table salt)
- Maple syrup (only pure will do)
- Marinated artichoke hearts
- Olive oil (extra-virgin for sauces, salads, and things that aren't going to be cooked; virgin for frying)
- Pine nuts
- Pure vanilla extract (if you have the fake stuff, pour it down the sink right now)
- Rice (Chinese white, healthful brown, and Italian arborio for the occasional risotto)
- Roasted red peppers (a jar goes a long way in pasta and Mediterranean dishes)
- Soy sauce, tamari, or shoyu (I happen

to prefer tamari because it has a lighter flavor, but the three are virtually interchangeable)
- **Spices** (curry powder, cinnamon, nutmeg, ground cumin, caraway seeds, ground coriander, turmeric, chili powder, paprika, you name it; just be sure to throw it out every other year and buy fresh)
- **Tahini**
- **Thai red curry paste** (a little can goes a long way)
- **Toasted sesame oil**
- **Unflavored gelatin**
- **Vegetable oil** (peanut is my preference, but I also use sunflower or safflower)
- **Vinegars** (a selection of balsamic, cider, sherry, red wine, rice wine, and white wine, so that you have one that fits your mood)

In the Refrigerator
- **Active dry yeast** (you never know when the mood to bake bread is going to hit)
- **Apples**
- **Bacon** (and if not, bacon fat)
- **Butter** (unsalted for cooking and baking, salted for eating)
- **Carrots**
- **Celery**
- **Eggs** (I buy only large)
- **Fresh herbs** (rosemary keeps the longest)
- **Imported Parmigiano-Reggiano (Parmesan) cheese** (always in block form to grate fresh; it keeps forever)
- **Italian flat-leaved parsley**
- **Lemons** (don't use bottled juice)
- **Mayonnaise** (only Hellman's)
- **Mesclun** (I hate cleaning lettuce)
- **Miso** (a good vegetarian substitute for stock)

- **Tofu** (I practically live on the stuff)
- **Vegetable shortening** (if I plan on making a lot of pie crust)
- **Watercress** (good to eat and good to garnish with)

In the Freezer
- **Chicken stock** (when I make a chicken soup or I order Chinese food and don't finish the wonton soup, I always freeze whatever's left so that I have some stock on hand for risotto and other things)
- **Coffee beans** (regular and decaf)
- **Häagen-Dazs vanilla ice cream** (for when you just don't feel like making dessert or when you feel like making dessert a little better)
- **Pizza dough** (if I feel industrious, I'll make it and freeze it in individual pizza-size pieces)
- **Smoked salmon** (it freezes well and you don't have to defrost it before you

cut it into pieces for a quiche or scrambled eggs)
- **Sourdough bread** (I like to have a backup loaf in the freezer in case there's an emergency and I can't buy fresh)

On the Counter
- **Eggplant** (my favorite vegetable; buy small, firm specimens; don't refrigerate)
- **Garlic** (you can never have too much; just be sure to throw it away if the cloves begin to grow)
- **Onions** (white and red)
- **Potatoes** (I prefer Yukon Gold or red-skinned potatoes for cooking)
- **Sourdough bread** (my fave)
- **Tomatoes** (when they're in season, tomato sandwiches with mayonnaise on toasted sourdough bread keep me alive)

Equipment

If you're going to start cooking a lot, you'll want to start buying kitchen equipment. That's not to say that you can't cook a good meal with a Swiss Army knife and a camping stove. But why make things hard on yourself?

The following lists contain the kitchen equipment I use most often when I cook. (That leaves out things like the French copper fish poacher I use to store gift wrap, the couscousière I schlepped back from Tunisia to collect dust, and the pizza stone that's too big to fit in my oven.)

I understand this is a wish list for most people, and that you probably won't have half of these things available to you. That shouldn't stop you from cooking. In fact, I tested many of these recipes in kitchens that barely had running water to see how well they would adapt. I mixed batters in pots, used chopsticks to flip chicken fingers, and strained soups through photographic developing equipment. Everything worked. Be inventive. If you don't have a lid for a pot, use a cookie sheet. If you don't have a grater, cut whatever it is you need grated into very small pieces. If money is a problem, I think it is better to acquire top-of-the-line equipment slowly than to run out and buy a lot of junk. The extra money you spend now will pay you back for years to come because good kitchen equipment should never need to be replaced.

Utensils

- **Carrot peeler** (make it a good one; the one with large rubber grip handles will change your life)
- **Chef's knife** (6-inch if you're timid, 8-inch if you're brave, and 10-inch if you like to show off)
- **Colander**
- **Corkscrew**
- **Cutting board** (I prefer wood, but some prefer plastic. I recently read there was no difference in terms of bacteria growth, but whichever you use, be sure to clean your board whenever raw meat or eggs come into contact with it.)
- **Glass jar with a tightly fitting lid** (for making dressings)
- **Grater** (box type with four different sides)
- **Measuring cups** (dry and liquid; if you have to choose one, choose liquid—measuring liquids in dry cups doesn't work.)
- **Measuring spoons**
- **Metal spatula**
- **Mixing bowls** (small, medium, and large, preferably made of stainless steel or heat-proof glass)
- **Paring knife** (3-inch)
- **Pepper mill**
- **Potato masher**
- **Rubber spatula**
- **Serrated knife** (10-inch)
- **Slotted spoon**
- **Strainer**
- **Whisk** (a balloon whisk, big and bulbous with lots of wires, works best)
- **Wooden spoons**

Pots and Pans

- **Baking dish, 2-quart**, glass or ceramic
- **Baking pans** (8 x 8-inch, 9 x 13-inch, 8 1/2-inch loaf pan, two 9-inch round pans)
- **Cookie sheets** (at least one should be like a jelly roll pan, with 1-inch sides)
- **Deep-dish pie plate, 9-inch** (which can double as a baking dish)
- **Roasting pan** (with rack)
- **Saucepan, small with lid** (2-quart; get a couple if you can afford them)
- **Saucepan, medium with lid** (5-quart)
- **Skillet, large** (10-inch)
- **Stock pot or large saucepan** (8-quart)

Staples

- **Aluminum foil**
- **Bamboo skewers** (to test for doneness)
- **Binder clips** (the ones from your office are great for closing bags)
- **Coffee filters** (they can come in handy)
- **Phone book** (just in case whatever you're cooking doesn't work and you have to order in)
- **Plastic wrap**
- **Resealable plastic bags** (in assorted sizes; I use them so much I buy them in bulk)
- **Waxed paper**

Other Useful Equipment

These are things that you will need less often, but that you'll want around if you begin cooking a lot.

- **Cast-iron skillet**
- **Cookie cutters** (you can use a variety of sizes for scones and tartlets and other yummy things)
- **Electric mixer** (as far as I'm concerned, the KitchenAid mixer is one of the marvels of not-so-modern science; attachments include the wire whip, the dough hook, and the paddle, each of which is indispensible)
- **Food processor** (seems like a luxury, but trust me, you'll love it. If you can't afford a big one, the minis are a fraction of the price and great for processing small quantities.)
- **Instant-read thermometer** (to test for doneness, nothing is more accurate)
- **Ladle**
- **Lemon reamer** (makes squeezing easier and more fun)
- **Muffin tin** (and paper muffin cups)
- **9-inch springform pan**
- **Nonstick skillet**
- **Parchment paper** (sometimes referred to as silicon paper, this is like an uncoated wax paper, but more versatile; great for baking cookies, lining cake pans, and making sure your baked goods don't stick)
- **Pastry brush** (you can also use an ordinary paint brush)
- **Rice cooker** (hard to believe there's an appliance dedicated to this, but if you eat a lot of rice or order a lot of take-out Chinese, this is a good thing to have around)
- **Sharpening steel** (to keep your knives in tip-top shape)
- **Slicing knife** (10-inch)
- **Stove-top grill** (cast-iron or nonstick both work well on gas ranges)
- **10-inch tart pan** (with removable bottom)
- **Tongs**
- **Vegetable mill** (for pureeing soups, sauces, etc.)
- **Wire cooling rack** (for cookies and other baked goods)
- **Wok** (with a gas stove, use a round-bottomed wok; with an electric stove, a flat-bottomed one is better)
- **Zester**

Recommended Reading

If the cooking bug gets you, you may want to do some additional reading. Here are a few books and a couple of magazines that I find indispensable when I'm cooking. Most of them are readily available in bookstores or on newsstands. A few of the books you might find on remainder tables or in used bookstores. If you have trouble putting your hands on them, check with New York City's great cookbook store Kitchen Arts and Letters (212/876-5550), or the mail order company Books for Cooks (718/796-1306).

On the Bookshelf

- *Classic Home Desserts* (Chapters) by Richard Sax
  A huge collection of recipes for home-style desserts that are foolproof and delicious.

- *La Varenne Pratique* (Crown) by Anne Willan
  A great general reference book with hundreds of pictures of ingredients, explanations of techniques, and basic recipes.

- *The Food Lover's Companion*, 2nd ed. (Barron's) by Sharon Tyler Herbst
  A dictionary of culinary terms with information about ingredient storage, seasonality, and use.

- *Sauces* (Van Nostrand Reinhold) and *Splendid Soups* (Bantam) by James Peterson
  Two comprehensive tomes on preparing sauces and soups.

- *Lighter, Quicker, Better* (Morrow) by Richard Sax and Marie Simmons
  Great recipes that are fast, light, and tasty.

- *Jacques Pépin's The Art of Cooking*, vols. 1 and 2 (Knopf) by Jacques Pépin
  Although many of the recipes in these picture-filled volumes are very complicated, I find these cookbooks to be among the most inspirational ever published.

- *How to Bake* (HarperCollins) by Nick Malgieri
  Straightforward and to the point.

- *The Complete Cookie* (Doubleday) by Barry Bluestein and Kevin Morrissey
  A great collection of recipes for cookies and related sweets, with a good low-fat section, too.

- *Mastering the Art of French Cooking*, vols. 1 and 2 (Knopf) by Julia Child, Simone Beck, and Luisette Bertholle (vol. 1, only)
  The title says it all. Comprehensive detailed recipes for all the classics.

- *The Surreal Gourmet* and *The Surreal Gourmet Entertains* (Chronicle) by Bob Blumer
  If you like the chatty, free-flowing tone of this book, you'll love the simple recipes in these two volumes.

- *The Good Cook Series* (TimeLife) by various editors and writers
  Though almost twenty years old, this twenty-five-book series is one of the best compendiums of recipes and techniques on an overwhelming number of culinary topics. Look for them in used book stores.

- *The Foods of the World Series* (TimeLife) by various editors and writers
  Even older than *The Good Cook Series*, this international collection of twenty-seven volumes still holds much value for people interested in the history, lore, and recipes of the world's cultures. Look for them in used-book stores.

In the Mailbox

- *Cooking Light*
  A serious food magazine despite the emphasis on low-fat and nutrition. Call 800/336-0125 for a subscription or send e-mail to CookingLight@time-inc.com.

- *Cook's Illustrated*
  A very opinionated magazine filled with step-by-step illustrations, helpful hints, foolproof recipes, tasting notes, equipment trials, wine information, and book reviews. Subscription inquiries should be sent to P.O. Box 59046, Boulder CO 80322-9046.

- *Fine Cooking*
  Like *Cook's Illustrated* but with glossy, color pictures, not line drawings, illustrating every technique and step in the recipes. Call 800/888-8286 for a subscription, or e-mail finecook@taunton.com.

- *Saveur*
  The most inspired food magazine on the newsstand today. Filled with beautiful pictures and personal journeys of culinary discovery, this magazine will whet your appetite. Call 800/462-0209 for subscription information.

The Basics

This section is intended as a reference for you to turn to when you come across a technique you are unsure about in any of the following recipes. Some of the techniques pertain to food in general, others are specific to certain recipes. I've divided them between Selecting Ingredients, Cooking, and Baking, so that you can just skip to the section that interests you. But because many principles apply to anything you do in the kitchen, it wouldn't hurt to read the whole thing through once to get the flavor of my approach. Photographs throughout the book illustrate most of these concepts and techniques.

Selecting Ingredients

Buying Fresh

I've said it before and I'll say it again, "You put in good, you get out good." (Actually it was my great-grandmother Eva who said it first.) When shopping, as when cooking, you have to employ all five of your senses (and a little of the sixth when you're just not sure about something). Always buy the freshest ingredients. One of the senses I rely on most in the grocery store, particularly in the produce section, is smell. I smell every fruit I buy to see if it has a sweet smell or any fragrance at all. I smell fish and meat to check for off odors. I don't let the stares I get from curious children dissuade me.

Your eyes are important, too. Ingredients should be free of any notice-able blemishes, dents, or other bruises. Touch fruits and vegetables and breads and anything you can get your hands on to make sure they feel right. Ripe fruits and vegetables should be firm, not mushy. Sometimes bruised is okay (and a lot cheaper). If you are making Banana Bread (page 63), you ought to

have spotty, overripe bananas. Sometimes you'll find them at the back of the produce section on the reduced rack. Buy them if you see them, the finished cake will taste better.

Use your head. I buy my meat from a shop that also sells fish. But while people are lined up five deep at the meat counter, no one is ever on line at the fish counter. This tells me the fish is probably not very fresh, so I buy it someplace else. Take the same approach to buying convenience products, too. Read the labels. Check for freshness. And most importantly, learn from your mistakes.

Convenience Foods

I'm all for using convenience foods like bottled sauces and prepared pie crusts. But you need to select them with the same care you would use to select fresh produce. Sometimes you have to experiment with different brands until you find one that you like. My rule of thumb is that the less processed and the fewer chemical additives, the better. Usually, things that need to be refrigerated and/or frozen are more

"real" than those that just sit on the shelf, but not always. Read the label.

Think of creative alternatives. Rather than use a salty, flavorless bouillon cube, if I'm out of stock, I order a couple of quarts of broth from my local Chinese restaurant. Ask at a bakery if they will sell you puff pastry, pie crust, or pizza dough. You'll be surprised what you can find if you open your mouth. Less processed foods also give you more control. Who knows what store-bought flavored bread crumbs are going to taste like. I prefer to buy unflavored bread crumbs and add my own seasonings. (That's the same reason I recommend using only unsalted butter. You never know how salty it's going to be. And besides, unsalted butter is usually fresher because the salt acts as a preservative, extending the shelf life.)

Go Ahead, Splurge

There are times when you just have to throw in the towel and pay a little more money for a better ingredient. This doesn't mean you can't be frugal. And it certainly doesn't mean you should be foolish. Shop around. Make smart choices. You will be surprised at the difference in your cooking a few strategically indulgent ingredients can make.

For example, no matter what anyone ever tells you, no domestic Parmesan cheese compares to imported Italian Parmigiano-Reggiano. Same holds true for dried porcini (mushrooms) and prosciutto di Parma (ham). Many American products are packaged to look as though they came from far-away places, so you have to read the labels carefully. Ask yourself, "Imported from where?" While you might think some of the prices of these higher quality items are outrageous, a little of them goes a lot longer than their less expensive alternatives (see "Less Is More" below).

Less Is More

Although the bulk-shopping craze may have you contemplating gallon-size jars of spices and other ingredients, I generally prefer to purchase only as much of something as I might be able to use in my lifetime. In fact, the flavor of your food will improve tremendously if you constantly replenish your larder with fresh ingredients. Estimate how often over the next few weeks or months you are going to be using a particular item, and then only buy as much as you think you'll need.

Buying dry goods from open bins in healthfood stores enables you to purchase only as much as you need. If you know that the store is busy (so that the bins are constantly being replenished with fresh ingredients), then this is a great alternative to shopping in grocery stores, where you are often forced to purchase things like nuts or baking soda in boxes and bags of large quantities. You'll also save valuable cupboard space. Just be sure to label everything carefully when you get home. Too many of my friends have ruined desserts because they mistook an unmarked bag of salt for sugar.

Cooking

Breading

I think just about everything is better when it's breaded and fried, although such treatment has fallen out of favor recently, what with the trend toward more healthful eating. Classic breading technique requires that the items to be breaded be dipped first in flour, then in beaten egg, then in bread crumbs, which I like to season with lots of salt and pepper (see Eggplant Parmesan, page 116). Sometimes other breading agents are used, such as cornmeal (see Fried Green Tomatoes, page 129), or matzo meal (see anything my mother ever breaded and fried), but the technique remains the same. (See Sautéing, Frying, and Stir-Frying below for more information about frying.)

Bringing to Room Temperature

Except when otherwise noted (Simple Pie Crust, page 226, or Whipped Cream, page 239, for example), it is always best to start cooking with your ingredients at room temperature. Granted, you don't always have the time to let your grocery items sit on the counter for an hour or two before you begin making dinner, but if you do, you should. For obvious reasons, chilled ingredients take longer to cook. They also respond differently to various techniques, particularly when baking. Eggs beat to a larger volume when at room temperature. Butter is impossible to cream out of the refrigerator. Pay attention to temperature notes in recipes.

Cleaning Produce

All produce needs to be cleaned and usually prepared in some way. Always rinse vegetables and fruit under cold running water (except for mushrooms, which should be cleaned with the blade of a small knife or a mushroom brush). A sharp paring knife is indispensable for cleaning vegetables. You don't always have to peel everything. For instance, if you are the only one who is going to eat a soup and you don't care how it looks, you don't have to peel the carrots. Same goes for tomatoes in a sauce. Generally, once something is peeled, it doesn't keep very long (eggplant, potatoes, apples, pears). Discard all seeds, which can make dishes bitter, and in some cases, even poisonous.

To clean leafy produce such as lettuce, greens, and herbs that have a tendency to be sandy, you have to soak them in cold water and lift them out of the water. Then use a salad spinner to dry them or pat them with paper towels. If you just dump them into a colander or strainer to drain, you run the risk of dumping the sand back onto the "cleaned" vegetables. Fresh spinach, arugula, parsley, and other very sandy greens should be soaked and lifted out of cold water several times before using.

Cooking Eggs

Though simple in concept, cooking eggs is not easy in practice. That's why I've included a recipe for Scrambled Eggs (page 220) and why I have instructions for boiling eggs in several recipes (Potato Salad, page 191, and Salade

Niçoise, page 211). The secret to hard-boiled eggs is not to overcook them, which causes that dark gray ring around the yolk. Place them cold in a saucepan, cover with water an inch above the eggs, and bring to a boil. The time from the point the eggs are placed on the burner to the time they are taken off should be no more than ten minutes. Rinse them under cold running water to cool them down before you peel them. (Note: old eggs peel easier than fresh eggs because they develop an air pocket that helps separate the shell from the white.)

When eggs are added to hot foods (see Cream Puffs, page 108) or used to thicken sauces (see Lemon Curd, page 153), you must be careful not to heat them too much or too quickly or they will cook and curdle whatever it is you are making. Remember that patience in the kitchen can be a virtue. If the eggs do curdle, you can strain out the cooked pieces and start again.

Cutting Up Things

This may sound like a stupid topic, but cutting up ingredients serves two purposes. The first is to make a dish look good. There are hundreds of different cuts of vegetables in classic French cooking that enhance the appearance of the final product. The second and most important purpose, however, is to ensure that ingredients cook uniformly. If you are making Mushroom Barley Soup (page 169) and you cut up the vegetables in all different sizes, they will be finished cooking at different times. By the time the largest piece is done, the smallest

piece will be falling apart. Therefore, when a recipe calls for dicing, cubing, or chunking, it is important to make sure all of the pieces are approximately the same size.

Emulsifying Demystified

Though it sounds rather scientific, emul-sification is a common physical reaction in the kitchen. Thick, creamy sauces like mayonnaise, hollandaise, and beurre blanc work because of the principles of emulsification, whereby liquid (usually the water in vinegar or wine) and fat (usually oil or butter) particles are suspended beside each other in some sort of emulsifying agent (usually egg yolks, as in the case of Aioli, page 53, or mustard, as in the case of French Vinaigrette, page 125). The secret of the emulsion is to beat the fat phase (to use the correct nomen-clature and bring you back to high school science class) into the liquid phase very slowly at first so that it is distrib-uted evenly. If the fat is added too quickly, the emulsion will break. A broken sauce looks like a disaster. But it's usually easy to fix by beating the whole mess into more of the emulsifying agent. In the case of the vinaigrette, the broken emulsion can be fixed by beating it into some more mustard. (Note that I didn't say, "by beating more mustard into it," which won't work.)

Freezing

Although most cooked foods cannot be frozen well in household freezers (which don't get cold enough to pro-duce results like Stouffer's and Weight Watchers can achieve), they are great

for long-term storage of ingredients and baked goods. Things like chicken soup or stock, pastry dough, bread, tomato sauce, opened cans of tomato paste, and so on, can all be frozen. Stay away from freezing fresh fruits and vegetables, and anything with potatoes in it. Everything that is frozen should be wrapped extremely well in plastic and labeled, so that when you go to throw it away in a year, you'll know what to mourn. Baked goods can be frozen up to three months without losing their integrity. Meats and vegetables up to six months. Stocks and other convenience foods will keep about one year.

Grilling, Barbecuing, and Broiling

Nothing says summer to me more than grilled or barbecued food. Although there are a number of kitchen appli-ances and gadgets that let you simulate grilling or barbecuing indoors, in my opinion nothing is as good as the real thing. The high heat, extra smoke, and burned fat generated by these methods are what give grilled and barbecued foods such a great flavor. I am not a fan of stove-top grills—either the cast-iron or the water-pan, nonstick variety—for anything other than grilling vegetables and the occasional piece of fish. Be sure the grill is good and hot before you lay anything on it. And don't forget to lightly oil whatever you are grilling to prevent it from sticking. I prefer to broil my meat than to grill it on top of the stove. Set it close to the flame and keep an eye on it so it doesn't scorch.

Increasing or Decreasing Recipes

Almost all of the recipes in this book can be increased or decreased proportionally. The only thing to be careful of is the seasoning. As a rule, doubled recipes don't take double the amount of salt and other spices. Don't ask me why, they just don't. The difficulty in increasing recipes too much is that they become harder to work with. Mixing is a problem (or, rather, not overmixing is a problem). For instance, if you double the Buttermilk Biscuit recipe on page 78, you will have to work twice as hard to combine all of the ingredients and the end result will be tough, over-worked biscuits. The size of the cooking equipment and the cooking times also have to be increased. You're almost always better off making multiple batches. Still, sometimes you just have to make a double batch or cut things in half. When decreasing a recipe, find the lowest common denominator (usually one egg), and divide everything proportionately. See also "Increasing or Decreasing Recipes" in the Baking section, page 24.

Lowering Fat

Whenever I felt I could lower the fat in a recipe and still maintain the integrity of the original dish, I have offered you a lighter variation. That's not to say that you couldn't probably use less fat in some of the other recipes, too. But that would go against my mother's oft-spoken rule that "If one stick of butter is good, two is better!"

That said, there are a couple of general low-fat cooking techniques that help reduce the amount of fat in a recipe. Using nonstick pans enables you to use less fat for frying. The recent preponderance of low-fat and nonfat dairy products (sour cream, ricotta, cheese, yogurt) also opens a world of fat-lowering alternatives. Wherever you feel like you could use less fat or substitute low-fat ingredients, feel free. But your results may be less than optimal. Experimenting with decreasing the amount of fat in recipes takes some time, but it's a challenge that some of my gym-loving friends have turned into a hobby. At the risk of sounding patronizing, why not just eat less?

Making a Sandwich

I'm sorry, but just putting a piece of cheese on a piece of bread does not a sandwich make. Ask my roommate Izabela, who will go to great pains to prepare a perfect sandwich even in the wee hours of the morning. There is an art to making a good sandwich (and if you go wait on line at a small Italian sandwich shop called Melampo in New York's SoHo area, you'll be able to see an artist at work). I like a lot of good bread in a sandwich, so it is important to make the flavor of the filling jump out and hit you. You should always have a condiment on the bread to make it moist (mayonnaise, mustard, olive oil and vinegar, rémoulade, aioli, olive paste, brisket gravy—use your imagination). And the filling should always be heavily seasoned. Contrasting flavors and textures are also welcome (crisp lettuce, soft cheese, spicy sprouts, crunchy cucumbers). Don't hold back. I recently invented a sandwich that I'm almost embarrassed to say I enjoyed: cold spaghetti with mayonnaise and radish sprouts on a soft roll. Don't knock it till you try it.

Marinating

Marinating serves two purposes. It imparts flavor to meats and vegetables and whatever else you are marinating, and it changes the texture. In the case of meats (such as the Beef Ribs, Korean Style on page 67), some ingredients in the marinade (the ginger) actually tenderize the meat. In some dishes, such as gravlax (cured salmon) and ceviche (marinated seafood), the marinade actually cooks the ingredients. I know some good cooks who don't ever cook a piece of meat, not even a chicken, without marinating it first, even if it's just in garlic, olive oil, and lemon juice. If you have the time, marinate. Experiment with different flavors and times to see what results you get.

Measuring

Measuring is most important in baking (see page 25). When cooking, measurements are much more a matter of taste. Still, I have provided you with measurements that best approximate the flavors and tastes I would be looking for if I were sitting down to eat. If you think something is going to be too salty or too sweet, feel free to adjust the recipe to your liking. But trust me the first time. Invest in a set of measuring spoons, dry measuring cups (for flours and other dry ingredients), and liquid measuring cups (which have a handle and a pour spout).

Mixing in a Jar

One of my favorite time- and dirty dish–saving techniques is to mix dressings in glass jars with tightly fitting lids. Put all of the ingredients in the jar, screw on the lid, grasp it with a finger or two on the top, and shake until the dressing is mixed. Any leftover dressing you can store in the same jar.

Nuking

I believe strongly that the microwave should be used as a tool in the kitchen, not as a cooking appliance (except in the case of Corn on the Cob, page 105). Use it to heat water, melt butter, defrost ingredients, and warm leftovers, but don't ever use it to finish cooking anything. You can cut off a considerable amount of baking time by starting a baked potato in the microwave for five minutes and then transferring it into a 400°F oven for thirty minutes or so to finish baking. Always err on the low side when estimating microwaving times. Check whatever's inside often, stir it up to distribute the heat, and remember never put anything metal or living inside.

Patience

Related to the technique of "Resting" (see page 17), patience is a very important thing for a cook to have in the kitchen. There are just some things, no matter what gadgets you have, that take time. (You'll know what I mean the first time you have to wait for one of the Flavored Oils on page 121 to pass through the coffee filter.) Waiting for things to cook or a sauce to thicken or whatever else needs to happen only

seems to take forever if you have nothing else to do. Don't sit and watch the Pizza Dough (page 187) rise. Read a book. Chat with someone online. Watch a *Mad About You* rerun. You'll be surprised how fast the time will fly.

Peeling and Seeding Tomatoes

If you want to use fresh tomatoes in soups and sauces (such as the Gazpacho on page 133 or the Fresh Tomato Sauce on page 127), you should peel and seed them first. Set a large pot of water on the stove to boil and set a large bowl of ice water on the counter. Using a paring knife, cut out the stem section of the tomato and make a little X in the skin on the opposite side. Drop the tomatoes into the boiling water and let them roll around for a minute or two until you can see the skin begin to peel back. Quickly lift the tomatoes out of the boiling water with a slotted spoon or tongs and plunge them into the ice water. The skin should lift right off. Slice the tomato in half, crosswise. With the tomato resting in the palm of your hand, cut side facing out, gently squeeze to press out the seeds. When all of your tomatoes are done, you are ready to proceed with your recipe.

Peeling Onions

A quick way to peel onions is to cut off about one-half inch from both ends and slice the onions in half, lengthwise through the center. With your fingers, peel back the outer layers of tough skin and slice or dice as directed in the recipe, keeping your fingers tucked underneath to avoid injury.

Preheating

This is one of those recipe directions you are apt to ignore until you realize that it can drastically affect your cooking success. When a recipe asks you to preheat an oven or heat a pan before adding an ingredient, this is a critical step. Ingredients respond very differently to a rapid burst of heat than they do to a gradual increase in temperature (of the type that occurs when you put a cake in a cold oven and turn the dial to 350). Pay attention to these preheating instructions, whether stir-frying watercress (page 228) or making Cream Puffs (page 108).

Presenting and Serving

We eat with our eyes before we eat with our mouths. Good food ought to look good. Even if you are just dining alone, take the time to make the dish look pretty. A sprinkle of chopped parsley and a spoon of sauce on a nice plate will tell people you care about what you are doing in the kitchen, even if it doesn't taste good.

Reheating

There is about as much an art to reheating as there is to cooking in the first place. If you can avoid using the microwave, do. It has the habit of zapping away all of the lovely texture that regular heat gave to the dishes in the first place. Nonstick pans are good for reheating sticky, gloppy things (such as leftover Risotto, page 200, or the Cheese Thing, page 87). Many liquid-based dishes, like soups and stews, thicken when they cool. To reheat them properly, add a little water to loosen them up and set them over a very low flame to avoid scorching. The oven does wonders for baked goods, even stale bread. But only reheat what you are going to eat because the oven doesn't give you a second chance (especially not with bread).

Resting

In many of the recipes you will be told to let things rest for anywhere from fifteen minutes to overnight. Resting is an important concept in cooking. Scientifically speaking, it enables molecules that were busy bouncing around because of heat or excessive motion to settle back down where they belong. Resting enables competing flavors to blend together. It is important to let roasted meats rest when you take them out of the oven (see Leg of Lamb, page 152) so that the juices settle before you carve. When working with doughs, resting allows the tough, elastic gluten in the flour to relax, which makes the doughs easier to handle. Baked goods should rest before they are unmolded from their pans so that they run less of a risk of breaking. Resting is also good for you, because a happy, well-rested cook is a good cook.

Roasting, Braising, and Steaming

Unlike, sautéing, frying, and stir-frying, roasting, braising, and steaming rely on a medium other than fat to conduct the heat to the food. Roasting uses hot air, braising uses hot liquid, and steaming uses, you guessed it, (hot) steam. The secret to good roasting is a high temperature and a lot of air

circulation. That's why roasts should be elevated off the roasting pan on racks (see Roasted Chicken, page 203, or Leg of Lamb, page 152). To braise, you need a liquid, usually wine, some aromatic vegetables, usually, onions, carrots, garlic, and celery, and a cover. You can braise on the stove or in the oven (see Osso Buco, page 172). Braised items are usually sautéed first to give them a nice browned color and flavor. To steam, you need simmering water, in a saucepan or a wok, and something through which the steam can pass, either a colander or a bamboo steamer. Steaming is great for vegetables because they retain a nice crunch and most of their nutrients.

Salting Water

Whenever anything is cooked in water (except beans and some grains) I'm an avid believer that the water should be salted. Pasta and rice cooked in unsalted water are tasteless. And mashed potatoes have a better flavor, in my opinion, if the potatoes are boiled in salted water. I suggest one teaspoon of salt per quart of water, although most good Italian cooks use more. You needn't worry that everything is going to be too salty, because most of it stays in the water anyway.

Saucing

A good sauce is the backbone to many great cuisines. The most exalted position in the classic French kitchen is the saucier, who is responsible for balancing all of the flavors in a dish with subtlety and finesse. But a good sauce doesn't have to be difficult to make.

The easiest way to start a classic meat sauce is with the pan juices and vegetables of a roast (see Leg of Lamb, page 152, or Roasted Chicken, page 203). Alternately, you can roast some vegetables (onions, carrots, celery), herbs (rosemary, parsley, thyme), and bones (veal, beef, chicken, turkey) in a very hot oven until well browned. Either way, skim or pour off all the fat. Set the pan on top of the stove over a low flame and pour in some wine. Scrape the bottom of the pan with a wooden spoon or metal spatula to lift off all of the flavorful bits stuck to the bottom. Add some water and seasonings and simmer for about 10 minutes. Strain into a saucepan. Now you can have some fun. Add green peppercorns or roasted red peppers or mushrooms, or whatever you think might go well with what you are preparing. You can add cream for a richer sauce, or just keep simmering what you've got until it has reduced to a good sauce consistency.

Other sauces are based on chopped or pureed vegetables or fruits. Chunky salsas made with tomatoes, onions, hot peppers, vinegar, olive oil, and lots of seasoning are popular. So are fruit salsas based on mango, papaya, or melon.

The important things to remember when saucing a dish are that the flavors of the sauce don't overpower everything else served with it and that the texture and appearance is appetizing. These days cornstarch or flour-and-butter-thickened sauces are less popular than lighter reduction sauces, except of course for turkey gravy (see Roasted Turkey, page 205).

Sautéing, Frying, and Stir-Frying

Most dishes cooked on top of the stove require you to sauté, fry, or stir-fry. To sauté means to cook quickly in hot fat (from the French sautér, "to jump"). Frying is like sautéing, only you use much more fat. Stir-frying requires more heat and a varying amount of fat depending on what you are cooking. The choice of fat depends on the dish and on the technique to be used.

Try never to fry or stir-fry anything in extra-virgin olive oil, if you can help it; it burns at a low temperature and is a waste of good oil. Use virgin olive oil instead. (If extra-virgin is all you've got, go ahead.) Butter is also a poor choice because the milk solids in it have a tendency to burn quickly. If you want the flavor of butter, combine it with oil, but you'll still have to be careful it doesn't burn. Peanut oil is my preference for sautéing, frying, or stir-frying anything because I like its rich flavor. But peanut oil can be expensive, unless you buy it in Chinatown or Asian food shops. Sunflower or safflower oils are also good because they have a light flavor. I am not a fan of corn oil or canola oil because I think they have a heavy flavor and an acidic aftertaste. If you really want to live a little, try using duck fat or bacon fat, or at least adding a little to the oil. Though rich in saturated fat, animal fats give sautéed and fried foods a great flavor.

Unless specified otherwise in the recipe, when sautéing, frying, or stir-frying you should be using medium-high to high heat. Fried foods should have an even, golden-brown color.

Drain them of any excess fat on paper towels or a clean brown paper bag before serving. Most home stoves do not get hot enough for woks—a good seasoned wok over a superhot flame gives Asian food a characteristic smoky flavor. But you can use a flat-bottomed wok or a cast-iron pan to produce acceptable results.

Seasoning to Taste

You never know how something will taste until you put it in your mouth. Often in the recipes you will see the instructions "season to taste" or "adjust the seasoning." This means you actually have to think about what is going on in whatever it is you're preparing, and make some decisions about what needs to be added. When you are working with raw ingredients, such as with a Meat Loaf to Be Proud Of (page 161) or Hamburgers (page 140), take the time to pinch off a little piece of seasoned meat and fry it up in a pan. If you take the time to season it correctly at the beginning, everyone will be happier at the end. I also feel it is important to season at every step of the cooking process (except when seasoning will affect the cooking process, such as when beans are cooked in salted water, see page 164). Just adding a dash of salt and pepper at the end doesn't generally cut it. As herbs and spices cook, their flavors go through many different incarnations. You can't simulate a slow-cooked dish by seasoning it at the end. Almost everything—salads, sandwiches, ripe tomatoes, you name it—should be seasoned a little to help bring out the natural flavors of the ingredients.

Simmering versus Boiling

Simmering is the sound of a quartet while boiling is a symphony. Water is just about the only thing you ever want to come to a rapid boil and stay there. Anything that needs to be cooked for a long period of time should be simmered over a low flame. Most soups, stews, and other liquid dishes are brought to a boil for a second and then turned down to a simmer to extract the maximum amount of flavor from the ingredients and to prevent the clouding that can result from the excessive motion of a boiling liquid. Simmering also helps prevent the bottoms of pots from burning. Only small bubbles should be seen on the surface of a properly simmering liquid. (The exception to this is tomato-based dishes because tomatoes boil at a low temperature.)

Skimming

To remove fat and other things that float to the top of simmering liquids, you need to skim them. Use a large, deep spoon or ladle. Hold the utensil upright and parallel with the surface of the liquid. Gently tilt the spoon or ladle down into the liquid to skim off the fat or scum, which should fall into the utensil. Dump in an empty can or the sink and continue until the surface is clean. The easiest and most effective way to remove fat from a soup or stew is to chill it overnight. The fat will coagulate at the surface and you can just lift it off with a spoon.

Smashing Garlic

No, smashing garlic is not a new rock band. It's a simple, quick technique used by professional chefs to peel garlic. To smash a clove of garlic, set it on a hard surface, such as a cutting board. Hold a chef's knife in one hand and lay the side of the knife on top of the clove. Give the knife a whack with your other fist so that the peel is broken and the flesh is smashed flat under the blade as a result of your blow. The peel should just lift off the smashed clove. Cut off the dark end and mince according to the directions in the recipe. The first time you smash a clove of garlic, you may send it across the kitchen, but you'll get the hang of it. If you have a lot of garlic to peel and mince, smashing makes the task much easier.

Squeezing Lemons

Since I won't let you use bottled lemon juice, you're going to have to learn how to squeeze a lemon. Sounds simple, but there's a trick. First, place the lemon on the counter and place the palm of your hand on top of it. Roll the lemon back and forth under your palm while putting all of your weight on top of it. The pressure helps break up the corpuscles of juice so that the lemon is easier to squeeze and you get more juice. Cut the lemon in half, crosswise through the center. Set a fine mesh strainer over a bowl, a measuring cup, or the dish in which you require the lemon juice. Insert the tines of a fork or a wooden lemon reamer into the center of the flesh and rock it back and forth while squeezing the lemon. Repeat until all of the juice is squeezed out. Force the juice through the strainer and discard the pits and the pulp.

Straining

One of the distinctions between refined cooking and peasant cooking is the texture of things. Although this is a large overgeneralization, it seems to me that more refined food is expected to be smoother. Smoothness is usually a function of straining. If you have a chunky soup and you puree it and pass it through a fine mesh sieve, all of a sudden it becomes an elegant potage. The same holds true for sauces.

One of the most amazing soups I've ever had was a garbure (a type of French soup) of different vegetable waters, made by separately pureeing a variety of vegetables, allowing the purees to drip individually through multiple layers of cheesecloth to produce clear vegetable "waters," and then combining them all in a bowl as a soup. The soup was completely clear, but full of flavor. It was truly amazing. If you have the time or inclination, strain away. Using the food processor, blender, or vegetable mill before you strain a soup or sauce will give you a more flavorful, richer result.

Tempering

A couple of recipes require you to temper ingredients before adding them. Tempering simply means bringing the ingredients closer to each other in temperature before you combine them. In the case of Chicken Paprikash (page 89), you simply spoon a couple of tablespoons of the hot cooking liquid into the sour cream or yogurt before you stir it into the pot to prevent it from curdling. Egg yolks are often tempered in the same way before they are added to hot milk for custards and other egg-thickened sauces.

Testing for Doneness

Of all the things you need to know to be able to cook, many people feel this is the one that is hardest to learn. Trial and error is really the only way to master it. Sight, touch, smell, and taste are all important senses when it comes to testing for doneness. A little intuition doesn't hurt either. Usually you should try to avoid overcooking anything to the point that it is unrecognizable. In fact, most things (rice, pasta, beans, grains, vegetables) should be ever so slightly undercooked, to the point that we now commonly call al dente, Italian for "to the tooth." The only way to know for sure if something is al dente is to put it in your mouth and test it.

With meats and other recipes that are cooked whole (such as the Savory Bread Pudding on page 215), putting a piece in your mouth is a little difficult. The most accurate way to test if roasted meats are done is to use an instant-read thermometer. All you do is stick the thermometer in a few places in the center of the meat or dish and read what it says. There are many different charts with temperatures for different doneness. As a rule, meats range from 120°F to 150°F and baked goods should be about 185°F (see the chart below for details). An instant-read thermometer costs about $10, so if you are going to be cooking a lot of meat, you should get one. Another technique is to prick the meat with a fork to check for the telltale tenderness that is characteristic of cooked meats. When the Roasted Chicken (page 203) is done, a fork should slide in and out with little effort. Poke it in a number of places to be sure it is done all around. The juices should also run clear, not pink, to indicate there's no raw blood about.

When in doubt cut open whatever it is you are testing for doneness to see what it looks like inside. Better there should be a cut in it than you should kill somebody. (Just kidding.)

Baked Goods

Done	185°F

Beef

Rare	125°F
Medium	155°F
Well Done	175°F

Lamb

Pink	135°F
Medium-rare	140°F
Well Done	160°F

Pork and Veal

Cooked	160°F

Poultry

Chicken Breast	170°F
Chicken Thigh	185°F

Using the Food Processor

As you will see by the number of recipes for which I recommend using a food processor, this is one of my favorite kitchen gadgets. Perhaps nothing saves as much time and effort in the kitchen as that small metal chopping blade (really the only blade you should ever be using) that whizzes around at breakneck speed. As with the microwave, the secret to using the food processor is not to use it too much. When chopping or blending things in the processor, use a technique called pulsing—a quick flick of the on/ off switch—to achieve the best results. Pulse something two or three times, open the lid, move everything around with a spoon, scrape down the sides, replace the lid, and pulse some more until your mixture has the desired consistency.

Don't overload the work bowl or the stuff on the bottom will turn to mush while the stuff on the top barely moves. If you have too much food to process in one batch, split it up and combine everything in a mixing bowl when you are done. I used to think the food processor was too much of a hassle to clean, but I got over that as soon as I started to use it on a regular basis.

Blenders are good for some things, but they are not nearly as versatile as the food processor. If you are using a blender to chop, you must work in very small batches and shake the whole machine around on the counter to be sure things stir up inside—you look possessed, but it works. Generally, blenders are better for blending liquids or pureeing.

Using Leftovers

Thinking up creative ways to use leftovers can be fun. I like to incorporate leftover sauces from take-out Chinese into new stir-fries or Fried Rice (page 131). I think that almost anything tastes good the next day in a sandwich (see Meat Loaf to Be Proud Of, page 161, or Brisket, page 76). My mother's general technique was to take leftovers and fry them in butter. (It works pretty well.) You can stir things into mashed potatoes (see Just-Between-You-and-Me Mashed Potatoes, page 149), boil leftover bones and veggies into soups (see Chicken Soup from a Roasted Chicken Carcass, page 93), or bake vegetables, roast fish, and turn them into quiches (see Real Man's Quiche, page 195). Use your imagination. And when that fails, fry in butter.

Working with Meat

Maybe because it's expensive or maybe because it was once alive, meat is intimidating to many novice cooks. It shouldn't be. What could be easier than cooking a prime rib roast. You put it on a rack in a roasting pan, crank up the oven, and bake it until it's done (see Testing for Doneness, page 20). As with most ingredients, buy the best meat you can afford. Despite the current trend, the best is almost always the meat with more fat. Fat interspersed in the muscle (called "marbling") of red meat adds flavor and moistness. If given the option, I prefer to cook most meat on the bone (even chicken and fish) because I think it imparts a better flavor. (And you can use the bones to make a soup or sauce.) Meat with a bone cooks a little faster than meat without because the bone conducts the heat to the center.

When choosing a cut of meat—chops, roast, shank, or whatever you like—you must consider the method of cooking. Tougher cuts require long, moist-heat cooking to soften the tough

tissue. What these cuts lack in tenderness they generally make up for in flavor. Conversely, it's a travesty to braise a tender filet. Whenever you have a question about meat, you should speak to a butcher. They are often surprisingly well informed about how to use the things they sell.

Whenever preparing or carving a large piece of meat, it is important to remember to "cut across the grain." Muscle fiber develops in long striations, the direction of which is referred to as the grain. In general, if you cut across the grain, your meat will be more tender. If you cut along the grain, your meat will be tough. Some meats (such as poultry) are so tender this distinction doesn't matter. But with larger cuts from bigger animals you will have to pay attention.

The old adage "less is more" generally holds true when seasoning meat, especially when you're working with showpieces such as a prime rib roast, a whole turkey, or a crown roast of pork. A little salt, some pepper, some aromatic vegetables, and a hot oven are all you need. Oh, and of course, a good sauce (see "Saucing," page 17).

Zesting

Many recipes call for the zest of oranges or lemons. There is a kitchen gadget called a zester that looks like a misshapen hand, with five holes where the fingernails would be. By pulling the zester down over the surface of the orange or lemon, you will get long, thin strands of zest. These strands need to be finely minced before they are added to a dish. If you don't have a zester, you can use the small, nubby side of a box grater. Rub the orange or lemon back and forth over the grater, being careful not to get any of the bitter white pith. Tap the grater hard on the side of the bowl or counter to loosen the grated zest. If you don't have a grater either, you can use a carrot peeler. Just be careful not to pick up any of the bitter white pith when you peel the fruit. (If you do, scrape it off with the sharp point of a knife.) Finely mince the zest before adding it to your recipe.

Baking

Beating Egg Whites and Whipping Cream

It's easiest to beat egg whites and whip cream with an electric mixer. But if you don't have one, you can use a good whisk, a large clean bowl, and a lot of elbow grease. For the egg whites, the whites and the bowl should be at room temperature. When you begin beating, the whites will start to froth. As you continue, the froth will become more stable, the color will turn from clear to white, and the mixture will stiffen. Any yolk or grease in the egg whites will prevent them from inflating, so make sure your utensils are very clean before you begin. Continue beating until the whites are stiff—when you lift the whisk, they should hold their shape. All in all, this should take about ten to fifteen minutes. A copper bowl makes the task easier.

To whip cream, the bowl, cream, and whisk should first be chilled. Follow the same process with the cream as you do with the whites. The cream should take less time. Stop as soon as it holds it shape because overwhipped cream turns into butter, and then there's nothing you can do with it; see Whipped Cream (page 239).

Bringing to Room Temperature

See Cooking section, page 12.

Buttering and Flouring

The best way to ensure that your baked goods will come out of the pan in one piece is to butter and flour the pan. Start with a tablespoon or so of soft butter held in a clean paper towel. Rub the butter over the entire inside surface of the baking dish. Now place a couple of tablespoons of flour in the dish and shake it around to coat the pan. Working over the sink or a garbage can, tilt the pan so that the flour falls to the side, and tap it around to coat the sides of the pan as well. When you are finished, turn the pan upside down and tap the bottom with your hand to remove any excess flour. Now the pan is ready to be filled with batter.

Alternately, you can purchase "buttering and flouring" sprays that coat the pan with a white film and prevent things from sticking. These sprays are easy to use, but they don't add a little buttery flavor to the crust of whatever you're making. Use whichever you prefer.

Chopping Nuts

Chopping nuts can be a pain, so I like to put them in a resealable plastic bag, seal it, and beat them with a rolling pin or hammer until they are the right size. It's clean, fast, effective, and it helps alleviate hostility. I use the same technique for making cookie crumbs. Alternately, you can use a miniprocessor or food processor and the pulsing action (see "Using the Food Processor," page 21). Just be sure not to over-process them into a paste.

Cooling

Almost all baked goods should be cooled thoroughly on a rack before being cut (the circulating air helps maintain the crust). I know it's tempting to cut right into a cake when it's warm out of the oven, but the texture of a freshly baked cake is generally not optimal. Also, many of the recipes in this book will tell you to let the cake cool for fifteen to thirty minutes in the pan before unmolding it to a rack. If you don't wait, you run the risk of the cake breaking apart when you handle it. It's your life.

Creaming

There are many meanings to the word cream. When a team looses a sporting event really badly they say they were creamed. On the other hand, when something's really terrific they call it the cream of the crop. Everyone knows the rich stuff that comes with your coffee, and I bet you've had whipped cream before (if not, see page 239). You've got creamed soups (page 106) and creamed corn (which usually doesn't have any cream in it at all). But you probably didn't know that cream also refers to the technique of beating butter and sugar together as a base for making cakes. Beating the butter

and sugar together and incorporating a lot of air makes cakes rise higher and imparts a fine texture. If you are creaming by hand, a wooden spoon works best. But get ready for a work-out. An electric mixer fitted with strong beaters or a paddle attachment produces the best results. When properly creamed, the butter and sugar mixture will have a light color and a smooth and creamy texture. If you're pooped and you just can't cream any more, start to beat the eggs, one at a time, into the butter and sugar mixture. The eggs will loosen the mixture so that you can really begin to incorporate some air. Proceed with the recipe as directed.

Cutting in Butter

Cutting in butter is one of the most common techniques used to shorten a dough (see "Shortening," page 27). It's what gives Blueberry Sour Cream Muffins (page 71), Buttermilk Biscuits (page 78), Scones (page 219), and Simple Pie Crust (page 226) their characteristic flaky and friable texture. To cut in butter, first cut the butter into chunks and chill. Combine all of the dry ingredients in the recipe in a large bowl and mix well. Add the chilled butter and break up the chunks with your hands so that they are all coated and buried in the dry ingredients. Using two knives (one held in each hand), the tines of a fork, a pastry cutter, or your fingertips, cut or break up the butter into small pieces, constantly keeping the butter covered with the flour mixture. Continue until the mixture resembles coarse crumbs.

Some people advise not using your

fingertips because your body heat has a tendency to melt the butter, which defeats the purpose of cutting it in. But I find that if I work fast enough, and if I'm constantly rubbing the big pieces between my finger tips with plenty of flour to break them up, then using my hands is the easiest way to cut in the butter. Alternately, you can use the metal chopping blade of the food processor to cut in the butter using on/off pulses (see "Using the Food Processor," page 21, and Light and Flaky Pie Crust, page 157). Don't worry if all of the pieces of butter are not the same size. The bigger pieces will melt when the pastry bakes, leaving large, lazy flakes.

Dusting with Powdered Sugar

A dusting of powdered sugar is beautiful on a cake, and it works like magic to cover any imperfections on the surface. Just before you are ready to serve, place a tablespoon or so of confectioner's sugar in a fine-mesh sieve and rub the spoon back and forth in the sieve while you are moving it over the surface of your cake. If you dust the cake too far in advance, it will absorb the sugar and you'll have to do it again. If you really feel creative, you can cut out a stencil and make pretty patterns on the cake. Very Martha Stewart.

Increasing or Decreasing Recipes

The recipes included in this book can all be increased or decreased pro-portionally, but when doubling cake recipes, you are almost always better off making two batches. (See "Increasing or Decreasing Recipes," page 15.) Just about the only exception is One-Pot Brownies (page 171), which I've made in multiples of ten.

Measuring

Measuring properly is very important in baking. Use dry measuring cups (the ones that come in individual sizes) for dry ingredients. Dip the measuring cup into the ingredient, except if you're measuring flour—you're supposed to spoon flour into the measuring cup—and then level it off with the back of a knife or another flat edge. Use liquid measuring cups (the calibrated ones with handles and pour spouts) for liquid ingredients. Hold the cups at eye level to increase your accuracy. Measuring spoons can be used for liquid or dry ingredients.

If you are going to be doing a lot of baking, you may want to invest in a scale. Weighing ingredients is the most accurate way of measuring them because volume varies. And many professional baking recipes will provide only weight measurements.

Liquid and Dry Measures

1 pinch	=	slightly less than $^1/_4$ teaspoon
a dash	=	a few drops
3 teaspoons	=	1 tablespoon
2 tablespoons	=	1 fluid ounce
4 tablespoons	=	$^1/_4$ cup
8 tablespoons	=	$^1/_2$ cup
	=	4 fluid ounces
2 cups	=	1 pint
2 pints	=	1 quart
4 quarts	=	1 gallon
1 pound	=	16 ounces

Some Helpful Equivalents

1 pound brown sugar	≈	2 $^1/_3$ cups
1 stick butter	=	$^1/_2$ cup
	=	$^1/_4$ pound
1 pound carrots	≈	3 cups sliced
1 cup flour	≈	5 ounces
1 pound flour	≈	3 $^1/_2$ cups
1 pound onions	≈	3 cups chopped
1 pound potatoes	≈	3 cups diced
1 cup sugar	≈	7 ounces

Melting

When melting butter or chocolate for a recipe, it is important not to cook the butter or chocolate because excessive heat will alter the flavor. I like to melt butter in the microwave. And I melt chocolate in a stainless steel or heat-proof bowl set over simmering water. Be careful never to get any water in the chocolate or it will seize up and become useless.

Mixing versus Overmixing

For the same reason that you should not handle pastry too much (see "Working with Pastry," page 27) you should not overmix batters and doughs, especially those for muffins and quick breads (such as Honey-Buttermilk Cornbread, page 144, or Banana Bread, page 63). Overmixing causes the gluten protein in the flour to develop, which makes baked goods tough. Stop mixing when all of the dry ingredients have been moistened by the wet and there are no visible lumps.

Preheating

Do it. Preheating your oven is even more important when you are baking than when you are cooking. See page 16.

Resting

The ingredients, not you. See discussion, page 17.

Separating Eggs

Some of the recipes in this book call for egg whites or egg yolks. To separate an egg, crack it on the side of a mixing bowl or the counter. Holding the cracked egg over a bowl if you need the white or over a garbage can if you don't, separate the shell into two roughly equal halves. The white will drip out of the shell, one hopes into the bowl. Transfer the yolk from one half to the other, letting more of the white drip off each time. Be careful not to break the yolk with your finger or on the edge of the shell or you might contaminate the whites; egg whites with yolk in them will not inflate properly and you'll have to start over. When most of the white is gone, drop the yolk into a separate bowl.

Alternately, you can separate the eggs using your hands, allowing the white to slip through your fingers as you pass the yolk from palm to palm. Also, if you're separating more than one egg, and don't feel too sure of your separating skills, you may want three bowls—two for the first egg (one for yolk, one for white), and one for any additional eggs (to place below to catch the white—or white and yolk). That way, if you screw up the second egg, you don't ruin the first one.

Shortening

The phenomenon of shortening is what makes biscuits pull apart and pie crusts flaky. When water is added to flour, the protein in the flour comes together to form gluten. As the dough is worked, the gluten builds up, making the dough elastic and resilient. Gluten is what makes bread hold its shape as it rises and gives it that great pull-apart consistency. When fat is added to the mix, however, the strands of gluten are shortened. Any fat can act as a shortening, but the most common fats in baked goods are butter, vegetable shortening, and lard. The higher the ratio of fat to flour in the dough, the shorter the dough. In contrast to elastic and dense doughs, short pastries are flaky and friable, as long as they aren't overworked. Biscuits and pie crust are the most common examples of short pastry. To be sure that they are not tough, just work the biscuit dough gently with a fork.

Tempering

See page 20.

Testing for Doneness

With cakes and baked goods, testing for doneness requires all of your senses. A cake is baked when it has pulled away from the sides, the center has risen, it is firm to the touch, and a bamboo skewer or toothpick inserted in the center comes out clean. It's important not to overbake anything, though, or the texture will be dry. Start checking five or ten minutes before the recipe says the baked good will be done. That way, you'll know you didn't overbake it. Fully baked goods should register between 185°F and 190°F on an instant-read thermometer. A strong sugary smell and a whiff of browned butter are signs that something is overbaking.

Working with Pastry

All doughs, except bread and pizza dough, need to be handled as little as possible. Overhandling causes the gluten in the flour to develop into tough strands that make the dough difficult to work with and become tough when it is baked. If a dough becomes difficult to handle or stubborn when you are trying to roll it out (meaning overelastic), let it rest in the refrigerator for fifteen to thirty minutes in order for the gluten to relax. Be sure to work pastry on a lightly floured surface to prevent sticking. Reflour the surface while you are working, as the dough will absorb the flour quickly. Pat out the dough with your hands (for scones or biscuits) or roll it out with a rolling pin (for pies and tarts) until the thickness indicated in the recipe. Always roll from the center out and try not to roll off the edge. If the rolling pin sticks, lightly flour the surface of the dough. If the dough tears, dab it with a drop or two of water and try to press the seam together with your fingertips. Roll over the seam to seal.

To transfer a rolled-out pie crust, roll it up on the rolling pin and position the rolling pin over the pie plate or baking sheet at one side. Unroll the crust from one end of the pie plate to the other, centering it as you go. Press the dough into the shell with your fingertips. If any tears appear, press them together. Trim the edges, leaving about 1/2-inch overhang around the circumference. Roll this overhang underneath the edge and press the edge with the floured tines of a fork or your thumb and forefinger to produce a pretty, fluted edge. If you are making a double-crusted pie (as for Apple Pie, page 55), don't prepare the edge until the pie is filled and the second crust is placed on top. Fold the lower overhang over the top crust and then press with a fork or your thumb and forefinger to seal the two crusts together.

To prebake a pie shell (called "blind baking") line the shell with aluminum foil and fill with dried beans or uncooked rice or ceramic pie weights to weigh it down. Bake in a preheated 425°F oven for fifteen minutes, until the dough begins to set and you can visibly see the fat melting. Remove the aluminum foil with the beans or rice, being careful not to spill any onto the crust, and return the crust to the oven to bake until light brown, about ten to fifteen minutes more. As it bakes, poke any bubbles with a small knife to deflate. Proceed with the recipe as directed.

Do's and Don'ts

Before you cook anything from this book, or any other book for that matter, you should read this section. There are some basic principles to good cooking and following a recipe that even many cooks don't know—what else would explain all the bad food in the world?

Do's

Do Taste

Your taste buds are your most important tool in the kitchen. Just because a recipe says to add the juice of one lemon doesn't mean you shouldn't add more if you can't taste the lemon in the dish. The incredible variance of flavors in nature makes even the best recipe only a guideline. Nobody knows how a particular tomato will taste until someone bites into it. (And even then one person will say it tastes sweet while another will think it tastes sour.) Learn to use your taste buds, not just when you're cooking, but also whenever you eat. Pay attention to things that you like, flavor combinations you find pleasing. Then when you go to cook something, remember those flavors. Try to simulate them. Until you are very experienced in the kitchen, there will be a lot of trial and error. I've been cooking since I was five years old (and eating for about five years before that) and I still get puzzled by the occasional odd flavor until I realize all I have to add is a little salt.

Do Approach a Recipe with an Open Mind

So many people I know who can't really cook go ahead and alter recipes before they've even tried them because they don't think they seem right. Go figure. The first time you try a new dish, you should be willing to let the recipe take you where it wants to go. Then if you realize you don't like where you are, change it to whatever suits you.

Do Read the Recipe Through Before You Begin

Unless you read the entire recipe before you begin, you may come across a surprise or two that can derail your whole cooking effort. And if you get frustrated by a dish once, the chances are it will be quite a while before you get back in the kitchen.

Do "Put in Good"

You're tired of hearing this phrase already, but my mother drilled it into my head so I'm going to drill it into yours. Her grandmother, Eva, who was apparently the first great cook in our family, always said, "You put in good, you get out good." The best ingredients are needed to make the best food. (Note that the corollary—all you need is good ingredients to make good food—is certainly not always true.) Grandma Eva's saying holds true for raw ingredients, such as produce and meats, and convenience foods, such as canned sauces and premade pie crusts. When

the difference in price of a mediocre bottle of olive oil and an excellent bottle of olive oil is only a couple of dollars, why hold back? You're not going to use it all at once. Use less, and you'll be more satisfied. Of course, there are extremes. You don't want the best olive oil if you are going to be using it in a deep-fryer. And now that the marketing world has caught on to the appeal of "gourmet" products, many foodstuffs are dressed up to look better than others and command a higher price, without any real qualitative differences. My advice is to shop in reputable stores, to develop good relationships with grocers, butchers, and bakers, to read labels carefully, to use your intuition, and if you make a mistake, to learn not to do it again.

Do Improvise

I know I've told you to read the recipe through and pay attention to what it says, but if a recipe calls for red wine vinegar and all you have is white wine vinegar, don't let that stop you. Sure there are some ingredients that would be difficult to substitute, especially if you're baking (baking soda has different chemical properties than baking powder), but in most instances substitution is the mother of invention. When I was testing the Blueberry Sour Cream Muffins (page 71) for the first time, for example, all I had was a couple of tablespoons of vanilla yogurt, some heavy cream, and some

buttermilk. I combined all three to give me the one cup milk and half cup sour cream the recipe called for. My ersatz muffins were delicious. There's as much to be learned from a substitution that doesn't work as there is from one that does.

Do Encourage Your Friends to Cook with You

If you don't view cooking as the chore you have to get out of the way before your friends arrive—a very 1950s mentality—then you'll find you'll have more fun doing it. For me, cooking has become a social activity, part of the evening's entertainment. My friends peel and chop and dice along with me while we listen to music or catch up on our lives. In the process, you'll encourage your friends to learn how to cook too. (In fact, why don't you buy them a copy of this book?) Another good way to get them to cook is to make every dinner party a potluck (see details about my potluck party on page 243). That way everybody has to make a dish and nobody has to worry about preparing an entire meal.

Don'ts

Don't Judge the Difficulty of a Recipe by the Length of the Ingredients List or the Method

I've made a conscious effort in this book to be explicit both with ingredients lists—which include things such as water and salt and pepper—and with methods—which will give you details such as "hold the spatula in your right hand." Don't let these extra words scare you away from the recipe. Many cookbooks distill information to the barest minimum in order to make the recipes look less daunting (for example, "...add 1 cup of pigeon stock..."). But I feel it is better to be honest, especially when I am referring to techniques with which you might not be familiar.

Don't Let a Word or Technique That You Don't Know Stop You

In The Basics section (page 11), I explain techniques that will help you get through most of the recipes in this book. But there may still be some things you are not familiar with, or some explanations you don't understand. Take the best educated guess you can, and proceed with the recipe. You are a smart person. And cooking is in the soul. Think of the times you've had the dish and what it was like. Be the recipe. Feel your way to the right dish. Remember, you are the cook.

Don't Be Afraid to Use Convenience Foods or Time-Saving Gadgets

There are people who believe that if something comes in a bottle or a can, then a good cook shouldn't use it. Similarly, people shun the use of "newfangled" gadgets like the microwave or the food processor. Hogwash. Anything you can do to save time, without skimping on flavor, is a good thing. Sure a tomato sauce tastes different if you use fresh, ripe tomatoes. But fresh tomatoes, if you can get them ripe, need to be peeled, seeded, and chopped (see page 16) before they can be used. Sometimes all you have the time to do is open a can (of top-quality Italian-style plum tomatoes, that is). The resulting sauce isn't worse than one made from fresh tomatoes, it's just a different type of sauce.

The same philosophy holds true for time-saving gadgets. Although I would rather eat Styrofoam than a piece of meat cooked in the microwave, I always use my microwave as a tool in the kitchen, for melting butter, boiling water, even cooking corn on the cob (see page 105). And you'll soon find out that I am the biggest fan of the food processor. The secret is to be creative.

Don't Be Afraid to Get Your Hands Dirty

Cooking is a contact sport. Roll up your sleeves and get in there. Pinch, tuck, taste, smell, and feel your way to a delicious meal. Clean your hands before you start and keep rinsing them while you cook. You'll improve your cooking tenfold if you cook with your heart and your hands, not just your head.

Don't Stress If Something Doesn't Work

There are some days when no matter what you do, nothing in the kitchen is going to work. You cooked the rice too long, the phone rang and you burned the hamburgers, you dropped a plate and glass splinters fall into the chicken salad, or you just can't seem to get that butter and flour to resemble coarse crumbs, whatever that means. Don't fret. Throw it out. Order in. Tomorrow is another day.

The Recipe Guide

Margaret Visser said it best: "We are ineradicably choosy about our food," she wrote in <u>The Rituals of Dinner</u> (HarperCollins, 1991). "Preference enters into every mouthful we consume. We play with food, show off with it, revere and disdain it. The main rules about eating are simple: If you do not eat you die; and no matter how large your dinner, you will soon be hungry again."

So you're psyched. You want to start cooking. But what to make? There are so many options. And everything sounds so good. Well, this section will help you decide. You may want to base your decision on a craving you have for something in particular. Or maybe you have a boneless chicken breast in the fridge that has one more day to live. Or you looked in the mirror this morning and felt fat. Or if you don't eat in less than a half an hour, you'll die of starvation. The recipes in this book have been categorized so that it's easy to find what you want to make.

Granted, some of the distinctions are arbitrary because there is a lot of crossover. Who's to say you can't eat mushroom barley soup for breakfast or pancakes for dinner? But I think that with this rough breakdown you'll be able to find something you want to make when you want to make it.

Remedial Course Work

And you thought you were done with courses when you finished college! These are courses of a different kind. At what point in the meal should you serve a particular dish? Here are some suggestions:

Hors d'Oeuvres

Almost anything can be served as an hors d'oeuvre if you make it small enough. But in this book most of the hors d'oeuvres are dips or spreads that should be served with vegetables, chips, bread, or anything you can think of that might taste good.

Appetizers

The best way to make the distinction between hors d'oeuvres and appetizers is how you eat them. Generally, hors d'oeuvres are eaten with your fingers, while appetizers are served on plates and eaten with knives and forks.

Main Courses

This category is pretty self explanatory. This is the thing that goes in the center of the plate with other things (side dishes) around it.

Side Dishes

Most side dishes can be main courses if you just serve them in larger portions. Many of them can also be served as appetizers. I like to mix and match ethnic cuisines, flavors, textures, colors, and temperatures to keep a meal interesting.

Condiments

One of the secrets of good cooking, well-flavored condiments (dressings, sauces, and other types of seasonings) are indispensable. Take the time to make them taste good and suddenly you're a good cook. There are many things that fall into the condiment category (like the gravy from a brisket spooned over mashed potatoes). Don't stop here.

Desserts

Eating sweet things at the end of the meal is, in my opinion, too limiting. I like to eat them all the time.

The Most Important Meal of the Day

If you wake up at four in the afternoon after a night of debauchery, is your first meal breakfast or dinner? What time of day should you eat something? Whenever you want it, I say. But just in case you need a little guidance, I've broken the recipes down into the following mealtimes.

Breakfast

Breakfast for some is often lunch or dinner for others, depending on when you start your day and what state your stomach is in when you wake up. I'm a fan of cold leftovers in the morning. Here are some suggestions to help wake you up gently.

Lunch

Your requirements for lunch are different if you pack it to go or if you enjoy it at home. Prepare accordingly. You can even use your old *Charlie's Angels* lunch box, if you like. What did we do before the earl of Sandwich made his revolutionary discovery? I think anything surrounded by two pieces of fresh sourdough bread tastes better.

Brunch

Since brunch is usually the first thing you eat on the days when you eat it, I lean toward more breakfast-type foods than lunch-type foods. But who am I to say? As long as you have Home Fries, serve whatever you want.

Dinner

It seems that among my friends these days, almost anything constitutes dinner (from roasted chicken to pretzels and mustard). Compressed between the gym, evening classes, late hours at the office, and other distractions, dinner has become less important than it used to be. Still, since you'll usually have more time to cook and eat in the evening, this is one of the biggest categories in the book. Besides, leftovers are good for lunch the next day.

Party

Everybody loves a party (except my introverted sister, Leslie). Foods in this category are easy to eat and easy to prepare for a crowd. But, as I've said before, almost anything can be adapted for almost any occasion. (Most of the recipes in this book can be increased to feed more people; see Increasing or Decreasing recipes in "The Basics" (page 15).

Whenever You Get the Urge

Some things, mostly desserts, I just want to eat anytime. What the hell, we're adults, aren't we?

Beat the Clock

So you want to eat something, and you want to eat it right now. This breakdown can save you from having one—it gives you an idea of how long it will take before you can put something in your mouth. Remember that the more often you cook, the faster you will get. I can have a four-course dinner for six ready in about forty-five minutes flat.

Zoom (About a Half Hour or Less)

Before It Grows Mold

You're looking at your refrigerator or cupboard and all you have is one celery stalk, three eggs, half a jar of maraschino cherries of dubious origin, a box of onion-flavored matzo, and a jar of Dijon that's running on fumes. Assess what you've got and look here to see what you can make.

I'm in the Mood For...

You can't explain it, but you have a craving for vegetarian mountain Korean cooking. Well, I can't help you there (except to give you the number of a restaurant on East 32nd Street in New York City), but I can direct you to these different types of food.

American

British

Chinese

Comfort

You've Got Time to Kill

So all of your friends are out of town for the weekend. Or the TV weather guy was right and you got four feet of snow. Or you just don't feel like getting out of your pajamas. Then it's the perfect time to stock up on those recipes that are often called for in other dishes throughout the book.

Just for a Laugh

It Doesn't End There...

With each recipe, you'll find some additional information to help guide you to culinary success.

Skill Level

Look for the piece of cake icon on supersimple recipes. Even though all of the recipes in this book are pretty easy, some are just so simple they're almost a joke. Note that difficulty is not always a function of the length of the ingredient list or the method, or the amount of time required to prepare a dish. Also, some of the more difficult recipes such as Apple Pie (page 55) can be made easier by substituting convenience foods such as ready-made pie crust.

Required Reading

At the end of the headnote for each recipe is a list of techniques that you should be familiar with before beginning. All of these techniques are explained in "The Basics" section. If you know them, skip them. Otherwise, I'm afraid you'll have some homework to do.

Yield

At the top of each ingredient list you will see an approximate yield for each recipe. This yield is based on a large portion because I like to eat a lot. You might find that you have a lot of leftovers. Save any leftovers and use them the next day. See "Reheating" (page 16) and "Using Leftovers" (page 21) for advice.

Ingredients

The ingredients list includes specifics about how to get everything ready so you can start cooking. Although some will require advance preparation, I've tried to explain the more difficult procedures in the method. More detailed ingredient information can also be found in the headnote.

Kitchen Stuff

These are the key pieces of equipment you will need on hand in order to be able to complete the recipe. But if you don't have something, try to think up an alternative. I've done wonders with a Swiss Army knife and a camping stove. Use your imagination and don't be afraid to try anything once. Just because someone has a gorgeous kitchen with the latest appliances doesn't mean he or she can cook and vice versa.

Links

At the end of each recipe you'll find a listing of related recipes. These are related for different reasons. Some of them go well together. Others share similar ingredients or techniques. Still others I just think you might want to try. I did a little free-associating to come up with these lists so they are a little quirky. The are not comprehensive, but I think they will point you to some other interesting stuff to try.

Adam's Big Pancake

My friend Adam likes to impress women with this big pancake on Sunday mornings. (I wonder if he tells them it's his mother's recipe.) Despite any implications, intended or otherwise, it's called Adam's Big Pancake because it puffs up three or four inches in the oven while it bakes. Required Reading: Dusting with Powdered Sugar (page 24), Melting (page 25), Mixing versus Overmixing (page 25), Preheating (page 25), Selecting Ingredients (page 11).

Preheat the oven to 425°F. Place the butter in a 9-inch pie plate and set in the oven to melt, about 5 minutes. Watch the butter carefully to make sure it doesn't burn. Meanwhile, in a medium mixing bowl, whisk together all of the remaining ingredients except the confectioner's sugar and lemon juice. When the butter is melted, pour this mixture into the hot pie plate, set the dish back in the oven, and bake for about 20 minutes, until the pancake has puffed up around the sides and has begun to brown. When the pancake is done, it will look like a weird cushion, with some butter floating in the depression in the center.

Remove from the oven, dust with confectioner's sugar, and sprinkle with lemon juice. Slice into wedges and serve immediately. The longer you wait to serve the pancake, the more it will deflate, and the less you will impress.

Links: French Toast (page 123), Pancakes (page 175).

Makes 2 to 4 servings

3 tablespoons unsalted butter

2 large eggs, beaten

$1/2$ cup unbleached all-purpose flour

$1/2$ cup milk

2 teaspoons sugar

Pinch salt

1 pinch nutmeg

Confectioner's sugar

Juice of $1/2$ lemon

Kitchen Stuff

9-inch pie plate

Liquid and dry measuring cups

Measuring spoons

Mixing bowl

Aioli

Aioli is one of the classic sauces (and meals, actually) of France, a specialty of sunny Provence. Like a supergarlicky mayonnaise, the pungent, creamy Aioli is served with everything from roast beef to fresh vegetables to boiled potatoes. It's also great on sandwiches and is particularly good as a condiment on Falafel Vegetable Burgers (see page 119). If your friends don't mind garlic breath, it makes a good dip for a party, too. Classic Aioli is made with a mortar and pestle, but I find the food processor produces good results. Just be sure your garlic is good and puréed before you begin to add the oil so that the finished Aioli doesn't have any unappetizing, large chunks of garlic in it. Required Reading: Emulsifying Demystified (page 13), Making a Sandwich (page 15), Selecting Ingredients (page 11), Smashing Garlic (page 19), Using the Food Processor (page 21).

Makes about 2 cups

1 head of garlic, about 8 to 10 cloves, separated and peeled

1 teaspoon salt

2 large egg yolks

2 cups extra-virgin olive oil

2 tablespoons water

Kitchen Stuff

Food processor

Liquid measuring cup

Measuring spoons

In the bowl of a food processor fitted with the metal blade, place the garlic cloves and salt. Pulse on and off 4 or 5 times to mince the garlic. If the garlic sticks to the sides of the bowl and won't mince, scrape it down and add a couple of tablespoons of the olive oil. Hold down the "on" button for a couple of minutes until the garlic has become a smooth paste. Add the egg yolks and process until frothy and smooth, a good 3 to 4 minutes.

With the machine running, slowly drizzle in the olive oil in a steady stream through the feed tube to form an emulsion. Stop after every $^1/_4$ cup or so to let the machine whip the oil into the egg yolks. When about 1 cup of the olive oil has been added, stop the machine and add the water.

Turn on the machine again and continue adding the oil in a steady stream until all of it is incorporated.

Store in a covered container in the refrigerator until ready to use. Aioli will keep about a week. If the top begins to darken, just stir it up before serving.

Variations
Mockoli
If the garlic flavor of the Aioli is just too overpowering, cut the number of garlic cloves in half and add only 1 cup of the olive oil. Follow the recipe as directed, omitting the water. When all of the oil is incorporated into the garlic yolk mixture, transfer the Aioli to a bowl and stir in 1 cup of prepared mayonnaise (use low-fat if you like).

Links: Avocado Sandwich (page 59), Falafel Vegetable Burgers (page 119), Fried Tofu Sandwiches (page 132), Grilled Vegetables (page 137), Leg of Lamb (page 152).

Apple Pie

Serve with vanilla ice cream. Enough said. Ask someone in the produce section for a good cooking apple. Stay away from Macintosh. Try Northern Spy, Empire, Cortland, Golden Delicious, or Gala. I only like cinnamon in my apple pie, but if you must, add some ground nutmeg or cloves. You can even buy something in the spice section of the grocery store called Apple Pie Spice. It's all in there.

Apple pie is one of those common, simple things that is easy if you know how to do it. About the only difficult part is handling the dough (see Working with Pastry, page 27). You can easily buy commercially produced frozen pie dough to get around the hard part. The result will still be better than any store-bought pie. Required Reading: Cooling (page 24), Cutting Up Things (page 13), Patience (page 16), Selecting Ingredients (page 11), Testing for Doneness (page 20), Working with Pastry (page 27).

Makes one 9-inch pie, serves 8 to 10

8 large cooking apples (see headnote)

Juice of 1 lemon

$^1/_4$ cup white or brown sugar

1 teaspoon ground cinnamon

2 teaspoons pure vanilla extract

$^1/_4$ cup unbleached all-purpose flour

$^1/_2$ cup raisins (optional)

$^1/_2$ cup chopped walnuts or pecans (optional)

3 tablespoons unsalted butter, cut into small pieces

Kitchen Stuff

Cookie sheet

Dry measuring cups

Large mixing bowl

Measuring spoons

9-inch pie plate (deep-dish if you have it) or tart pan

Paring knife

Rolling pin

On a lightly floured work surface, roll out half of the pie crust to at least an 11-inch-diameter circle, slightly less than $^1/_4$ inch thick. Drape the crust on the rolling pin and transfer to a 9-inch pie plate (deep-dish if you have it). Leave the overhang and set in the refrigerator to rest.

Preheat the oven to 425°F. One at a time, peel, core, and slice the apples and place in a large mixing bowl. To prevent browning, after slicing each apple, drizzle some of the lemon juice on the slices and toss them around. Repeat until all of the apples are sliced and coated with lemon.

Add all of the remaining ingredients except the butter to the apples. Mix with a wooden spoon or fork until all of the apples are coated with the flour and spices. Remove the pastry-lined pie plate from the refrigerator. Transfer

the filling into the crust. Pack the apples in. Don't worry if it looks like there's too much filling, it will cook down as the pie bakes. Dot the top of the apples with $^1/_2$-inch pieces of the butter.

Roll out the remaining half of the dough into a circle slightly smaller than the first. Transfer it to the top of the pie by rolling it up on the rolling pin and unrolling it on top of the apples. Fold up the overhang of crust from the bottom to seal the edges all the way around the pie. Trim off any excess crust so that the seam is an even thickness all the way around. Press the seam of the crust with the tines of a fork dipped in flour. Alternately, you can pinch the crust between your thumb and forefinger to make a pretty, fluted edge. Poke 2 or 3 holes in the top of the crust with the point of a knife to allow the steam to escape during baking.

A freshly baked, properly made pie is a triumph. Nearly every-one loves the combination of a good, flaky crust, and a tender filling, whether it's fresh fruit, delicate custard, or rich cream. Pies are remarkably easy to make. You won't have to rely on instant fillings, pie-crust mixes, or frozen pies.

—MARION CUNNINGHAM, *THE FANNIE FARMER BAKING BOOK*
(KNOPF, 1984)

Place the pie on a cookie sheet and set in the middle of the preheated oven. Reduce the heat to 400°F and bake for 30 minutes, until the crust begins to turn light brown. Turn down the heat to 350°F and continue baking for 35 minutes. If the crust begins to burn around the edges, cover the edges with strips of aluminum foil. If you aren't sure if the pie is done, stick a small knife through one of the holes in the top crust and poke around to see if the apples inside are tender.

Remove from the oven. You really should allow the pie to cool completely before serving, otherwise the filling will be runny and serving it will be a mess. If you can't wait, just spoon some of the filling run off onto the pieces of pie as you serve them.

Variations

Apple Tart

In general, there are three differences between a tart and a pie. One is that a tart is usually shallower. It is also most often baked without a top crust. And because tarts are open-faced, the fruit is usually arranged more artistically. Tart pans have removable bottoms to make the finished product easier to serve. To turn this apple pie into an apple tart, roll out the bottom layer of crust as for the apple pie and transfer it to a shallow pie plate or tart pan. Press the dough on the bottom around the edge to be sure it sits flush against the pan. Trim the edge to be even with the pan. Follow the procedure for preparing the apple filling, but instead of dumping it into the center of the crust, arrange the spice-coated apple slices one at a time in concentric circles to fill the tart. Fill in any gaps with additional apple slices. Dot with butter and bake as directed, checking to make sure the apples are cooked through by inserting the point of a knife into a slice or two to see if they are tender. Cool and serve.

Links: Applesauce (page 57), Light and Flaky Pie Crust (page 157), Pecan Pie (page 182), Simple Pie Crust (page 226).

Applesauce

Making your own applesauce is so simple, once you do it, you'll never buy applesauce again. Use a good cooking apple such as Northern Spy, Cortland, Golden Delicious, or Gala. If you have a food mill (see Straining, page 20), you don't even have to peel and core the apples. Just cook them until they are soft and pass the whole mess through the mill. Without a mill, you will have a chunkier sauce, which I happen to prefer. Serve applesauce as it is, warm with a drizzle of heavy cream, or as an accompaniment to Latkes (page 151). Required Reading: Cutting Up Things (page 13), Selecting Ingredients (page 11), Straining (page 20).

Put all of the ingredients in a medium saucepan, cover, and set over a low flame. Simmer until the apples are soft, 20 to 25 minutes. Mash with a fork until the mixture is the texture of a chunky puree. Cool.

If using a food mill, do not peel, core, or seed the apples. Place all of the ingredients in the saucepan and simmer until the apples are tender, 20 to 25 minutes. Pass the apples, peels, cores, seeds, and all, through the food mill to puree. Adjust the seasoning with lemon and more cinnamon.

Links: Apple Pie (page 55), Bran Muffin on a Diet (page 73), Latkes (page 151).

Makes 2 to 3 cups

5 to 6 cooking apples
(see headnote), peeled, cored, and cut into chunks

2 tablespoons water

1 teaspoon cinnamon

1 teaspoon pure vanilla extract

2 tablespoons sugar (optional)

Juice of $^1/_2$ lemon

Kitchen Stuff

Food mill (optional)

Measuring spoons

Paring knife

Saucepan with cover

Aunt Josephine's Chocolate Cake

Makes one 9 x 13-inch cake,
or two 9-inch rounds,
or two 8^1/2-inch loaves,
serves 10 or more

Butter and flour for pan(s)

4 ounces (4 squares) unsweetened baking chocolate

^{1}/4 pound (1 stick) unsalted butter

1 cup water

1 teaspoon baking soda

^{1}/2 pint sour cream

2 cups sugar

2 large eggs

2 cups unbleached all-purpose flour

1 teaspoon baking powder

Kitchen Stuff

Cooling rack

Dry and liquid measuring cups

Measuring spoons

Mixing bowls

9 x 13-inch cake pan, or two
9-inch round pans, or two
8^1/2 x 4^1/2 x 2^1/2-inch loaf pans

Rubber spatula

Small saucepan

A classic sour cream chocolate cake, this is the only cake my siblings and I ever requested for our birthdays. It's dense and chocolaty and delicious. Whipped cream (page 239) and fresh raspberries are the best accompaniments, but I like it just plain, too.

We were devastated when as children we learned that Aunt Josephine wasn't our real aunt, just a childhood friend of my mother's. So don't worry about calling this Aunt Josephine's Chocolate Cake when you serve it because obviously it doesn't matter if she's related to you or not. If anyone asks who Aunt Josephine is, tell them she's a small Italian woman who lives in Ridgefield, New Jersey. Required Reading: Buttering and Flouring (page 23), Cooling (page 24), Dusting with Powdered Sugar (page 24), Measuring (page 25), Melting (page 25), Mixing versus Overmixing (page 25), Preheating (page 25), Selecting Ingredients (page 11), Testing for Doneness (page 27).

Preheat the oven to 350°F. Butter and flour a 9 x13-inch cake pan or two 9-inch round cake tins, or two 8^1/2-inch loaf pans. In a small saucepan, place the chocolate, butter, and water and melt over medium heat. Stir to combine and set aside to cool. Meanwhile, in the sour cream container, stir the baking soda into the sour cream. The soda will begin to react and the mixture will froth and expand. Don't be alarmed, just make sure it doesn't overflow onto the counter. Set aside.

In a large mixing bowl combine the sugar, the cooled chocolate mixture, and the eggs. Add the sour cream mixture, alternating it with the flour. After you've added 1 cup of the flour, add the baking powder. Continue alternating the ingredients and stir until well combined.

Pour into the buttered and floured pan(s) and tap on the counter to remove any air bubbles. Set on the middle rack of the preheated oven and bake for about 35 minutes, or until the middle springs back to the touch and the sides have pulled away from the pan. The loaf pans will take about 50 minutes. Don't overbake the cake or it will be dry.

Remove from the oven and let cool on a rack for about 1 hour. Run a knife around the edge of the pan and invert onto a cooling rack or serving plate. Allow the cake to cool completely before serving.

Links: Whipped Cream (page 239).

Avocado Sandwich

During the phase of my life when I was a vegetarian, this sandwich saw me through the tough times. The combination of toasted multigrain bread, mayonnaise, and tomatoes is as close to the flavor of a BLT as you can get (see BLT Tartlets on page 69 for the real thing). Look for ripe Haas avocados (the small, dark, nubby ones) that are firm but soft to the touch. If they feel like rocks, let them sit on the counter for a few days to ripen. Use any combination of vegetables that pleases you. Required Reading: Cleaning Produce (page 12), Making a Sandwich (page 15), Selecting Ingredients (page 11).

Spread 1 side of each piece of toast with mayonnaise. Holding the avocado in one hand, run a sharp paring knife around the avocado pit, and twist the avocado to separate the fruit into halves. With a spoon, scoop out the avocado flesh and divide it among 2 pieces of the bread. Mash the avocado with a fork to make sure it stays put. Sprinkle with salt and pepper. Layer on the remaining ingredients, top with the remaining pieces of bread, cut in half, and enjoy.

Variations

Guacamole Sandwich

Use leftover Guacamole (page 139) instead of the avocado and proceed as directed.

Rémoulade Twist

If you want a slightly more exciting sandwich—although it's hard for me to believe that anything could be more exciting than the original—use Aioli (page 53) or Rémoulade (page 197) instead of mayonnaise.

Links: Aioli (page 53), BLT Tartlets (page 69), Guacamole (page 139), Rémoulade (page 197).

Makes 2 sandwiches

4 slices multigrain bread, toasted

2 tablespoons mayonnaise

1 ripe Haas avocado (see headnote)

Pinch of salt

3 to 4 grinds black pepper

4 slices tomato

6 to 10 slices cucumber

1 handful sprouts

3 to 4 leaves lettuce

Kitchen Stuff

Fork

Sharp knife

Wide mouth

Badda-Bing Chicken

Makes 4 servings

¹/₂ cup unbleached all-purpose flour

1 teaspoon salt

10 grinds black pepper

4 large skinless and boneless chicken breasts

3 to 4 tablespoons virgin olive oil

2 tablespoons unsalted butter

1 shallot, minced, or 1 tablespoon chopped onion

¹/₄ pound fresh mushrooms, sliced

About ¹/₄ cup chopped fresh herbs (Italian parsley, thyme, oregano, or a combination)

¹/₄ pound prosciutto or other ham or salami, thinly sliced

¹/₄ pound fresh mozzarella or other cheese, thinly sliced

¹/₂ cup dry white wine

¹/₂ cup chicken stock (if canned, use salt-free)

Kitchen Stuff

Large skillet with a lid (or you can use a cookie sheet to cover the pan)

Liquid and dry measuring cups

Measuring spoons

Plate or wide soup bowl

This is a recipe from my friend Tom, who also happens to be the main photographer for this book. It was devised by Tom's late friend Mike, who described the last step in the preparation by saying, "You hit the pan with stock and white wine and badda-bing, that's the dish." Don't be fooled by the long list of ingredients—it's really that simple. Required Reading: Preheating (page 16), Saucing (page 17), Sautéing, Frying, and Stir-Frying (page 19), Seasoning to Taste (page 19), Selecting Ingredients (page 11), Testing for Doneness (page 27).

On a plate or in a wide soup bowl, place the flour and season it with the salt and pepper. Mix well. Dredge the chicken breasts on both sides in the seasoned flour and dust off any excess. The breasts should have a very fine coating of flour. In a large skillet (that has a cover), heat the olive oil and butter over medium-high heat. Lay the chicken breasts in the hot pan and sauté until golden brown on the bottom, 8 to 10 minutes. Turn over the breasts and repeat on the second side. Remove the breasts from the pan and set aside on a plate. Don't worry if the chicken isn't fully cooked, it will be cooked again in the sauce.

Return the pan with the oil and butter still in it to the flame. Add the shallot or onion and mushrooms and sauté until soft. Add the fresh herbs. Push the mushroom mixture off to the side of the pan and return the chicken breasts to the pan. On top of each breast lay a slice of prosciutto and a piece of mozzarella. Pour the white wine and chicken stock into the pan and place the cover on. The steam from the liquid will cause the cheese to melt. When the cheese is sufficiently melted and the chicken is cooked through, 5 to 8 minutes, remove the chicken to serving plates. If you are not sure if the chicken is cooked, cut one of the breasts open and peek inside. The melted cheese will cover up the incision. Stir the mushrooms around in the sauce. Allow the juices in the pan to continue boiling until they reduce slightly, and pour over the breasts, being sure to divide the mushroom mixture evenly among the 4 portions. Serve hot.

Links: Cabbage Sauté with Caraway (page 79), Chickpea Salad (page 94), Yogurt Curried Chicken (page 240).

Baked Artichoke Hearts

Everybody serves marinated artichoke hearts for company. Why not spruce them up a little? This is an easy side dish that says you...um...care.

Required Reading: Selecting Ingredients (page 11).

Preheat the oven to 350°F. In a small baking dish, arrange the rinsed and drained artichokes in a single layer. Lay the strips of roasted red pepper, if using, on the artichoke hearts and sprinkle with pine nuts. Sprinkle with bread crumbs, Parmesan cheese, and black pepper. Set in the middle of the oven and bake for 20 minutes, until the cheese and bread crumbs have browned and the artichokes are heated through. Serve warm.

Links: Roasted Vegetables (page 209).

Makes 4 side dish servings

2 small (6-ounce) jars marinated artichoke hearts, rinsed in cold water and drained

1 roasted red pepper, peeled and cut into thin strips (optional), see page 209

3 tablespoons pine nuts

$1/2$ cup unflavored bread crumbs

$1/4$ cup freshly grated imported Parmesan cheese

4 to 5 grinds black pepper, or to taste

Kitchen Stuff

Baking dish

Dry measuring cups

Measuring spoons

Baked Beans While You Sleep

Makes 8 cups, serves 6 to 8

2 cups dried small white beans (such as cannellini or great northern beans)

6 to 8 ounces salt pork (available in the meat section of the supermarket) or meaty bacon, rinsed under cold water and cut into thin strips

6 cups water

1½ teaspoons salt

2 onions, finely sliced

2 large cloves garlic, minced

2 tablespoons unsulphured molasses (usually near the pancake syrup in the grocery store)

2 tablespoons Dijon mustard

2 bay leaves

1 teaspoon minced fresh ginger, or a scant ¼ teaspoon ground ginger

10 to 12 grinds black pepper

Kitchen Stuff

Large oven-proof dish or pot with a tightly fitting lid

Liquid measuring cups

Measuring spoons

Why bake beans when you can just open a can? Because the flavor doesn't compare. And people will be so impressed that you made them. Little do they know you did it while you were sleeping. That's right, these beans bake through the night. Put them up before you go to bed, take them out of the oven in the morning, and you will have delicious baked beans for dinner that night, if you don't eat them for breakfast, that is. Pretty cool, eh? Required Reading: Patience (page 16), Peeling Onions (page 16), Selecting Ingredients (page 11), Smashing Garlic (page 19).

Pick over the beans to be sure there are no stones (see Mister Bean on page 164). Rinse twice in cold water. In a heavy oven-proof casserole with a tightly fitting lid, combine all of the ingredients. If you have a pot with handles that can go in the oven (made of metal, not plastic or wood), use that. Turn the oven to 250°F, set the beans inside, and sleep tight for 12 hours. When you come back after 12 hours, the beans will have turned a dark reddish brown and the delicious smell will be overwhelming. Eat some for breakfast and save the rest for dinner.

Links: Hamburgers—they go really well (page 140), Mister Bean (page 164).

Banana Bread

About those rotting bananas and that sour milk: if you aren't diligent about cleaning out your refrigerator, here is a recipe for you. Banana Bread is different from Banana Cake (see page 64) because it's baked in a loaf pan and it has a denser, coarser texture. It's actually a part of a family of baked goods called quick breads (so named because they take less time to prepare than breads raised with yeast.) Banana bread is terrific for breakfast or with a cup of coffee in the afternoon. Required Reading: Bringing to Room Temperature (page 12), Buttering and Flouring (page 23), Chopping Nuts (page 23), Cooling (page 24), Creaming (page 24), Measuring (page 25), Mixing versus Overmixing (page 25), Preheating (page 16), Selecting Ingredients (page 11), Testing for Doneness (page 20).

Preheat the oven to 325°F. Butter and flour an 8^1/$_2$ x 4^1/$_2$ x 2^1/$_2$-inch loaf pan. In a large mixing bowl, cream together the butter and the sugar. Add the eggs and beat until blended. In a separate bowl, combine the flours, salt, and baking powder. Add the flour mixture to the butter mixture, alternating with the mashed banana and the sour milk. Just before the last of the flour is stirred in, add the walnuts and chocolate chips, if using. Pour into the buttered and floured loaf pan and bake in the preheated oven for 1 hour and 15 minutes or until the top cracks and a small knife inserted in the center comes out clean (except for some streaks of chocolate and banana). Allow to cool for 20 minutes. Run the tip of a knife around the edge of the pan and invert onto a rack to cool to room temperature.

Links: Banana Cake (page 64), Honey-Buttermilk Cornbread (page 144).

Makes one 8^1/$_2$-inch loaf

Butter and flour for pan

^{1}/$_4$ pound (1 stick) unsalted butter, at room temperature

1 cup sugar

2 large eggs

1 cup unbleached all-purpose flour

1 cup whole-wheat flour

^{1}/$_2$ teaspoon salt

1 teaspoon baking powder

1 cup mashed very ripe banana (about 4 bananas)

^{1}/$_2$ cup sour milk

^{1}/$_2$ cup chopped walnuts, optional

^{3}/$_4$ cup chocolate chips, optional

Kitchen Stuff

Cooling rack

8^1/$_2$ x 4^1/$_2$ x 2^1/$_2$-inch loaf pan

Liquid and dry measuring cups

Measuring spoons

Mixing bowls

Banana Cake

Makes one 9 x 12-inch cake,
or two 9-inch cake rounds,
serves 8 to 10

Butter and flour for pans

1 teaspoon baking soda

$^3/_4$ cup sour or regular milk

$^1/_4$ pound (1 stick) unsalted
butter, at room temperature

$1^1/_2$ cups sugar

3 large eggs

2 cups unbleached all-purpose
flour

1 teaspoon baking powder

$^1/_2$ teaspoon cinnamon

3 very ripe bananas, the more
spotty the better, mashed with
a fork

Kitchen Stuff

Cooling rack

Liquid and dry measuring cups

Measuring spoons

Mixing bowls

9 x 12-inch cake pan or
two 9-inch round pans

Mrs. Cooper was our neighbor in Toronto while I was growing up. Born in Poland, Mrs. Cooper was a good cook and an excellent baker. There was always a cake cooling on the windowsill at the Cooper house. If it wasn't this banana cake, it was her "famous" apple cake (which is a secret recipe). I got the banana cake recipe, which I now share with you.

Required Reading: Bringing to Room Temperature (page 12), Cooling (page 24), Creaming (page 24), Mixing versus Overmixing (page 25), Preheating (page 16), Selecting Ingredients (page 11), Testing for Doneness (page 27).

Preheat the oven to 350°F. Butter and flour a 9 x 12-inch cake pan or two 9-inch round pans. In a small soup bowl or other container, combine the baking soda and the sour milk. In a large mixing bowl, cream the butter and sugar by beating with a wooden spoon to form a smooth, light, creamy paste. If you have an electric mixer with strong beaters or a paddle attachment, use that. Once you are finished, or if you are having some trouble achieving a smooth paste, add the eggs and continue beating. In a small bowl, stir together the flour, baking powder, and cinnamon, and add to the creamed butter mixture,

alternating with the mashed bananas and the milk mixture. Continue stirring to form a smooth batter. Pour into the prepared pan(s) and bake in the preheated oven for 30 minutes or until the center springs back when touched and the sides of the cake have pulled away from the pan. Cool for 20 minutes on a rack. Run the tip of a knife around the edge of the pan and invert the cake onto a rack to finish cooling.

Links: Banana Bread (page 63), Chocolate Sauce—it's delicious served with the cake (page 98).

Beans from the Girl from Ipanema

I met my friend Dorothea Ellman-Winston on a whirlwind culinary tour through Brazil. A native of Ipanema who now lives in Westchester, New York, Donna Dorothea led a group of food and travel writers on a mind-opening journey through the great regional cuisines of the world's fifth-largest country. It was a trip I will never forget, partly because Dorothea and I have become good friends. Dorothea is a wonderful cook. And when I asked her for a simple Brazilian recipe to include in this collection, these beans from the area called Ceará are what she offered. I've adapted the recipe to make it a little easier. Dorothea suggests serving the beans with brown rice (see Waves of Grain, page 236) and Sautéed Greens (see page 214). Almost like a soup, these beans are an excellent alternative to chili when you have a crowd to feed. Required Reading: Cutting Up Things (page 13), Patience (page 16), Resting (page 17), Seasoning to Taste (page 19), Selecting Ingredients (page 11), Simmering versus Boiling (page 19), Skimming (page 19), Smashing Garlic (page 19), Testing for Doneness (page 20).

The night before you make this dish, pick through the beans to remove any stones or broken beans and soak in enough cold water to cover (see Mister Bean on page 164). The following day, drain the beans and begin preparing the dish. In the bottom of a large saucepan, heat the oil over medium-high heat. Add the bacon and sauté for 5 to 8 minutes, until it begins to give off some of its fat. Add the garlic and onion and sauté until translucent. Add the water and the chuck and bring to a boil. Lower the heat and simmer for about 1 hour. Add the beans. If there isn't enough liquid to cover the beans, add more water. Return the mixture to the boil, lower the heat, and simmer for another 40 minutes. Add more water as necessary to keep the beans wet. Add the butternut squash and salt and continue simmering until the squash, the beans, and the meat are tender, about 1 hour, depending on the tenderness of the meat. Add the scallions and black pepper and turn off the heat. Allow the beans to sit for 10 minutes before serving.

Links: Baked Beans While You Sleep (page 62), Mister Bean (page 164), Sautéed Greens—for the greens on the side (page 214), Waves of Grain—for the rice on the side (page 236).

Makes 6 to 8 main course servings

1 pound dried pink or white beans (such as pinto or cannellini beans)

1 tablespoon vegetable oil

1/2 pound slab bacon, cut into 3/4-inch cubes, or 1/2 pound bacon slices, chopped

5 large cloves garlic, minced

1 medium onion, finely chopped

6 cups water

1 pound lean beef chuck, cut into 1 x 2-inch cubes

1 medium butternut squash, peeled, seeded, and cut into 1-inch cubes

2 teaspoons salt, or to taste

2 scallions, finely sliced, white and green parts

10 to 15 grinds black pepper

Kitchen Stuff

Large saucepan or stock pot with cover

Mixing bowl

Beef Ribs, Korean-Style

If you ever plan to have a barbecue, serve these ribs. When my sister Carrie and I used to cater together, we once served these ribs (known as <u>bulgolgi</u> in Korean) as an hors d'oeuvre for an outdoor wedding. The guests literally came running to the grill when they saw the ribs were ready.

Because the meat marinates for three days, the ginger, garlic, and soy perfume and tenderize the beef. Barbecuing over a hot flame caramelizes the marinade and makes the ribs crispy. You can also broil the ribs until crisp. The recipe takes a little forethought, but aside from knowing what you are going to eat a few days in advance, it couldn't be any easier. The ribs are also great for a crowd because you can increase the recipe for however much you need. Required Reading: Grilling, Barbecueing, and Broiling (page 13), Increasing or Decreasing Recipes (page 15), Marinating (page 15), Patience (page 16), Selecting Ingredients (page 11), Working with Meat (page 21).

Three days before you are planning to grill the ribs, combine all of the ingredients in a mixing bowl or other container. Mix to be sure the meat is covered with the marinade. Cover and set in the refrigerator for 3 days. On the third day, lift the meat out of the marinade and barbecue over hot coals or broil under a very hot, preheated broiler. The ribs will only take a few minutes on each side to be cooked through. Serve with rice.

Links: Chop Suey, Korean–Style (page 99), Waves of Grain— for the rice on the side (page 236).

Makes 5 to 6 servings

One 4- to 5-inch piece fresh ginger, peeled and minced, ($^1/_4$ cup)

2 cloves garlic, minced

$^1/_2$ cup brown sugar

$^1/_2$ cup dry sherry (drinking sherry, not cooking sherry)

$^1/_2$ cup soy sauce

$2^1/_2$ pounds thinly sliced beef short ribs (aka Miami ribs)

Kitchen Stuff

Aluminum foil

Barbecue grill or broiler

Large bowl

Measuring cups

Beef Stew

Makes 4 to 6 servings

3 tablespoons vegetable oil

2 pounds stewing beef,
cut into 1-inch chunks

1 to 2 large onions, thinly sliced

3 tablespoons unbleached
all-purpose flour

2 cups red wine

3 cups water

1 bay leaf

1 tablespoon salt

10 to 15 grinds black pepper

2 large russet or red potatoes,
peeled and cut into chunks

3 carrots, peeled and cut into
thick slices

1/4 pound mushrooms, sliced

Kitchen Stuff

Large saucepan with lid

Liquid measuring cups

Measuring spoons

Anything that gets better as it sits should be part of your culinary repertoire. There's nothing like having people over for dinner and having everything ready long before they get there, or making a large pot of something that's terrific as leftovers. Beef Stew is one of the best make-ahead entrées. It's easy. It only takes one pot. And as it sits in the refrigerator the flavors blend and become even better than when it was originally made. Add any vegetables you like, but put quicker cooking ones in toward the end so that they do not overcook. Serve the stew with buttered egg noodles and a glass of hearty red wine. Required Reading: Cleaning Produce (page 12), Cutting Up Things (page 13), Patience (page 16), Peeling Onions (page 16), Preheating (page 16), Seasoning to Taste (page 19), Selecting Ingredients (page 11), Simmering versus Boiling (page 19), Working with Meat (page 21).

In a large saucepan (with a lid), heat the oil over medium-high heat. Add the beef and toss to brown the cubes of meat on all sides, about 5 minutes. Add the onion and continue sautéing until the onion is translucent. Add the flour and continue cooking for 3 to 4 minutes. Pour in the red wine and water and stir to make sure there are no lumps of flour.

Add the bay leaf, salt, and pepper, cover the pot with the lid just slightly ajar, turn down the heat, and simmer for 1 hour. Check the stew occasionally to be sure it isn't burning. If the liquid evaporates, add more wine or water to be sure the meat is covered with liquid.

After one hour, add the potatoes and the carrots and mix well. Cover and cook for another 20 minutes. Add the mushrooms and continue simmering, covered, until the vegetables are tender and the meat falls apart, about 30

more minutes. The stew will have thickened considerably. If it gets too thick (begins to stick to the bottom of the pot and burn) add some more water.

Adjust the seasoning with salt and pepper and remove from the heat. If you are planning to serve the stew on another day, cool it to room temperature, cover, and refrigerate. Reheat on top of the stove, adding some more water if it has thickened too much. Serve over buttered egg noodles.

Links: Beans from the Girl from Ipanema (page 65), Braised Red Cabbage (page 72), Just-Between-You-and-Me Mashed Potatoes (page 149), Pasta Primer—for the accompanying noodles (page 177).

BLT Tartlets

This recipe was developed by my friend Bonnie for the first Thanksgiving dinner served at The James Beard House in New York City. Bonnie wanted to make every aspect of the menu as all-American as possible, so she devised this hors d'oeuvre, based on the classic BLT sandwich. The tartlets were an instant success and they became the signature dish of Bonnie's catering company. At my prebook party (see details on page 243) they disappeared before they left the kitchen. After my party, Jeff Steingarten, the food editor of <u>Vogue</u>, called them a "brilliant innovation." They are so kitschy and so delicious that you'll make them again and again. Required Reading: Making a Sandwich (page 15), Seasoning to Taste (page 19), Selecting Ingredients (page 11).

Preheat the oven to 350°F. With a rolling pin, working one slice at a time, flatten the bread to the thickness of a floppy diskette and cut a round from each slice with a 2-inch diameter cookie cutter or a wine glass. Press the rounds gently into mini muffin tins to form the shape of small cups. Toast in the preheated oven until the bread is pale golden and firm, about 10 minutes. Remove from the oven and cool on a rack. (These toast cups can be prepared several days in advance and stored in an airtight container.)

In a medium bowl, combine approximately equal amounts of the finely chopped lettuce, crumbled bacon, and finely diced tomatoes. Add enough of the mayonnaise to bind the mixture. Season with salt and plenty of black pepper. (The mixture should taste exactly like the filling of a BLT sandwich.) Fill each toast cup with a spoonful of the filling mixture and serve immediately.

Links: Avocado Sandwich—similar flavors (page 59).

Makes about 30 hors d'oeuvres

1 loaf Pepperidge Farm or Arnold white thinly sliced sandwich bread

1/2 head iceberg lettuce, finely chopped

1/2 pound sliced bacon, cooked, drained, and finely crumbled

1 pound ripe tomatoes, seeded and finely diced

1/4 cup Hellman's mayonnaise, no low-fat or fat-free allowed

1/4 teaspoon salt

10 to 12 grinds black pepper, or to taste

Kitchen Stuff

Cookie cutter or wine glass

Measuring cups

Measuring spoons

Mini muffin tins

Mixing bowl

Rolling pin

Blueberry Sour Cream Muffins

A good muffin is hard to find. Almost all the muffins sold commercially come from mixes. This is an easy recipe for a rich muffin that will make the morning a little easier to deal with. Keep them in the freezer and microwave one or two for 15 to 25 seconds for a satisfying breakfast.

Required Reading: Cooling (page 24), Cutting in Butter (page 24), Measuring (page 25), Mixing versus Overmixing (page 25), Preheating (page 25), Selecting Ingredients (page 11), Testing for Doneness (page 27), Using the Food Processor (page 21).

Preheat the oven to 350°F. Line muffin tins with paper muffin cups or grease the tins with softened butter. In a large mixing bowl, combine the flour, sugar, baking powder, and salt. Cut in the butter until the mixture resembles small crumbs. Alternately, you can pulse this mixture in the food processor to get the right consistency. In a separate bowl, beat together the milk, sour cream, and eggs. Pour the liquid mixture into the dry ingredients and stir with a wooden spoon just until the batter comes together. It will be almost as stiff as cookie dough, but lighter in consistency. Be careful not to overmix or the muffins will be tough. Stir the blueberries into the batter.

Spoon the batter into the prepared muffin tins—use your fingers if you have to—filling them to the top. Bake for about 40 minutes or until a knife or skewer inserted into the center comes out clean and the top of the muffin bounces back to your touch. Allow the muffins to cool for 10 minutes in the tins before removing them to wire racks to cool to room temperature. Store in an airtight container or freeze.

Variations

Berry Good Muffins
Substitute other berries such as raspberries or blackberries. Or use a combination.

Blueberry Cornmeal Muffins
Reduce the flour to $2^3/_4$ cups and add $^3/_4$ cup yellow cornmeal. Proceed with the recipe as directed.

Lemon Blueberry Muffins
Add the juice and grated zest of a lemon to the liquid mixture and proceed with the recipe as directed.

Links: Banana Bread—it's like a big muffin (page 63), Bran Muffins (page 73).

Makes 12 muffins

$3^1/_2$ cups unbleached all-purpose flour

1 cup white or brown sugar

$1^1/_2$ tablespoons baking powder

Pinch salt

$^3/_4$ cup ($1^1/_2$ sticks) unsalted butter, chilled

1 cup milk

$^1/_2$ cup sour cream or plain or vanilla-flavored yogurt

2 large eggs, slightly beaten

2 cups fresh blueberries

Kitchen Stuff

Food processor (optional)

Measuring cups

Measuring spoons

Mixing bowls

Muffin tins

Paper muffin cups (optional, but easier than buttering the tins)

Braised Red Cabbage

Makes 4 side dish servings

2 tablespoons butter, bacon fat, or duck fat (no comments, please)

1 onion, peeled and roughly chopped

3 tablespoons red wine vinegar

3 tablespoons sugar

1 small head red cabbage, roughly sliced (5 to 6 cups)

1 bay leaf

$1/2$ teaspoon salt, or to taste

7 to 8 grinds black pepper, or $1/2$ teaspoon cracked red peppercorns (available in specialty food shops)

Kitchen Stuff

Hammer (to crack red peppercorns, if using)

Measuring spoons

Saucepan with a lid or other suitable cover

When I was in college in Ithaca, New York, I used to gather a group of my friends at least once a month—sometimes I was left to go it alone—to dine at a terrific local restaurant called Dano's on Cayuga. It was the only place within a hundred miles where you could get a decent meal. Even now that I live in the Big Apple, Dano remains one of my favorite chefs. Since graduation, Dano and his wife, Karen, and I have become good friends. My favorite dish is still one of the first things Dano ever served me—Braised Red Cabbage. This is a perfect side dish for a warming Beef Stew (see page 68). It's also delicious with Just-Between-You-and-Me Mashed Potatoes (see page 149). Required Reading: Cutting Up Things (page 13), Patience (page 16), Peeling Onions (page 16), Reheating (page 16), Sautéing, Frying, and Stir-Frying (page 19), Seasoning to Taste (page 19), Selecting Ingredients (page 11), Testing for Doneness (page 20).

In a medium-sized saucepan, heat the butter or fat over medium-high heat. Sauté the onion in the butter for 2 to 3 minutes. Add the vinegar, sugar, cabbage, bay leaf, salt, and the black or red pepper. It looks like you will have too much cabbage, but the volume decreases considerably as it cooks. Cover the pot until the cabbage has given off some of its liquid, 4 to 5 minutes.

Remove the cover and continue to cook the cabbage, pushing it from one side of the pan to the other to enable the liquid at the bottom of the pan to evaporate. The cooking process should take about 25 minutes total. Be careful not to overcook the cabbage—it should not be mushy. The cabbage is best if it is prepared 1 or 2 days in advance. Reheat in a small saucepan before serving.

Links: Beef Stew—goes well (page 68), Cabbage Sauté with Caraway (page 79), Just-Between-You-and-Me Mashed Potatoes (page 149), Osso Buco (page 172).

Bran Muffins

While my sister Carrie was writing a cookbook on naturally sweetened desserts called <u>The Naturally Sweet Baker</u>, also published by Macmillan, I helped her by copyediting the manuscript and by testing a few recipes. I particularly liked this bran muffin recipe because of the intense flavor and the moist texture, neither of which are typical of most bran muffins. If you want to make a muffin with less fat, I've given you a variation that substitutes applesauce for some of the oil. Required Reading: Cooling (page 24), Lowering Fat (page 15), Measuring (page 15), Mixing versus Overmixing (page 25), Selecting Ingredients (page 11).

Preheat the oven to 375°F. Line muffin tins with paper muffin cups or generously grease the tins with softened butter. In a large mixing bowl, whisk together the buttermilk, oil, molasses, eggs, and vanilla. In a separate bowl, combine the flours, baking soda, salt, and bran. Stir the dry ingredients into the wet ingredients with a wooden spoon. Be careful not to overmix or the muffins will be tough. Stir in the raisins.

Divide the batter equally among the prepared muffin tins, filling them to the top. Bake for 25 to 30 minutes, until they are firm to the touch and a knife tip or skewer inserted in the center of a muffin comes out clean. Let cool for 10 minutes in the tins before transferring to a wire rack to cool to room temperature.

Variation

Bran Muffin on a Diet
Substitute $^1/_2$ cup applesauce (see page 57 or use store-bought) for $^1/_2$ cup of the vegetable oil. Proceed with the recipe as directed.

Links: Blueberry Sour Cream Muffins (page 71).

Makes 16 large muffins

2 cups buttermilk

1 cup vegetable oil

1 cup unsulphured molasses, blackstrap if available (usually near the pancake syrup in the grocery store)

3 large eggs

1 teaspoon vanilla

$2^2/_3$ cups unbleached all-purpose flour

1 cup cake flour (available in the baking section of the grocery store)

1 tablespoon baking soda

$^1/_2$ teaspoon salt

2 cups wheat bran

1 cup raisins

Kitchen Stuff

Measuring cups

Measuring spoons

Mixing bowls

Muffin tins

Paper muffin cups (optional, but easier than buttering the tins)

Bread Pudding

I must make a bread pudding at least once a month because I almost never finish a loaf of bread and I hate to throw anything out. There are about a million variations (see Savory Bread Pudding on page 215), but this one, based on a recipe by my late friend and great cookbook writer Richard Sax, is easy and, better yet, it works with a variety of breads (challah and brioche are best). For a good bread pudding your bread must be stale, otherwise it won't soak up the custard mixture. Serve it with Caramel Sauce (page 84) or Chocolate Sauce (page 98), and you will never throw away a piece of stale bread again, either. Required Reading: Cooling (page 24), Selecting Ingredients (page 11), Separating Eggs (page 25), Testing for Doneness (page 27).

Preheat the oven to 375°F. In a large mixing bowl, whisk together the eggs, egg yolks, and sugar. Beat in the milk, vanilla, and cinnamon. Add the bread cubes and raisins or currants, if using, and stir to combine.

Pour this mixture into a 2-quart baking dish (a soufflé dish or deep-dish pie plate works well). The custard mixture should come close to the top of the dish. If it doesn't, mix up some more using the same proportions of milk to egg, and pour it on the top. Set in the middle of the preheated oven, and bake until the pudding is set, about 1 hour, depending on the depth of the dish. (Insert a butter knife or skewer into the center and it should come out clean when the pudding is done.) The bread pudding will be all puffed up like a soufflé when it comes out of the oven, but it will fall as it cools. Allow the pudding to cool to room temperature or chill it in the refrigerator before serving.

Links: Caramel Sauce (page 84), Chocolate Sauce (page 98), Savory Bread Pudding (page 215).

Makes about 6 servings

5 large eggs

2 large egg yolks

$^2/_3$ cup sugar

3 cups milk

2 teaspoons pure vanilla extract

1 teaspoon cinnamon

$^1/_2$ to $^3/_4$ loaf (depending on size) stale bread, cut into $^3/_4$-inch cubes to produce about $3^1/_2$ cups

$^1/_2$ cup raisins or dried currants (optional)

Kitchen Stuff

Large mixing bowl

Liquid measuring cups and spoons

2-quart baking dish, such as a soufflé dish, deep-dish pie plate, or gratin dish

Brisket

Makes 6 to 8 servings,
with plenty of leftovers

3 onions, chopped

3 carrots, chopped

One 4- to 5-pound brisket,
trimmed of excess fat

About 2 tablespoons salt

About 20 grinds black pepper

1 tablespoon paprika

5 cloves garlic, smashed but
not peeled (see Smashing Garlic,
page 19)

One 3-ounce can tomato paste

³/₄ cup water

Kitchen Stuff

Large roasting pan

Liquid measuring cups

Measuring spoons

Sharp knife for slicing

My friend Adam insisted that I include a recipe for brisket in my book because not only is it easy to make, it tastes better left over (particularly on sandwiches). Brisket is a traditional Jewish cut of beef that's easy to find in most grocery stores or butcher shops. As long as you're cooking, you may as well make a big one (about five pounds) so you'll have it around. It shrinks almost by half when it cooks, so don't be alarmed by how big it looks. If you have a smaller piece of meat than I specify in the recipe, just decrease the other ingredients in proportion. Brisket is best if it's made over two days, so that the meat has time to chill before you slice it. But in a pinch you can do it all in one day. Required Reading: Cooling (page 24), Cutting Up Things (page 13), Making a Sandwich (page 15), Peeling Onions (page 16), Reheating (page 16), Roasting, Braising, and Steaming (page 17), Selecting Ingredients (page 11), Smashing Garlic (page 19), Working with Meat (page 21).

Preheat the oven to 350°F. In the bottom of a roasting pan, place the chopped onions and carrots. Set the brisket on top, fat-side down. Season liberally with about half of the salt, pepper, and paprika. Turn the brisket over and season the other side the same way. Place the smashed garlic in the pan. Spread the top of the brisket with the tomato paste. Pour the water over the meat and into the pan.

Cover tightly with aluminum foil and set in the middle of the preheated oven. Bake, covered, for about 2¹/₂ hours. The brisket should have turned a grayish color, shrunk considerably, and given off a lot of juice. Remove the roasting pan from the oven and allow it to cool. If you have the time, chill the brisket overnight. Otherwise, proceed with the recipe when the brisket is cool enough to handle.

Preheat the oven to 350°F again. Remove any fat that has coagulated at the top of the pan or around the brisket. Remove the brisket from the juice and slice it into ¹/₄-inch-thick slices against the grain. (The grain is the direction of the ridges or striations of the meat. Usually, you should be slicing along the short side of the brisket.)

Return the slices to the pan with the juice, cover again with aluminum foil, and set back in the oven. The brisket should cook for an additional 1¹/₂ to 2 hours, until the meat is tender enough to cut with a fork. Serve hot with some of the pan juices to pour over. Store and reheat the leftovers in the pan juices so the meat stays moist.

Links: Just-Between-You-and-Me Mashed Potatoes—on the side (page 149), Sautéed Greens—ditto (page 214).

Brown Sugar Shortbread

This is a deceivingly simple recipe from my friend Karla. There isn't much to say about these cookies except that if you can't make them, you should get out of the kitchen. For fun, drizzle melted semisweet chocolate on top. Required Reading: Bringing to Room Temperature (page 23), Cooling (page 24), Creaming (page 24), Melting (page 25), Preheating (page 25), Resting (page 25), Selecting Ingredients (page 11).

Preheat the oven to 325°F. In a large mixing bowl, cream together the butter and brown sugar, beating with a wooden spoon until smooth. Add the vanilla and salt. Stir in the flour. The mixture will be crumbly, sort of the consistency of wet sand. Transfer the mixture to a baking dish (9-inch pie plate, springform pan, or square baking pan) and press it with your fingertips to make a smooth, even layer.

Bake in the preheated oven for 35 to 45 minutes, depending on the thickness, until the edges have begun to brown. Remove from the oven, cool for 15 minutes, and cut into the desired shapes while still warm (wedges or squares are easiest to handle). Continue cooling to room temperature before you attempt to get the shortbread cookies out of the pan, or they are likely to fall apart and crumble. Store in an airtight container. The cookies are actually better after they have sat for a day.

Links: Macaroons—the only easier cookie (page 158).

Makes 16 to 24 cookies, depending on how you cut them

1 cup (2 sticks) unsalted butter, at room temperature

1 cup brown sugar

$^{1}/_{2}$ teaspoon pure vanilla extract

Pinch salt

2 cups unbleached all-purpose flour

Kitchen Stuff

Dry measuring cups

Measuring spoons

Mixing bowl

9-inch pie plate, springform pan, or square baking dish

Buttermilk Biscuits

**Makes approximately
twenty-four 1¹/₂-inch biscuits**

4 cups unbleached all-purpose
flour

1 teaspoon salt

2 tablespoons sugar

2 tablespoons baking powder

10 tablespoons (1¹/₄ sticks)
unsalted butter, chilled and
cut into small cubes

1¹/₂ cups buttermilk

Kitchen Stuff

Cookie sheet

Food processor (optional)

Large mixing bowl

Liquid and dry measuring cups

Measuring spoons

1¹/₂-inch cookie cutter or wine
glass

**The first time you make your own biscuits, you'll never again be able to
stomach those hockey pucks they serve at KFC. The secret to a great
biscuit is to handle the dough as little as possible. This recipe, one of my
brother Sheldon's standbys, is completely reliable. The buttermilk gives
these biscuits a great flavor. Once you get it right, try some additions
such as chocolate chips or grated orange zest and currants.** Required
Reading: Cutting in Butter (page 24), Measuring (page 25), Mixing versus
Overmixing (page 25), Preheating (page 25), Resting (page 25), Selecting
Ingredients (page 11), Shortening (page 27), Using the Food Processor
(page 21), Working with Pastry (page 27), Zesting (page 23).

Preheat the oven to 350°F. In a large mixing bowl, combine the flour, salt, sugar, and baking powder. Add the chilled butter to the dry ingredients and toss around to coat the cubes well. With the tines of a fork or two knives—one held in each hand with the blades crossed in the bowl—cut the butter into small pea-sized pieces. Alternately, you can use your fingertips to break up the butter, or process the mixture in two batches in the food processor using on/off pulses. Be sure to keep the butter buried in enough of the flour and butter mixture so that the heat from your hands doesn't melt it. Work quickly. When you are finished, the mixture should resemble coarse crumbs.

Make a well in the center of the flour and pour in the buttermilk. Using a fork, stir the mixture gently until it begins to form a soft dough. Continue mixing until almost all of the flour is incorporated. Dump out onto a clean counter and knead 2 or 3 times until the dough is almost smooth. Don't worry if it looks a little rough around the edges. Let the dough rest for 10 minutes.

With the palm of your hand, pat the dough out until it is about ¹/₂ to ³/₄ inch thick. Using a cookie cutter or a wine glass dipped in flour, cut the dough into 1¹/₂-inch circles. Keep dipping the cutter into flour so that the dough doesn't stick. Bunch up the remaining dough and pat it out again. Cut the remaining dough into circles and discard the scraps (it will be worked too much the third time to produce a good biscuit).

Place the biscuits on an ungreased cookie sheet and bake in the preheated oven for about 15 minutes, or until the biscuits are light brown and have almost doubled in height. To be sure they are done, split a biscuit in half. Serve at once.

Links: Light and Flaky Pie Crust (page 157), Scones (page 219), Shortcake (page 225), Simple Pie Crust (page 226).

Cabbage Sauté with Caraway

This is a quick, easy, and cheap side dish that people love. It's another adaptation of a recipe from my friend Dano, whose restaurant in Ithaca was like a second home to me during college (see Braised Red Cabbage, page 72). It's in the category of dishes that are impressive to people because they have no idea how to do them. The cabbage is great with any kind of meat, salmon, potatoes, or grains. It's kind of wintry, but I eat it in the summer, too. It's also really cheap to make. Required Reading: Cutting Up Things (page 13), Peeling Onions (page 16), Reheating (page 16), Sautéing, Frying, and Stir-Frying (page 19), Seasoning to Taste (page 19), Selecting Ingredients (page 11).

In a large sauté pan or wide saucepan, heat the oil and butter over medium-high heat. Add the onion and sauté until it becomes translucent, 4 to 5 minutes. Add the cabbage and vinegar and sauté until the cabbage wilts and gives off some of its water, about 10 to 15 minutes. Push the cabbage to one side of the pan as it cooks so that the liquid evaporates. Then spread the cabbage out over the bottom of the pan to let it cook some more and push it to the other side to let the liquid evaporate again. Don't worry if it looks like there is a ton of cabbage when you start because it will cook down quite a bit.

Once the cabbage has softened, add the caraway, turn down the heat, and continue cooking until the cabbage is tender, but not mushy, 5 to 8 minutes more. Adjust the seasoning with salt and pepper. The cabbage can be made in advance and reheated as needed.

Links: Beef Stew (page 68), Braised Red Cabbage (page 72), Salmon Fillets with Mustard Sauce (page 212).

Makes 4 to 6 side dish servings

2 tablespoons vegetable oil

2 tablespoons unsalted butter

1 onion, thinly sliced

1 small head white cabbage, cored and thinly sliced

1 tablespoon vinegar (white, cider, white wine, or what have you)

1 tablespoon caraway seeds

1/2 teaspoon salt

8 to 10 grinds black pepper

Kitchen Stuff

Large sauté pan or wide saucepan

Measuring spoons

Caesar Salad

Veni, vidi, mangi. (I came, I saw, I ate.) Before you make a toga out of your bed sheet and a garland out of romaine lettuce to serve this salad at your next theme party, you should know that this garlicky, crouton-adorned classic has nothing to do with the Roman emperor, or even Italy for that matter. It is believed to have been created in 1924 by Caesar Cardini, an Italian chef who owned a restaurant in Tijuana, Mexico (see quote, page 83). As such, it probably makes a perfect accompaniment to barbecued iguana, but I wouldn't know. Actually, it's fine all by itself. Or you can add the ubiquitous neoclassic garnish of grilled chicken breast. The variations are endless. I've suggested a few, but use your imagination. Just be sure that anything you add can stand up to the strong garlic flavor of the dressing. I've included the technique for making your own croutons, but you could easily buy them. Required Reading: Cleaning Produce (page 12), Emulsifying Demystified (page 13), Grilling, Barbecuing, and Broiling (page 13), Selecting Ingredients (page 11), Separating Eggs (page 25), Smashing Garlic (page 19), Using the Food Processor (page 21).

Makes 4 main course servings, or 6 side dish servings, with a little extra dressing left over for another salad

For the croutons

3 tablespoons olive oil

1 clove garlic, smashed

2 to 3 slices stale bread, cut into cubes (a country loaf or dense sourdough bread is best)

Pinch salt

5 to 6 grinds black pepper, or to taste

For the dressing

6 anchovy fillets, or 4 teaspoons anchovy paste

2 small cloves garlic, peeled

2 large egg yolks

Juice of 1 to 2 lemons, to taste

1 cup extra-virgin olive oil

To assemble the salad

1 head romaine lettuce, washed and torn into bite-sized pieces

1/4 cup freshly grated imported Parmesan cheese

5 to 6 grinds black pepper

If you are going to make your own croutons, you need to start with some stale bread. If you do not have stale bread, use fresh, but cut it into cubes and toast it very lightly in the oven before you proceed with the recipe.

In a medium frying pan (if you have nonstick, use it), heat the oil. Add the smashed garlic clove and gently sauté it for 3 to 4 minutes. Add the cubed bread and toss. Continue to sauté the bread cubes, tossing them frequently, until they take on a golden brown color, 5 to 8 minutes. Watch them closely because they burn quickly. As long as the bread soaks up the oil evenly, you shouldn't need to add any more. When the croutons are golden brown, discard the garlic clove, pour off any excess oil, toss with the salt and pepper, and set aside to cool.

For the dressing, it's easiest to use a food processor or blender. In the bowl of the processor fitted with the metal chopping blade, place the anchovies and garlic. Process with on/off pulses until the garlic is minced and the mixture has begun to form a paste. Add the egg yolks and the juice of one lemon and blend until mixed.

With the processor running, slowly drizzle the oil through the feed tube in a constant stream. The dressing should begin to emulsify, becoming thick and creamy. Continue pouring the oil in a slow, steady stream until it is all incorporated. If the mixture is getting too thick (it looks more like a paste than a dressing), thin it down with some more lemon juice or water. Set aside until ready to serve.

Kitchen Stuff

Food processor or blender
(it makes it easier)

Frying pan (to make croutons)

Large mixing bowl

Liquid and dry measuring cups

If you don't have a food processor, you can use a mortar and pestle or a small mixing bowl, a fork, and a small whisk. For this method, you are probably better off using the anchovy paste instead of the fillets.

Finely mince the garlic. Work the garlic into the anchovies in the mortar or mixing bowl with the pestle or the fork to form a paste. Add the egg yolks and the juice of one lemon. Begin to beat in the olive oil in droplets using a whisk or a fork, until all of the oil is incorporated before adding more. Once you have built a sturdy emulsion, you can begin to drizzle in the olive oil in a steady stream. Be sure all of the oil is incorporated. And if it looks like the emulsion might break, thin out the mixture with additional lemon juice and/or water. Set aside.

Just before you are ready to eat, assemble the salad. (The salt in the anchovies in the dressing will wilt the lettuce if you mix it in advance.) Place the romaine in a large salad or mixing bowl. Add the croutons, Parmesan cheese, black pepper, and about half of the dressing. Add more dressing to taste, or allow your guests to add additional dressing to their taste.

Parmesan shavings—made by taking a carrot peeler to the block of cheese—make a sophisticated garnish. Some people like to drape whole anchovy fillets on top of the salad. At any time, if the dressing is too thick, it can be thinned down with lemon juice or a little water. Leftover dressing made

with the food processor will last about three or four days in the refrigerator. The handmade version will only keep about a day because the emulsion is weaker.

Variations

Caesar Dressing, Hold the Anchovies

If the thought of anchovies is just too much for you to take, or you're a strict vegetarian, try this creamy version, which substitutes the strong flavors of capers, Dijon, and Worcestershire sauce to simulate the anchovy flavor (actually this is even closer to the original, which didn't have anchovies in it).

3 small cloves garlic

2 tablespoons capers

1 egg yolk

1 lemon, juiced

Dash Worcestershire sauce

Dash Tabasco sauce

1 tablespoon Dijon mustard

$^3/_4$ cup extra-virgin olive oil

$^3/_4$ cup mayonnaise

Additional capers to taste, chopped

For this version you need to use the food processor. Combine the garlic with the capers in the bowl of the processor and use on/off pulses to mince finely. Add the egg yolk, lemon juice, Worcestershire sauce, Tabasco, and Dijon. Pulse once to blend. With the machine running, add the extra-virgin olive oil in a slow steady stream (as

1924—The Caesar salad is created by some accounts at Tijuana, Mexico, where Italian Air Force veteran Alex Cardini has joined his brother, Caesar, in the hotel (or restaurant) owned by Caesar. When a party of Californians arrives to celebrate July 4, Alex finds little in the cupboard to feed them other than eggs, romaine lettuce, dry bread, Parmesan cheese, garlic, olive oil, lemon juice, and pepper. He makes croutons of the dry bread, mixes them with the other ingredients, calls the result Aviator Salad, and will rename it after his brother (anchovies will later be added).

—James Trager, *The Food Chronology* (Holt, 1995)

explained above) to form a stiff emulsion. Transfer to a mixing bowl and stir in the mayonnaise. For a stronger flavor, stir in more capers that have been finely chopped. Assemble the salad as above.

Caesar on a Diet

Instead of sautéing the croutons in the garlic-flavored oil, toss with salt and pepper and spread them out on a cookie sheet in a single layer. Toast in a preheated 300°F oven until golden brown, about 10 to 15 minutes. Toss the croutons frequently and keep an eye on them because they have a tendency to burn suddenly.

For the dressing, follow the directions, but use only 1 egg yolk and 1/2 cup of extra-virgin olive oil. Once all of the oil is incorporated, spoon in 1/2 cup of low-fat mayonnaise and stir until blended. Assemble the salad the same way.

Grilled Chicken Caesar

With a rubber mallet or the back of a frying pan, gently pound 2 skinless and boneless chicken breasts between two sheets of waxed paper or plastic wrap until the thickness of the flesh is a uniform 1/2 inch. Rub the chicken breasts with olive oil. Cut a clove of garlic in half and rub the cut surface over the breasts. Season with salt, pepper, and assorted herbs (oregano, basil, rosemary, herbes de Provence). Grill on a barbecue or broil until cooked through, about 6 minutes per side. Cut into strips and lay over the Caesar salad as a garnish.

Grilled Lamb Caesar

Skewer 1-inch cubes of lamb shoulder on bamboo skewers and rub with olive oil. Season with salt, pepper, and assorted herbs (oregano, basil, rosemary, herbes de Provence) and grill or broil to desired doneness, 10 to 12 minutes for medium. Remove from skewers and arrange around the Caesar salad just before serving.

Roasted Vegetable Caesar

In addition to the romaine, add an assortment of roasted vegetables when you toss the salad (see page 209).

Links: Aioli—the dressing is very similar (page 53), Roasted Vegetables (page 209).

Caramel Sauce

This is a simple dessert sauce that's great poured over Bread Pudding (page 75) or vanilla ice cream. Required Reading: Saucing (page 17), Selecting Ingredients (page 11).

Makes about 1 cup

$^1/_3$ cup sugar

2 tablespoons water

2 tablespoons unsalted butter

$^3/_4$ cup heavy cream
(aka whipping cream)

Kitchen Stuff

Frying pan or small saucepan

Liquid and dry measuring cups

Measuring spoons

In a heavy frying pan or a small saucepan, combine the sugar, water, and butter and set over medium-high heat. Bring the mixture to a boil, stir to dissolve the sugar, and continue cooking. As the mixture boils, it will froth and take on the consistency of marshmallow fluff. Continue boiling until the fluff turns the color of deep caramel, 8 to 10 minutes.

Pour in the heavy cream and stir with a wooden spoon. The caramel will harden into lumps when it comes into contact with the cold cream, and then melt and dissolve as it continues cooking. When no lumps remain, after about another 5 minutes of cooking, remove from the heat and serve.

Links: Bread Pudding (page 75).

Cheesecake Brownies

My friends Kathleen and Blake offered me this recipe because they make these brownies all the time and people love them. I love them, too. They are a little more complicated than One-Pot Brownies (page 171), but when you get bored making just your basic brownie, give these creamy, cheesy desserts a try. Required Reading: Cooling (page 24), Melting (page 25), Mixing versus Overmixing (page 25), Preheating (page 25), Selecting Ingredients (page 11), Testing for Doneness (page 27).

Preheat the oven to 350°F. Butter a 9-inch square baking pan. To prepare the brownie base, melt the chocolate in the top of a double boiler or in a stainless-steel bowl set over simmering water. Stir until smooth and set aside to cool. In a large mixing bowl, combine the sugar and butter and beat with a wooden spoon until creamy. Add the eggs, vanilla extract, and salt. Mix well. Add the melted chocolate and flour and stir until blended. Pour into the prepared pan and set aside.

In another large bowl, combine the cream cheese, sugar, and butter, and beat until creamy. Add the eggs, milk, and flour, and mix well. Pour this mixture over the brownie base. Bake in the preheated oven for about 35 minutes, until the cheesecake layer is set. Cool completely before cutting into squares.

Links: One-Pot Brownies (page 171), You Gotta Try These Blondies (page 241).

Makes 9 large, rich brownies

For the brownie base
12 ounces semisweet chocolate

$^2/_3$ cup sugar

6 tablespoons unsalted butter

2 large eggs

1 teaspoon pure vanilla extract

$^1/_2$ teaspoon salt

1 cup unbleached all-purpose flour

For the cheesecake topping
1 pound cream cheese, at room temperature

1 cup sugar

5 tablespoons unsalted butter

4 large eggs

$^1/_4$ cup milk

2 tablespoons unbleached all-purpose flour

Kitchen Stuff

Double boiler or stainless-steel bowl set over a saucepan

Liquid and dry measuring cups

Measuring spoons

Mixing bowls

9-inch square baking dish

Cheese Thing

thing, n. 1. some entity, object, or creature that is not or cannot be specifically designated or precisely described.

My mother has been making this dish for so long, you'd think it would have a real name by now. "Cheese Thing" doesn't really do it justice, what with the gooey, crispy melted cheddar and tomatoes and crunchy noodles, but that's all we've ever called it. It is the ultimate comfort food.

Cheese Thing is good to eat at every stage—sitting on the counter raw waiting to bake, hot out of the oven, or reheated in a frying pan for breakfast the next day. Although it can be made in a matter of minutes, it's best if it sits for a few hours or overnight before baking.

My siblings and I have tried to modify the recipe, but we always prefer the original. You may be tempted to substitute one pound medium cheddar for the half pound each of mild and sharp, but trust me, the result is not as good. I have been known to make and eat an entire Cheese Thing myself after an emotionally taxing day. Heat leftovers in a nonstick frying pan. Required Reading: Cutting Up Things (page 13), Reheating (page 16), Selecting Ingredients (page 11).

Bring a large pot of salted water (at least five quarts) to a boil. Add the penne and cook until al dente, about 8 minutes. Don't worry if the pasta is a little undercooked, it will be finished in the oven. Meanwhile, cut both cheeses into 1/2-inch cubes. Leave the tomatoes in their juice and cut them into bite-sized pieces with a knife or for fun, squeeze them with your hands.

When the pasta is done, drain and return it to the pot. Add the butter and stir until almost melted. Add the cheese, tomatoes, sugar, and salt and stir well. Pour the mixture into a 2-quart baking dish—glass or ceramic is best. For optimal results, the Cheese Thing should sit for 12 to 24 hours before baking, although it can be baked right away. It can stay covered in the refrigerator for up to three days or it can be frozen at this point for up to a month.

When ready to bake, preheat the oven to 400°F. Set the Cheese Thing on a rack in the middle of the oven and bake for about 1 hour or until it is bubbly and the noodles poking out of the top have browned considerably. Serve hot as an entrée with a salad, or as a side dish for meat, or cold for breakfast the next morning.

Links: Pasta Primer (page 177).

Makes 1 to 8 servings, with leftovers

1 pound penne rigatte or similar tubular pasta (rigatoni or regular penne work well)

1/2 pound (1 brick) sharp cheddar cheese

1/2 pound (1 brick) mild cheddar cheese

One 28-ounce can whole, peeled tomatoes with juice

1/4 pound (1 stick) unsalted butter

2 tablespoons sugar

1 teaspoon salt

Kitchen Stuff

Large pot

Measuring spoons

2-quart baking dish, preferably not more than 2 inches deep

Cherry Tomatoes with Butter and Parsley

Makes 4 side dish servings

3 tablespoons butter

1 pint cherry tomatoes,
stems removed and washed

Pinch salt

6 to 8 sprigs Italian parsley,
rinsed, dried, and finely chopped

Kitchen Stuff

Medium skillet

When it's hard to find ripe tomatoes, which is almost always, ripe cherry tomatoes are usually available (for the most part they are grown in greenhouses). Not just for salads, cherry tomatoes also make a good vegetable side dish. Required Reading: Sautéing, Frying, and Stir-Frying (page 19), Selecting Ingredients (page 11).

In a medium skillet, heat the butter. Add the cherry tomatoes, and sauté until the skin begins to wrinkle, 5 to 8 minutes. Toss in the salt and chopped parsley and cook for another minute or two. Serve warm.

Links: Anything for dinner.

Chicken Paprikash

"Paprikash schmaprikash," you say? Just because this classic Hungarian dish was bastardized by homemaker magazines in the fifties doesn't mean it isn't delicious. In fact, Hungarian food authority George Lang considers it one of the pillars of Hungarian cuisine. The secret is to use the best paprika you can find. If yours has been sitting on the shelf since you moved into your apartment five years ago, do yourself a favor and throw it out. Hungarian paprika, made without the seeds and ribs of the chile peppers so that the flavor is sweeter, works better than the more common Spanish variety. This dish is traditionally served over egg noodles that have been tossed with butter, salt, and freshly ground pepper.

Required Reading: Saucing (page 17), Sautéing, Frying, and Stir-Frying (page 19), Selecting Ingredients (page 11), Tempering (page 20), Testing for Doneness (page 20), Working with Meat (page 21).

In a large soup bowl or small baking dish, combine the flour for dredging with the teaspoon of salt and the black pepper. If you are using whole chicken pieces, separate the wings from the breasts and cut the breasts in half with a sharp, heavy knife. Also separate the legs from the thighs, and if the thighs are very large, cut them in half. Dredge the chicken pieces in the flour mixture so that they are well coated. Tap off any excess flour.

In a saucepan or high-sided frying pan that is big enough to hold all of the chicken in one layer (and that has a tightly fitting cover), heat the oil over a medium-high flame. Fry the chicken on all sides until golden brown, 7 to 8 minutes.

Add the onion and the garlic and continue cooking until the onion is translucent, 3 to 4 more minutes. Add the additional flour and the paprika

and fry for another 3 or 4 minutes. Pour in the chicken stock, the wine, if using, and season with salt and pepper.

Turn down the heat, cover, and let simmer until the chicken is cooked through and has pulled away from the bone, about 1 hour. (If you want to make the dish in advance, you can refrigerate it for a day or two. Before serving, bring the chicken to a simmer.)

Spoon a couple of tablespoons of the hot gravy into the sour cream—a technique called "tempering"—and pour the sour cream back into the chicken, stirring until blended. Serve over egg noodles tossed in butter and seasoned with salt and pepper.

Links: Pasta Primer—for the noodle accompaniment (page 177).

Makes 4 servings

About 1 cup unbleached all-purpose flour for dredging, plus 2 tablespoons

1 teaspoon salt

About 10 grinds black pepper

3 pounds chicken parts, or 1 whole 3- to 4-pound fryer chicken, cut into 10 pieces

1/3 cup vegetable oil

1 large onion, sliced

1 clove garlic, minced

2 tablespoons Hungarian paprika, the best and freshest available (see headnote)

2 1/2 cups chicken stock (if using canned, make sure it's salt-free)

1/2 cup white wine (optional)

Additional salt and freshly ground black pepper to taste

1/2 cup sour cream or plain yogurt

Kitchen Stuff

Large sauté pan or deep frying pan with a tightly fitting lid

Large soup bowl or small baking dish

Liquid and dry measuring cups

Measuring spoons

Chicken Salad

Since Jack Nicholson immortalized the chicken salad sandwich on toast in <u>Five Easy Pieces</u>, how can a hip, rad, fly cookbook (like this one) be without a recipe for it? Use leftovers from a Roasted Chicken (page 203) or the boiled chicken from a Chicken Soup (page 92). If you have less chicken than the recipe calls for, use less mayonnaise. As with most salads, any combination of vegetables and condiments will do—pickles, peanuts, raisins, mustard, fresh herbs, capers. Use what you have on hand. And don't hold the chicken salad. Required Reading: Increasing or Decreasing Recipes (page 15), Making a Sandwich (page 15), Selecting Ingredients (page 11).

In a medium mixing bowl, combine all of the ingredients. If necessary, adjust the consistency with more mayonnaise—sometimes if the chicken is dry, the salad will require more mayonnaise, and some people prefer their chicken salad gloppy. Adjust the seasoning with salt and pepper. Serve on toasted bread with lettuce, tomato, sprouts, or whatever you like on a sandwich.

Variations

Chicken Salad on a Diet
If you would rather not eat so much mayonnaise, substitute 3 tablespoons of nonfat yogurt for 3 tablespoons of the mayonnaise.

Chicken Salad Vinaigrette
Omit the mayonnaise and Dijon mustard and substitute $1/4$ cup of French Vinaigrette (page 125).

Links: Chicken Soup (page 92), Classic Tuna Salad (page 103), Curried Chicken Salad (page 113), French Vinaigrette (page 125), Roasted Chicken (page 203).

Makes enough filling for 4 to 6 hefty sandwiches

2 cups cooked, diced white and dark chicken meat

1 rib celery, diced

$1/4$ medium red onion, chopped (optional)

1 tablespoon capers, chopped

1 dill pickle, diced

2 teaspoons Dijon mustard

$1/4$ cup mayonnaise

Squirt of fresh lemon juice

Pinch salt

5 to 6 grinds black pepper, or to taste

Kitchen Stuff

Dry measuring cups

Measuring spoons

Mixing bowl

Chicken Soup

Makes 5 quarts, about 16 bowls of soup

One 4 to 5 pound soup chicken, stewing hen, or other old bird rinsed under cold water and cut into quarters

5 large carrots, peeled and cut into large chunks

4 large onions, cut into large chunks

Top half of a bunch of celery, with the leaves

10 sprigs Italian parsley

5 sprigs fresh dill (optional)

2 turnips, peeled and cut into chunks (optional)

10 black peppercorns

2 tablespoons salt (omit if making stock)

Water to cover, about 6 to 8 quarts

Kitchen Stuff

Large 10- or 12-quart stock pot with cover

Strainer

I've included this recipe because it's delicious and sometimes when you are sick, all you want is a bowl of chicken soup. If you don't have anyone to make it for you, and you are too far away to have New York's Second Avenue Deli deliver, you just have to do it yourself.

There are many different techniques, but my mother just always put everything in a pot and let it simmer. If you can find something called a soup chicken, stewing hen, or pullet, use it. In a pinch, any chicken will do. Save the chicken meat for Chicken Salad (see page 91). The dill and the turnips make a sweet, flavorful broth, but if you don't have them, don't worry. If you leave out the dill and, more importantly, the salt, the strained soup can be used in any recipe that calls for chicken stock. Just salt the soup to taste before you serve it. Required Reading: Seasoning to Taste (page 19), Selecting Ingredients (page 11), Working with Meat (page 21).

In a large stock pot, place all of the ingredients and add enough cold water to cover. Bring to a boil and skim off any white scum that rises to the surface. Cover with the lid slightly ajar, turn down the heat to a simmer, and cook until the broth has taken on a deep golden color and a rich taste, at least 2^1/$_2$ hours. If you prefer a clear soup, strain the broth into a large container or another pot.

Remove the boiled chicken and some of the vegetables. If you don't mind overcooked carrots and onions in your chicken soup, cut the vegetables into small pieces and serve them in the soup. Skim the fat and adjust the seasoning. If you have the time, the best way to remove all of the fat is to chill the soup in the refrigerator overnight. The fat will congeal at the surface and you can just lift it off with a spoon.

Serve with boiled egg noodles, rice, or pasta, or use the soup as a base for other soups. If you freeze the soup in ice cube trays or small containers, you can always have it on hand for a bowl of soup or to use in other recipes.

Variations

Mamacita Rosenberg's Chicken Soup Oaxacena
My friend Barbara Ann created this recipe one winter while she and her husband, Bob, were staying in Oaxaca, Mexico. To the basic chicken soup recipe, add 3 large cloves garlic, peeled and left whole; 3 fresh jalapeño peppers, seeded and chopped; and 2 or 3 small dried chiles. Omit the dill. Proceed with the recipe as directed. Serve the spicy broth with small shapes of egg pasta, cut-up fresh avocado, chunks of fresh ripe tomato, chopped fresh cilantro, and a squirt of lime. It's a little spicy, a little unusual, but it's really good.

My mother tended to evaluate women on their soup, and her verdict that "she can't even make a decent chicken soup" left no room for doubt about the unfortunate woman's worth in other areas. In our home, chicken soup was the answer to everything, never mind the question. It appeared to celebrate triumphs and it brought comfort in sadness. It was offered when we were in blooming health and when we were ill. Yet it was special enough to distinguish wedding dinners.

—MIMI SHERATON, *THE WHOLE WORLD LOVES CHICKEN SOUP* (WARNER, 1995)

Chicken Soup from a Roasted Chicken or Turkey Carcass

If you have the carcass of a Roasted Chicken (page 203) or turkey left over, you can easily turn it into a soup. Place the carcass and any leftover chicken in a pot (cut it up if you have to make it fit). Add 3 carrots, 2 onions, 2 whole cloves, the top of a bunch of celery, 10 peppercorns, 1 bay leaf, and 1/2 parsnip. Cover with water (about 8 cups), bring to a boil, turn down the heat, and simmer for 1 to 2 hours. Strain the soup and use it as stock or as a base for other soups.

Chicken, Rice, and Tomato Soup

To 6 cups of strained chicken soup (regular or roasted-chicken based), add 2 diced carrots, 2 chopped stalks of celery, 1/2 diced parsnip, 6 diced plum or roma tomatoes, and 3/4 cup white rice that's been rinsed twice in cold water. Bring to a boil, turn down the heat, and simmer until the rice is tender, about 30 minutes. Adjust the seasoning with salt and freshly ground pepper.

Links: Anything that uses broth or stock, Chicken Salad (page 91), Pasta Primer (page 177), Roasted Chicken (page 203).

Chickpea Salad

Makes 2 to 3 side dish servings

One 14-ounce can (about 1$^1/_2$ cups) chickpeas, drained

$^1/_2$ medium red pepper, seeded and diced

$^1/_2$ cup black olives, pitted

3 scallions, thinly sliced

$^1/_4$ cup French Vinaigrette (page 125)

Salt and freshly ground black pepper to taste

Kitchen Stuff

Dry and liquid measuring cups

Medium mixing bowl

Almost like Hummus before it's pureed (see page 148), this is a good side dish for a sandwich or a topping for greens. Purists would insist on cooking your own chickpeas (aka garbanzo beans), but I think canned beans are fine when you want to eat the salad today. (Actually, it tastes even better if it sits overnight.) As with other salads, use whatever vegetables you have on hand. Required Reading: Seasoning to Taste (page 19), Selecting Ingredients (page 11).

In a medium bowl, combine all of the ingredients. Adjust the seasoning and chill.

Links: French Vinaigrette (page 125), Hummus (page 148), Mister Bean (page 164).

Chocolate Chip Cookies

When I lived with my friend Matt, who helped me test a lot of the recipes for this book, he was forever making chocolate chip cookies. Well, that's not exactly true. He was forever making chocolate chip cookie batter. I'm not sure he ever got around to baking them because he preferred them raw. As everyone will tell you, the best recipe is on the chocolate chip package. In case you buy your chips in bulk or you threw away the package, here is the one I use. Required Reading: Bringing to Room Temperature (page 12), Cooling (page 24), Creaming (page 24), Selecting Ingredients (page 11).

Preheat the oven to 375°F. In a large mixing bowl, beat the butter with a wooden spoon to soften. Add both sugars and continue beating until the mixture is blended. If you have the strength, keep beating until the mixture is light and fluffy. This is called creaming. Otherwise, add the vanilla and eggs and beat until smooth.

Stir in the flour, baking soda, and salt until blended. Add the chocolate chips and nuts, if using. Drop the batter by tablespoonfuls onto cookie sheets, about 2 inches apart to allow room for spreading. Bake 9 to 10 minutes if you like a chewy cookie, 12 minutes for a crunchy cookie.

Remove from the oven and cool slightly so the cookies harden a little before you gently remove them from the pan with a metal spatula. Store in an airtight container, if they last, or freeze them.

Links: Chocolate Nut Biscotti—they're like chocolate chip cookies, only harder (page 97), You Gotta Try These Blondies—they're like chocolate chip cookies, only thicker (page 241).

Makes 2 to 3 dozen cookies, depending on how big you like them

$^1/_2$ pound (2 sticks) unsalted butter, at room temperature

$^3/_4$ cup brown sugar (light or dark, doesn't really matter)

$^3/_4$ cup white sugar

1 teaspoon pure vanilla extract

2 large eggs

2$^1/_3$ cups unbleached all-purpose flour

1 teaspoon baking soda

1 teaspoon salt

2 cups (12-ounce package) chocolate chips

1 cup chopped walnuts or pecans (optional)

Kitchen Stuff

Cookie sheets

Dry measuring cups

Measuring spoons

Metal spatula

Mixing bowl

Wooden spoon

Chocolate Cloud Cake

Makes one 8-inch cake, serves 8 to 12 (because it's so rich)

$^1/_2$ pound top-quality bittersweet chocolate (Lindt, Valrhona, or Callebaut, for example), coarsely chopped

$^1/_2$ cup (1 stick) unsalted butter, cut into chunks

6 large eggs

1 cup sugar

2 tablespoons cognac or Grand Marnier (optional, but delicious)

Grated zest of 1 orange (ditto)

Kitchen Stuff

Double boiler or stainless-steel bowl set over a small saucepan

Dry measuring cups and spoons

8-inch springform pan

Mixing bowls

Waxed paper

Whisk or electric mixer

This recipe was given to me by Richard Sax, one of my dearest friends in the food business, who died in 1995. Richard was a warm, generous person and a prolific writer. He gave me this recipe one day when I asked for a suggestion for a chocolate dessert to bring to a party. It is an easy, elegant cake that everybody loves. This recipe appeared in Richard's masterpiece, <u>Classic Home Desserts</u> (Chapters), published just before his death. Required Reading: Beating Egg Whites and Whipping Cream (page 23), Selecting Ingredients (page 11), Separating Eggs (page 25), Testing for Doneness (page 27).

Preheat the oven to 350°F. Line the bottom of an 8-inch springform pan with a round of waxed paper; do not butter the pan. In the top of a double boiler or in a stainless-steel bowl set over simmering water, place chocolate to melt. Remove from the heat and whisk in the butter.

Into separate mixing bowls, separate 4 of the eggs. Add the remaining 2 whole eggs to the yolks along with $^1/_2$ cup of the sugar. Whisk until blended. Add the melted chocolate and butter mixture to the yolks. Whisk in the cognac or Grand Marnier, and orange zest, if using, beating until blended.

Using an electric beater or a good whisk and a strong arm, beat the egg whites until foamy. Gradually add the remaining $^1/_2$ cup of sugar and continue to beat the whites until they form soft mounds that hold their shape, but are not stiff. Stir about $^1/_4$ of the beaten egg whites into the chocolate mixture to lighten it, then gently fold in the remaining whites. Pour the filling into the prepared pan. Bake the cake in the oven 35 to 40 minutes, until the top is puffed and cracked, and the mixture is no longer wobbly. Do not overbake or the cake will be dry. Cool in the pan on a wire rack (leave the sides of the pan on). The cake will sink as it cools, forming a crater in the center with high sides. At serving time—the cake should be served warm or at room temperature—run a knife around the edges of the cake, then carefully remove the sides of the pan. If you like, fill the crater with Whipped Cream (see page 239), and dust with cocoa or cinnamon.

Links: Whipped Cream (page 239).

Chocolate Nut Biscotti

The James Beard Foundation's pastry pontiff Nick Malgieri brought these biscotti to my prebook party (see page 243). Although the desserts were supposed to be set to the side and put out once everyone tasted the other food, when I went to arrange these cookies on a serving plate, there was only one left in the tin. That tells you how good they are.

In Italian, the word <u>biscotti</u> literally means "twice-cooked." So like almost all biscotti recipes (see also Crunchy Poppy Seed Biscotti, page 111), these cookies are baked once, cut, then baked again until crisp. Don't let that extra step fool you into thinking they are complicated. It's easy, but it just takes a little more time. Required Reading: Chopping Nuts (page 23), Patience (page 16), Preheating (page 16), Selecting Ingredients (page 11), Testing for Doneness (page 20).

Set the rack in the center of the oven and preheat the oven to 350°F. Line a cookie sheet with aluminum foil. (You will need a second cookie sheet lined with foil later to rebake the biscotti.) In a large mixing bowl, whisk together the eggs and salt until liquid. Whisk in the sugar and vanilla. Beat in the butter, then stir in the nuts and chocolate chips.

In another bowl, combine the flour with the cocoa, baking powder, and cinnamon. Fold the flour mixture into the egg mixture until all of the flour is absorbed—the dough will be pretty sticky.

Spoon the dough onto the foil-lined pans in the shape of two separate logs, each about 1 inch thick by 2^1/$_2$ inches wide by about 15 inches long. Use a rubber or metal spatula to adjust the shape, if necessary. Bake the logs of dough about 30 minutes, or until risen and firm when pressed with your fingertips. Remove from the oven and cool to room temperature.

Lower the oven to 300°F. Using a sharp serrated knife, slice the baked logs crosswise, diagonally, about ^{1}/$_4$ to ^{1}/$_2$ inch thick. The thickness you choose doesn't matter as long as all of the biscotti are cut uniformly. Return the biscotti to the pan (you'll need the second pan to fit them all), cut side down, and bake about 20 minutes on each side (40 minutes in total), until the biscotti are dry and crisp. Pay close attention to make sure they don't burn (you'll have to look closely because the cookies are dark to begin with. I rely on my nose in this case.) Remove from the oven and cool to room temperature on the pans. Store in an airtight container.

Links: Chocolate Chip Cookies (page 95), Crunchy Poppy Seed Biscotti (page 111).

Makes about 4 dozen cookies, depending on how thinly they are sliced

3 large eggs

Pinch salt

1 cup sugar

1 teaspoon pure vanilla extract

^{1}/$_2$ cup (1 stick) unsalted butter, melted and cooled to room temperature

1 cup coarsely chopped hazelnuts or macadamia nuts

2 cups (12-ounce package) semisweet chocolate chips

2^1/$_4$ cups unbleached all-purpose flour

^{1}/$_4$ cup unsweetened cocoa powder

1 tablespoon baking powder

1 teaspoon cinnamon

Kitchen Stuff

Aluminum foil

Cookie sheets

Dry measuring cups

Measuring spoons

Mixing bowl

Rubber spatula

Serrated knife

Chocolate Sauce

Makes about 2 cups

$^1/_2$ cup (1 stick) unsalted butter

4 ounces ($^1/_4$ pound) semisweet chocolate (the better the quality, the better the sauce)

$^1/_2$ cup sugar

$^1/_2$ cup unsweetened cocoa powder

3 tablespoons strong coffee

$^1/_3$ cup corn syrup (light or dark, doesn't matter)

$^3/_4$ cup heavy cream

Pinch cinnamon

Pinch salt

Kitchen Stuff

Double boiler or a stainless-steel bowl set over a pot of simmering water

Liquid and dry measuring cups

Measuring spoons

This is one of the richest, chocolatiest sauces you'll ever taste. I first came across it while I was executive editor of <u>Art Culinaire</u>. We did a feature of Dawn Rose, who was then pastry chef of Olives in Boston. I've been making a variation of it ever since. There is so much chocolate in it that the sauce hardens when it cools, so you should gently heat it in the microwave or in a metal bowl set over boiling water if you're not going to use it right away. (To be honest, it tastes pretty good straight out of the refrigerator.) Just be careful not to turn the flame up too high when you are reheating the sauce because it has a tendency to scorch. Required Reading: Melting (page 25), Reheating (page 16), Saucing (page 17), Selecting Ingredients (page 11).

In the top of a double boiler or in a stainless-steel bowl set over a pot of simmering water, melt the butter and chocolate together. In a separate saucepan, combine the sugar, cocoa powder, and coffee and whisk together over low heat. Add the melted chocolate and the remaining ingredients. Continue whisking over low heat until the sugar has dissolved and the sauce develops a smooth consistency. (Rub a dab between your thumb and forefinger to test it. If you still feel the granules of sugar, the sauce is not yet done.)

Remove from the heat. You can use the sauce right away, but if not, you should store it in an airtight container in the refrigerator (it will last for about a month). Then, when you go to use it, gently heat the sauce up in the microwave, or in a stainless-steel bowl set over a pot of simmering water.

Links: Anything that might taste better with some chocolate sauce on it.

Chop Suey, Korean-Style

Ed Kim's Korean Chop Suey has become a favorite dish among a small group of my friends. The Korean name is <u>jab chai</u>, pronounced "chop cheh," and your success rests on your ability to find the noodles. If you are in New York, Ed suggests going to Sam Bok, a little Asian grocery store next to Town Hall on 43rd Street. In the back, you'll find a clear package of long, thin, transparent noodles made from sweet potato starch. Everything will be in Korean, but, as Ed explains, these are the consequences of living in a multicultural society. Anyway, in very small print on the back of the package, it will say for "jab chai" or sometimes "jab chae." The noodles are also available at most Asian grocery stores or large grocery stores with Asian food sections. If you cannot find the noodles, you can substitute bean threads or rice threads. Required Reading: Sautéing, Frying, and Stir-Frying (page 19), Seasoning to Taste (page 19), Selecting Ingredients (page 11).

In a pot of cold water, soak the noodles until they are soft, about 1 hour. Meanwhile, heat a large frying pan or wok over high heat until very hot. Add 1 tablespoon of the vegetable oil and 1 tablespoon of the sesame oil. Lightly brown a pinch of the garlic. Add the onion, stirring quickly, and add a dash of the soy sauce and a dash of the oyster sauce. Transfer to a large bowl.

Repeat this process with the peppers, mushrooms, watercress, snow peas, baby corn, and water chestnuts, cooking each vegetable separately, but adding oil, garlic, soy sauce, and oyster sauce each time. Add a little more oyster sauce to the baby corn and water chestnuts. For the carrots, add 1 tablespoon of ginger along with the garlic, and the orange juice along with the soy and oyster sauces. When each vegetable is

done, add it to the large bowl. Cook the noodles according to the directions on the package usually by boiling them 5 minutes in salt water. They should be soft, but chewy. When they are done, drain the water and set the noodles aside. Dry the pot. Place the remaining sesame oil and vegetable oil in the pot and set over a medium flame. Add 1 tablespoon of oyster sauce and the remaining garlic and ginger and sauté until tender. Add the noodles and the stir-fried vegetables. Stir to mix well. Adjust the seasoning with salt and pepper. Serve warm with *kim chee* (Korean pickled cabbage). It's even better the next day.

Links: Beef Ribs, Korean-Style (page 67), Stir Fried Watercress or Bok Choy (page 228).

Makes 4 to 6 servings

1 bag sweet potato starch noodles—jab chai (see headnote)

³/4 cup peanut oil

³/4 cup toasted sesame oil

3 cloves garlic, minced

1 onion, chopped

¹/4 cup soy sauce

¹/4 cup oyster sauce

2 bell peppers, 1 red and 1 yellow, seeded and cut into thin strips

1 handful fresh shiitake mushrooms, sliced

1 bunch watercress

1 handful snow peas, cleaned

1 can baby corn

1 small can sliced water chestnuts

2 carrots, cut into thin strips

One 2-inch piece ginger, minced

2 tablespoons orange juice

Salt and black pepper to taste

Kitchen Stuff

Large frying pan or wok

Liquid measuring cups

Measuring spoons

Clafoutis

Not a disease, but a sweet, custardy dessert native to France, clafoutis (pronounced klah-foo-tee) is a simple and impressive dessert that's kind of like a sweet quiche. Sour cherry clafoutis is traditional, but you can substitute anything from blueberries to mango with delicious results. Sometimes clafoutis is baked in a pie crust. Other times it is just baked in a flat dish, much like a crème brûlée, but without the brûlée. Required Reading: Preheating (page 25), Selecting Ingredients (page 11), Testing for Doneness (page 27), Working with Pastry (page 27).

Makes one 10-inch tart, serves 8 to 10

²/₃ recipe Light and Flaky Pie Crust (page 157) or Simple Pie Crust (page 226) or store-bought pie crust (optional)

3 large eggs

³/₄ cup sugar

1 teaspoon pure vanilla extract, or 1 tablespoon flavored liqueur (such as Grand Marnier, Kirsch, or Canton Ginger Liqueur)

1 cup heavy cream (aka whipping cream)

³/₄ cup unbleached all-purpose flour

1 pint fresh sour cherries, pitted, or 2 cups other fruit such as blueberries, chopped mango, or fresh figs

Kitchen Stuff

Liquid and dry measuring cups

Measuring spoons

Mixing bowl

Rolling pin (if using the crust)

10-inch tart pan with a removable bottom or a 9-inch deep-dish pie plate

Whisk

Preheat the oven to 425°F. If you intend to use a crust, roll out the dough on a lightly floured surface to an 11- or 12-inch circle, less than ¹/₄ inch thick. Transfer the dough to a 10-inch tart pan with a removable bottom or a 9-inch deep dish pie plate. Trim the edges. Line with aluminum foil, fill with rice or dried beans to weigh down the crust, and set in the preheated oven for 10 to 15 minutes, until the crust begins to set. Lift out the aluminum with the beans or rice (being careful not to leave any behind in the crust) and bake for an additional 10 minutes, or until the crust begins to lightly brown. Remove from the oven and cool. Turn down the oven temperature to 400°F.

In a medium-sized bowl, beat together the eggs and sugar with a whisk until the mixture takes on a pale yellow color and becomes thick and ribbony (when you lift up the whisk, the mixture should fall in a slow, steady stream). Beat in the vanilla or liqueur. Add the heavy cream and stir in the flour with a wooden spoon. If using a crust, spread the cherries or other fruit in an even layer on the bottom of the prebaked crust. If not using a crust, spread the fruit directly on the bottom of the pan. Pour over the batter, being careful not to let it overflow.

Set the tart in the middle of the preheated oven and bake for 30 to 45 minutes, until the filling has set, browned, and risen. If you are unsure whether the clafoutis is done, gently insert a bamboo skewer or butter knife in the center and pull it out. The skewer will be clean when the clafoutis is done. The clafoutis without the crust will take about 10 minutes less time to cook. If the crust or the top begins to brown too much, set a piece of aluminum foil on top, turn down the oven temperature to 350°F, and continue baking until set. Remove from the oven and cool. The filling will fall, but don't worry, this is natural. Slice and serve at room temperature.

Links: Light and Flaky Crust (page 157), Real Man's Quiche—it's like a savory clafoutis (page 195), Simple Pie Crust (page 226).

Clam Dip

My friend Marion brought this dip to my prebook party with an array of fresh vegetables. It's easy and it stumps people when they try to figure out what's in it. For a richer dip, substitute cream cheese for the ricotta.

Required Reading: Convenience Foods (page 11), Seasoning to Taste (page 19), Selecting Ingredients (page 11).

Drain the clams, reserving 2 to 3 tablespoons of the liquid. In a small mixing bowl, combine all of the ingredients and stir well. If the dip is too thick, thin it out with some of the reserved clam juice. Refrigerate the dip for several hours before serving so that the flavors blend. Serve with fresh vegetables, crackers, or chips.

Links: Curried Carrot Spread (page 112), Mediterranean Potato Dip (page 162), Roasted Eggplant Spread (page 206).

Makes about 3 cups

1 large can (10^1/$_2$ ounces) minced clams, or 1 cup chopped fresh cooked clams (see Pasta with Seafood, page 179)

1 pound ricotta or cream cheese, at room temperature

Juice of 1 lemon

2 large cloves garlic, minced

6 sprigs Italian parsley, finely chopped

2 tablespoons finely chopped fresh chives

1 teaspoon Worcestershire sauce

^{1}/$_2$ teaspoon Tabasco sauce

Salt and freshly ground black pepper to taste

Kitchen Stuff

Measuring spoons

Mixing bowl

Classic Tuna Salad

There's a gourmet store in my neighborhood that sells what they call "Tuna Salad—The Classic" for $9.99 a pound. When people come to visit me, I always take them by the store to show them the sign. When you figure a can of tuna costs about ninety-nine cents and tuna salad is one of the easiest things in the world to make, spending $10 a pound for it is unfathomable. (Besides, the overpriced salad isn't even any good!) This is my mother's recipe for tuna. It's very lemony. Sometimes she adds onion, other times chopped hard-boiled egg. I like it best plain. Use it to make a comforting sandwich on toasted rye with lettuce and tomato, or use it as the basis of a Tuna Melt. Required Reading: Making a Sandwich (page 15), Seasoning to Taste (page 19), Selecting Ingredients (page 11).

In a small mixing bowl, place the drained tuna and flake with a fork to break up the big chunks. Add the remaining ingredients and mix well. The tuna salad tastes best if it sits for a couple of hours in the refrigerator before serving.

Variations

Tuna Melt

I know, I know, you think a tuna melt is so easy, who needs a recipe? The secret is to toast the bread first. And to start with a good Classic Tuna Salad. It also helps to use top-quality cheddar cheese, but I understand if, for nostalgia's sake, you have to use processed cheese slices. Preheat the oven to 425°F. Toast 4 slices of bread in a toaster or toaster oven until light brown. Lay out the bread on a cookie sheet. Using a fork or a slotted spoon, pick up the tuna and press with the back of another spoon to drain any excess liquid. Mound the tuna on the toasted bread. Lay the sliced cheese on top of the tuna and set the baking sheet in the preheated oven. Bake until the cheese has melted and begins to brown, 10 to 15 minutes. Garnish with curly parsley for a truly authentic diner look and serve immediately.

Tuna Salad on a Diet

I make a surprisingly good low-fat tuna salad by substituting plain, nonfat yogurt for some or all of the mayonnaise. Proceed with the recipe as directed.

Links: Chicken Salad (page 91), Salade Niçoise (page 211).

Makes 3 to 4 sandwiches, depending on how thick you fill them

Two 6-ounce cans white-meat tuna packed in oil or water, drained

2 ribs celery, finely chopped

1/4 cup mayonnaise

Juice of 1 to 2 lemons

1/2 small onion, finely chopped (optional)

1 hard-boiled egg, finely chopped (optional)

Freshly ground black pepper

Kitchen Stuff

Can opener

Small bowl

Coconut Curry

Makes 4 servings

2 tablespoons vegetable oil

1 pound meat (cut-up chicken parts, lamb stewing meat, beef stewing meat) or assorted vegetables (carrots, potatoes, turnips, eggplant)

1 large onion, finely sliced

One 4-ounce can Thai red curry paste (aka Penang curry paste)

One 13$1/2$-ounce can unsweetened coconut milk

3 cups water

4 sprigs fresh Thai or opal basil

Kitchen Stuff

Can opener

Liquid measuring cups

Measuring spoons

Saucepan

When I once worked for a Thai chef, the family meal always consisted of either Fried Rice (page 131) or this fiery Coconut Curry, made with anything from chicken to lamb to veal to vegetables. Similar in preparation to Chicken Paprikash (page 89), the secret is to find a good Thai red curry paste. Then there's nothin' to it. Required Reading: Cutting Up Things (page 13), Lowering Fat (page 15), Seasoning to Taste (page 19), Selecting Ingredients (page 11), Simmering versus Boiling (page 19), Tempering (page 20), Working with Meat (page 21).

In a large saucepan, heat the vegetable oil over medium-high heat. Add the meat and brown on all sides. (If using vegetables, they should be added with the coconut milk and simmered for about 45 minutes.) Add the onion and continue cooking until the onion has turned translucent, 5 to 8 minutes. Add the curry paste (use the whole can for nuclear heat, half the can for a superspicy dish, and only 1 tablespoon for a lightly spicy curry) and continue cooking for another 5 minutes.

Pour in the coconut milk and water and bring to a boil. Reduce the heat and simmer until the meat is tender, 1 to 2 hours, depending on the cut. If the liquid boils down so that some of the meat is no longer submerged, add more water. Just before the meat is done, add the basil leaves and return to the boil. Serve over steamed rice.

Links: Chicken Paprikash—similar technique (page 89), Fried Rice—goes well (page 131).

Corn on the Cob

Why a recipe for corn on the cob? Well, I wrote most of this book during the summer and I probably ate more corn on the cob during that time than in my whole life. When it is freshly picked, there is nothing better than a sweet ear of corn (or four). I know it's sacrilegious, but I don't even put butter or salt on my corn. The secret, and the real reason I'm including instructions for making corn, is that one of my biggest pet peeves in life is overcooked corn. If the corn is cooked too long it looses its sweetness and becomes tough. Pay attention! Required Reading: Nuking (page 16), Selecting Ingredients (page 11).

Bring a large pot of salted water, large enough to hold the corn, to a boil. (If you don't have a big enough pot, you can break the ears of corn in half.) Pull back the husks and break them off at the bottom of each ear. Remove as much of the silk from the ears as you can and rinse under cold water. Once the salted water is boiling, add the corn. When the water comes back up to a boil, let the corn cook for 1 minute. Turn off the heat and let the corn sit in the hot water for 5 minutes. Serve with butter and salt.

Variations

Microwave Method

This is my favorite thing to do in the microwave because it makes it so easy to eat an ear of corn (and you don't have a pot to clean). Clean the ears and rinse in cold water. Be sure the corn is wet. Wrap each ear individually in waxed paper by rolling it up and tucking in the edges. Place the corn in the microwave and nuke for $1^1/_2$ minutes per ear (if you have 1 ear, set the timer for $1^1/_2$ minutes, 4 ears, 6 minutes). Remove, unwrap, and enjoy.

Fiery Corn on the Cob

Why stop at butter and salt? Add cayenne pepper or red pepper flakes.

Links: Hamburgers (page 140), Potato Salad (page 191).

Makes 4 ears of corn

4 ears of corn, husked and cleaned of all silk

Butter

Salt

Kitchen Stuff

Large pot or microwave

Waxed paper

Cream of Broccoli Soup

Makes about 2 quarts, serves 6 to 8

2 tablespoons unsalted butter

1 onion, roughly chopped

2 to 3 stalks broccoli, roughly chopped

Water or stock to cover, about 6 cups (see Chicken Soup, page 92)

1 to 1½ cups half-and-half (if you want a richer soup with more calories, use all or part heavy cream)

About 1 tablespoon salt

10 grinds black pepper, or to taste

Kitchen Stuff

Food processor, blender, vegetable mill, or hand-held blender

Large saucepan or stock pot

Liquid measuring cups

Measuring spoons

Sieve (for a smoother soup)

This is another recipe that is really easy to make, but impresses people nonetheless. You can turn almost anything into a creamed soup—chicken, tomatoes, zucchini, asparagus, celery—once you understand the principles. The secret is to make a very flavorful puree that will still retain a strong taste once it is diluted with cream. And the secret to a flavorful puree is to use a lot of good, fresh ingredients. Once you make this recipe the first time, try your own variations or ingredients. Required Reading: Reheating (page 16), Selecting Ingredients (page 11), Simmering versus Boiling (page 19), Skimming (page 19), Straining (page 20), Using the Food Processor (page 21).

In a large saucepan, heat the butter. Add the onion and sauté until translucent, but not brown. Add the broccoli and sauté just until the broccoli is slightly wilted, another 3 to 5 minutes.

Cover the vegetables with water or stock—no more than 6 cups. Bring to a boil, turn down the heat, and simmer until the broccoli is very tender, 25 to 30 minutes. Using a blender, food processor, or vegetable mill, or one of those hand-held blending sticks that you got as a gift once but that you're never quite sure about how to use, puree the soup mixture in small batches until smooth. For a more refined soup, pass this mixture through a fine sieve, using the back of a ladle to press out all of the juices. If you don't care about how smooth the end result is, forget the sieve and leave the puree as is.

Stir in the cream until you have the desired consistency (some people prefer a thicker soup than others). Adjust the seasoning with the salt and pepper. To serve, return to a simmer over a medium heat, making sure the soup doesn't burn on the bottom of the pan. Don't worry if a cream "scum" forms on top of the soup. Skim it off and discard.

Variations

Cream of Asparagus Soup

Substitute 1 large bunch of asparagus for the broccoli. Remove the tips about 1 inch down the stalk and set aside to garnish the soup. Proceed with the recipe as directed for the broccoli, substituting the trimmed asparagus stems. Strain the soup. When you go to reheat the soup after you've added the cream, add the reserved asparagus tips. Simmer until the tips are tender, 5 to 6 minutes, and serve.

Cream of Carrot Soup

Use the technique outlined for the Cream of Broccoli Soup, only substitute two pounds of carrots, peeled and thinly sliced, for the broccoli and simmer until the carrots are tender,

I rarely prepare dishes according to an exact recipe because I never like to cook the same thing twice—I need to invent as I go along, or I get bored. Whether your dishes are authentic or not, you'll have more fun playing around with flavors and ingredients, adding things here and there, than you will by methodically following a recipe.

—JAMES PETERSON, *SPLENDID SOUPS* (BANTAM, 1993)

about 45 minutes to an hour. Add a dash of nutmeg to the puree before you add the cream. Follow the rest of the recipe as directed.

Curried Cauliflower Soup
Use the technique outlined above, only add 1 to 2 tablespoons of curry powder to the sautéing onions. Cook the curry powder for 3 to 5 minutes before adding $1/2$ medium-sized head of cauliflower (instead of the broccoli) that has been roughly chopped. Cover with the water or stock, simmer until the cauliflower is tender, puree, and follow the recipe as directed.

Links: Chicken Soup—should you want to use stock instead of water (page 92), Mushroom Barley Soup (page 169).

Cream Puffs

Makes about 14 large puffs

For the cream puff paste

$1/4$ pound (1 stick) butter

1 cup water

1 cup unbleached all-purpose flour

4 large eggs

For the filling

1 cup milk

$1/2$ cup sugar

3 large egg yolks

Pinch of salt

3 tablespoons unbleached
all-purpose flour

1 tablespoon pure vanilla extract

2 tablespoons unsalted butter

1 cup heavy cream
(aka whipping cream)

Kitchen Stuff

Cookie sheets

Measuring cups

Measuring spoons

Mixing bowls

Small saucepan

Whisk or electric mixer

Wooden spoon

If you learn one thing from this book that will impress your friends, this is it. The basis for those elegant and sophisticated desserts you see on menus with fancy names like profiteroles, gâteau St. Honoré, cream puffs, or éclairs is really a simple dough called pâté à choux, or cream puff paste, that is one of the easiest things to make. Master the technique, which should only take one try, and a whole world of sweet and savory dishes can be yours. Required Reading: Measuring (page 15), Melting (page 25), Preheating (page 16), Selecting Ingredients (page 11), Tempering (page 20), Testing for Doneness (page 20).

In a medium-sized saucepan, combine the butter and water and set over medium-high heat. Take a wooden spoon in one hand and the flour in the other. Once the butter has melted and the mixture has begun to boil rapidly and froth, add the flour. Immediately stir the mixture with the wooden spoon to form a stiff paste. Continue stirring for 3 minutes while the mixture begins to cook. Remove from the heat and allow to cool until the mixture is luke-warm to the touch, about 10 minutes.

Preheat the oven to 425°F. Crack one egg into the cooked flour and water paste and quickly beat with the wooden spoon to incorporate. If the pan is still very hot, be sure the egg doesn't fall to the bottom or it will start to cook. As you stir, the dough will separate into little slimy blobs that are sort of hard to handle. Be patient and strong and continue beating until the mixture comes back together to form a paste.

Add the next egg and continue the beating process through the slimy blob stage until the paste has come back

again. Repeat this procedure with the remaining eggs. If you are having trouble getting the mixture to come together again after the last egg has been added, crack a fifth egg, beat it in a small bowl, and beat in additional droplets of egg to the paste until it comes back together to form a smooth, shiny paste. There you have it, you have just mastered one of the basic techniques of French cooking.

Using two large spoons, drop the mixture onto an ungreased cookie sheet into balls about $1^1/2$ inches in diameter, with enough room between them to allow them to double in size without touching. You can make them any size you wish, just be sure to adjust the baking time accordingly. (Tiny puffs dropped from teaspoons are great for hors d'oeuvres.) Bake in the preheated oven for 15 minutes, until they have puffed. Lower the oven to 350°F and bake until golden brown and firm, 20 to 25 more minutes for the $1^1/2$-inch puffs. Cut one open to check if it is cooked inside. Cool. The puffs can be stored in an airtight container for two to three days or frozen for up to one month.

Prepare the filling. In a small saucepan, combine the milk and $1/4$ cup of the sugar and bring to a boil. In a small mixing bowl, whisk together egg yolks with a pinch of salt and another $1/4$ cup sugar. Stir in the flour. Whisk $1/3$ of the hot milk into the egg mixture and pour it back into the saucepan with the milk. Continue whisking until the cream thickens and comes to a boil.

Remove from the heat and whisk in the vanilla extract and unsalted butter. Pour into a bowl and cover with plastic wrap, pressing it right against the cream. Chill. In a large mixing bowl, beat the whipping cream with a whisk until stiff (see page 239). Using a fork, break up the stiff pastry cream into small pieces and add to the whipped cream. Mix well. The cream filling should be lumpy, with pieces of the pastry cream in every bite. Use this mixture to fill the cooled cream puffs. Cover with chocolate sauce and serve.

Sweet Variations

Cappuccino Filling

Prepare a coffee pastry cream filling as follows. In a small saucepan, bring $1 1/2$ cups milk to a boil with $1/4$ cup of sugar. In a small mixing bowl, beat four egg yolks with another $1/4$ cup of sugar, a pinch of salt, and $1/4$ cup of flour. Whisk half of the hot milk into the egg mixture and whisk this mixture back

into the milk in the saucepan. Return to the heat and continue whisking until the cream thickens and comes to a boil.

Remove from the heat and whisk in 2 teaspoons pure vanilla extract, 2 tablespoons butter, and 2 tablespoons instant coffee dissolved in 1 tablespoon of water. Pour into a bowl and cover with plastic wrap, pressing it right against the cream. Chill. Use this cream to fill the cream puffs or éclairs. Cover with chocolate sauce and sprinkle with cinnamon and cocoa powder.

Eclairs

Use the same pastry and filling as for cream puffs, but form the dough into long cigar shapes before baking.

Profiteroles

To serve, cut the puffs in half crosswise with a sharp knife. Fill with a scoop of vanilla ice cream, top with the other half, and cover with Chocolate Sauce (page 98). Your guests will be amazed.

Savory Variations

Cheese Puffs

Stir $3/4$ cup of grated Swiss cheese (Emmenthal or Gruyère) and 8 grinds black pepper into the cream puff paste after the last egg is incorporated. Drop onto a cookie sheet as for cream puffs, but only 1 inch in diameter. Sprinkle the tops with additional grated cheese and bake as for cream puffs. Serve hot out of the oven.

Herb Puffs

Add 2 tablespoons of assorted chopped fresh herbs, $1/2$ teaspoon of salt, and freshly ground black pepper to the pâté à choux after the last egg is incorporated. Shape and bake as for cream puffs.

Jalapeño Cheddar Puffs

Stir $3/4$ cup of grated cheddar cheese and 1 finely diced jalapeño pepper into the finished cream puff paste. Drop onto a cookie sheet as for cream puffs, but only 1 inch in diameter. Sprinkle the tops with additional grated cheddar and bake as directed above. Serve hot out of the oven.

Mushroom Puffs

Add $1/2$ teaspoon of salt and some freshly ground pepper to the cream puff paste. Drop the batter in small teaspoonfuls onto cookies sheets and bake as directed (cutting the time by about 10 minutes because of the smaller size). Fill the puffs with Mom's Mushrooms and Onions (page 166), that have been drained well. Reheat in the oven before serving.

Links: Chocolate Sauce (page 98), Mom's Mushrooms and Onions (page 166), Whipped Cream (page 239).

Crunchy Poppy Seed Biscotti

Before she worked at The James Beard Foundation and after she worked on Wall Street, my friend Carrie was a pastry chef. The first time I ever had her desserts was when my roommates and I decided to have a tea party—about sixty-five people showed up. Carrie baked up a storm. And one of my favorite things were these crunchy, buttery biscotti. Required Reading: Bringing to Room Temperature (page 23), Cooling (page 24), Creaming (page 24), Patience (page 16), Selecting Ingredients (page 11), Testing for Doneness (page 27), Zesting (page 23).

In a large mixing bowl with a wooden spoon, or in an electric mixer, cream together the butter, sugar, and zests. The mixture should become smooth and, if you have enough stamina, fluffy. Add the vanilla and the eggs, one at a time, beating after each until it is well incorporated.

In a separate bowl, combine the flour, cornmeal, baking powder, and salt, and mix until blended. Stir the dry ingredients into the butter mixture. Add the poppy seeds.

Preheat the oven to 325°F. On 2 cookie sheets, shape the dough into 4 equal logs, about 1 1/2 to 2 inches across and 1 inch thick. If the dough is too soft to handle or shape with a spatula, refrigerate it for about 30 minutes. Leave 3 to 4 inches between the logs because they will spread to about double their width and they shouldn't touch. Bake the logs until they are light golden brown on the outside and firm to the touch, about 25 minutes depending on the thickness. Keep watching the oven to be sure they do not overbake.

Remove from the oven and let the logs come to room temperature. If you do not want to finish baking the biscotti right away, they can be left in logs for several hours. When you are ready to finish the cookies, preheat the oven to 275°F. Slice the logs about 1/2 inch thick on an angle—it doesn't matter how thick, as long as they are all uniform—and lay the cookies cut side down on cookie sheets. Sometimes if the biscotti are too thin they break in half. You can finish baking them anyway. Place in the preheated oven and bake until lightly toasted, about 30 minutes. Turn over and toast on the other side for about 15 more minutes. Remove from the oven and cool. Store in an airtight container or freeze.

Links: Chocolate Nut Biscotti (page 97).

Makes 4 to 5 dozen cookies, depending on how they are cut

1 cup (2 sticks) unsalted butter, at room temperature

2 cups sugar

Zest of 1 orange and 1 lemon, minced

1 teaspoon vanilla

4 large eggs

3 cups unbleached all-purpose flour

1 cup yellow cornmeal

1 tablespoon baking powder

1 teaspoon salt

3 tablespoons poppy seeds

Kitchen Stuff

Electric mixer (optional)

Measuring cups

Measuring spoons

Rubber spatula

2 large mixing bowls

2 or 3 cookie sheets

Wooden spoon

Curried Carrot Spread

Makes about 3 cups

2 pounds carrots, peeled and cut into chunks

About $^1/_2$ cup olive oil

2 medium onions, chopped

1 clove garlic, minced

1 fresh jalapeño or other chile, seeded and chopped

1 tablespoon plus 1 teaspoon curry powder

$^1/_4$ cup chicken stock or water

About 1 teaspoon salt

7 grinds black pepper, or to taste

Kitchen Stuff

Food processor

Liquid measuring cup

Measuring spoons

Roasting pan or baking dish

This is a dish my friend Kerri devised to bring to a party at my house some time ago. She just threw it together for the do, but I've been making it ever since. It's sweet and spicy and everyone always loves it.
Required Reading: Roasting, Braising, and Steaming (page 17), Sautéing, Frying, and Stir-Frying (page 19), Seasoning to Taste (page 19), Selecting Ingredients (page 11), Using the Food Processor (page 21).

Preheat the oven to 400°F. In a roasting pan or on a baking dish, place the carrot chunks and drizzle with about 2 tablespoons of the olive oil. Set in the preheated oven and roast for 1 hour to 1 hour 15 minutes, until the carrots are browned and tender when poked with a fork. Stir the carrots once or twice while they are roasting to be sure they brown evenly.

Meanwhile, in a medium sauté pan, heat 2 to 3 tablespoons of the olive oil. Add the onions, garlic, and jalapeño, and sauté until wilted, 5 to 6 minutes. Add the curry powder and continue cooking until the vegetables are tender and the curry powder has darkened and cooked through, 7 to 8 minutes. Stir frequently to prevent the curry powder from burning on the bottom of the pan.

Transfer the curried mixture to the bowl of a food processor fitted with the metal chopping blade. Pour about $^1/_4$ cup of chicken stock or water into the pan to scrape out any curried

mixture that is stuck to the pan and add it to the food processor. Add the roasted carrots, 3 tablespoons of olive oil, and the salt and pepper. Process using on/off pulses until the mixture has turned into a chunky spread. Adjust the texture if necessary with more olive oil or stock and adjust the seasoning with more salt and pepper. The spread is best served the next day, after the flavors have had a chance to blend. It will keep in the refrigerator for up to a week. Serve at room temperature with bread or toast.

Variation

Curried Any Vegetable Spread
Almost any vegetable will work with this technique. Be sure to roast until tender and puree as directed.

Links: Curried Chicken Salad (page 113), Roasted Eggplant Spread (page 206), Roasted Vegetables (page 209), Yogurt Curried Chicken (page 240).

Curried Chicken Salad

Here's another simple salad recipe that works as a light entrée or as a sandwich filling. Use leftover Yogurt Curried Chicken (page 240) or roast a chicken especially for this dish, following the technique on page 203, but seasoning the chicken with about one tablespoon of curry powder instead of garlic powder and paprika. Use any combination of garnishes that you like in a chicken salad. Required Reading: Lowering Fat (page 15), Making a Sandwich (page 15), Seasoning to Taste (page 19), Selecting Ingredients (page 11), Using Leftovers (page 21).

In a mixing bowl, combine all of the ingredients and mix until well blended. Adjust the curry flavor by adding more curry powder if you feel the flavor isn't strong enough. If you have some Curry Oil on hand, add 1 to 2 teaspoons, to taste. Serve chilled over greens or use as a filling for sandwiches.

Variation

Curried Chicken Salad on a Diet
Substitute $1/4$ cup nonfat yogurt for the mayonnaise and proceed with the recipe as directed.

Links: Chicken Salad (page 91), Curried Cauliflower Soup (page 107), Roasted Chicken (page 203), Yogurt Curried Chicken (page 240).

Makes 4 servings

2 to 4 pieces cooked curried chicken, cubed to produce about $1^1/2$ cups meat (see headnote)

2 ribs celery, diced

$1/2$ red bell pepper, seeded and diced

3 scallions, thinly sliced, white and green parts

2 tablespoons chopped nuts (almonds, cashews, or peanuts)

2 tablespoons raisins or currants

1 teaspoon chopped cilantro

$1/4$ cup mayonnaise

About $1/2$ teaspoon curry powder, or to taste

Curry Oil (page 121), to taste (optional)

Kitchen Stuff

Measuring cups

Measuring spoons

Mixing bowl

Date Nut Cake

Makes one 9 x 12-inch cake, or two 8^1/$_2$ x 4^1/$_2$ x 2^1/$_2$-inch loaves

Butter and flour for pans

^{1}/$_2$ pound (8 ounces) pitted dates, chopped

1 cup hot water

1 teaspoon baking soda

^{1}/$_2$ pound (2 sticks) unsalted butter, at room temperature

1 cup sugar

3 large eggs

1 teaspoon pure vanilla extract

2 cups unbleached all-purpose flour

^{3}/$_4$ cup chopped walnuts, pecans, or hazelnuts

Confectioner's sugar for garnish

Kitchen Stuff

Cooling rack

Liquid and dry measuring cups

Measuring spoons

Mixing bowls

9 x 12-inch cake pan or two 8^1/$_2$ x 4^1/$_2$ x 2^1/$_2$-inch loaf pans

I defy you to find a recipe for a moister, more delicious cake. Lighter than a quick bread, this cake is sweet and moist and buttery. Use the best dates you can find, pitted are easiest. Required Reading: Buttering and Flouring (page 23), Bringing to Room Temperature (page 12), Chopping Nuts (page 23), Cooling (page 24), Creaming (page 24), Dusting with Powdered Sugar (page 24), Selecting Ingredients (page 11), Testing for Doneness (page 20).

Preheat the oven to 375°F. Butter and flour a 9 x 12-inch cake pan, or two 8^1/$_2$ x 4^1/$_2$ x 2^1/$_2$-inch loaf pans. In a small bowl, combine the dates, hot water, and baking soda, and allow to soak until the dates have softened, about 2 hours.

Once they are ready, in a large mixing bowl, cream the butter and sugar. Add the eggs and the vanilla extract and beat until smooth. Stir in the flour along with the dates (and their soaking water) and the chopped nuts.

When everything is incorporated, pour the batter into the prepared pan(s) and bake in the preheated oven for 30 to 35 minutes, or until the center bounces back when touched and the sides have pulled away from the pan. (The loaf pans will take about 50 minutes to an hour.) Allow to cool for 15 minutes. Run a knife around the edge of the pan(s) and invert on a cake rack to finish cooling. Cut into squares. Just before serving, sprinkle each piece with confectioner's sugar.

Links: Banana Bread (page 63), Banana Cake (page 64), You Gotta Try These Blondies (page 241).

Dill Sauce

This is a great sauce to serve with fish (hot or cold). It goes particularly well with the Salmon Mousse on page 213. If you leave out the milk and keep the sauce a little on the thick side, it also makes a good dip for chips. Required Reading: Saucing (page 17), Seasoning to Taste (page 19), Selecting Ingredients (page 11), Using the Food Processor (page 21).

Into a blender or the bowl of a food processor, dump all of the ingredients and process until smooth. If the sauce is too thick, adjust the consistency with a tablespoon or so of milk. If you do not have a food processor, finely mince the onion and the dill and combine all of the ingredients in a small bowl. Serve chilled.

Links: Salmon Mousse (page 213).

Makes about 1¼ cups

1 cup sour cream

Juice of 1 lemon

½ onion, chopped

4 to 5 sprigs fresh dill

½ teaspoon salt

5 grinds black pepper, or to taste

1 to 2 tablespoons milk

Kitchen Stuff

Food processor or blender

Measuring spoons

Small bowl

Eggplant Parmesan

**Makes 4 to 6 servings,
with leftovers**

2 small, firm eggplants,
peeled if you prefer

1 to 2 tablespoons salt

1^1/$_2$ to 2^1/$_2$ cups unflavored
bread crumbs

1 teaspoon salt

^{1}/$_2$ teaspoon garlic powder

15 grinds black pepper

2 large eggs

^{3}/$_4$ cup all-purpose flour

Vegetable oil for frying

1 double recipe Fresh Tomato
Sauce (page 127) or 1 recipe
Spaghetti Sauce (page 227), or
your favorite store-bought sauce

2 cups (1 pound) grated
mozzarella cheese

^{1}/$_3$ cup freshly grated
Parmesan cheese

Kitchen Stuff

Baking dish

Cheese grater

Measuring cups

Measuring spoons

Paper towel or brown paper bag

Sauté pan

**Good hot for dinner, cold for breakfast, or on a sandwich for lunch,
Eggplant Parmesan is a versatile thing. Though it takes a little more time,
I prefer to slice my eggplant very thinly and layer it with tomato sauce
and grated cheese. I also prefer it without the peel, but that's a matter of
personal taste. You can treat other vegetables, such as zucchini or yellow
squash, and veal and chicken, for that matter, the same way. Just be sure
to pound the meat thinly and cook it through.** Required Reading: Breading
(page 12), Cutting Up Things (page 13), Grilling, Barbecuing, and
Broiling (page 13), Lowering Fat (page 15), Making a Sandwich (page 15),
Sautéing, Frying, and Stir-Frying (page 19), Selecting Ingredients (page 11),
Using Leftovers (page 21).

Whether using peeled or unpeeled
eggplants, slice them into thin slices, no
more than ^{1}/$_8$ to ^{1}/$_4$ inch thick,
vertically from the top to the bottom. I
prefer the longer slices to rounds cut
crosswise because they cook more
evenly and they layer better. Sprinkle
both sides of the eggplant slices with 1
to 2 tablespoons of salt and set aside
on a plate for 20 to 30 minutes. The
salt will draw out some of the moisture
that makes the eggplant bitter.

Meanwhile, in a wide, shallow bowl or
on a large plate—a soup bowl or rimmed
dinner plate works well—place the
bread crumbs and combine with about
1 teaspoon of salt, the garlic powder,
and black pepper. Mix well. In another
bowl, beat the eggs with a fork until
frothy. Place the flour in a third dish.

In a large frying pan, heat about ^{1}/$_8$
inch of vegetable oil over medium-high
heat. Rinse the eggplant slices under
cold water to remove the salt and
bitter moisture and pat dry with paper

towel. Lay some paper towel or a clean
brown paper bag on a clean plate to
drain the fried eggplant slices later.

When the oil is hot, dip an eggplant
slice in the flour to lightly coat on all
sides. Tap the slice with your finger to
remove any excess flour. Dip the floured
slice in the beaten egg to coat and
then lay it on the seasoned bread crumbs.
Move the crumbs around with a fork to
coat the entire slice on all sides.

Place the breaded slice in the hot oil
and repeat with the other slices until
the pan is full. Cook until golden brown
on the bottom, turn over with tongs, a
fork, or a small spatula, and cook the
second side until brown. Remove from
the oil and lay on the paper towel or
brown paper bag to drain. Repeat with
the remaining slices of eggplant until
all of them are fried.

If you need to add more oil to the pan,
which you probably will after the
second batch, be sure to let it heat up

In the 17th century, legend has it that fishermen in Naples fished up from the sea what they thought was a treasure, and it turned out to be a picture of the Madonna. Filled with religious fervor, King Carlo III constructed a church around it at the beach, and August 15 became the Festa della Nzegna...Food served on the occasion included a dessert that derived from eggplant alla parmigiana, although chocolate cream was substituted for the tomatoes, cream and basil took the place of Parmesan cheese, and raisins, citron and cinnamon flavored the slices of eggplant.

—CAROL FIELD, *CELEBRATING ITALY* (MORROW, 1990)

before you add the next round of breaded eggplant slices. Also, if you need more bread crumbs, egg, or flour, do not hesitate to dump some more in. Just be sure to season any additional bread crumbs.

Preheat the oven to 400°F. When all of the eggplant is fried and drained you are ready to layer it in a baking dish. Use a small lasagne pan, deep brownie pan, square Pyrex dish, or a loaf pan. Place a couple of the tablespoons of tomato sauce on the bottom of the pan and arrange about 1/3 of the eggplant slices in a thick layer over top. Spoon on a layer of sauce and sprinkle about 1/3 of the grated mozzarella and Parmesan. Repeat the layers until all of the ingredients are used up and you end with a layer of cheese. If you have leftovers, you can arrange them in

another dish or on a cookie sheet and use them for sandwiches. Bake in the preheated oven for 45 minutes to an hour, until the cheese has melted and browned and the sauce is bubbling. Cut into squares to serve.

Variation

Eggplant Parmesan on a Diet
My sister Leslie makes a terrific low-fat version of Eggplant Parmesan by grilling the eggplant instead of breading and frying it. After the eggplant has been salted and rinsed, brush the slices with a little olive oil and season with salt and freshly ground black pepper. Grill over hot coals or in a stove-top grill just until tender. Continue with the recipe as directed, substituting the grilled eggplant slices for the fried eggplant slices.

Links: Fresh Tomato Sauce (page 127), Grilled Vegetables (page 137), Spaghetti Sauce (page 227).

Falafel Vegetable Burgers

A terrific vegetarian burger, this recipe is adapted from my friend Bonnie Stern's <u>Simply HeartSmart Cooking</u> (Random House, 1994) cookbook. The burgers are great in a pita with lettuce, tomato, cucumber, sprouts, and the Lemon Tahini Dressing on page 155, the Aioli on page 53, or the Rémoulade on page 197. If you have a food processor, the whole thing takes a matter of minutes to make. If you have to chop everything by hand, making the burgers becomes a chore I wouldn't advise. Required Reading: Convenience Foods (page 11), Seasoning to Taste (page 19), Selecting Ingredients (page 11), Separating Eggs (page 25), Using the Food Processor (page 21).

Makes 10 burgers

6 slices white bread

2 small cloves garlic

10 sprigs Italian parsley

1 small onion

1 small carrot

One 6-ounce can mushrooms, drained, or $^1/_2$ pound fresh, sautéed in butter and drained

Two 16-ounce cans chickpeas, rinsed and drained

2 egg whites

1 teaspoon baking soda

1 tablespoon ground cumin

1 teaspoon ground coriander

1 teaspoon hot pepper sauce

1 teaspoon salt

1 teaspoon freshly ground black pepper

Vegetable oil for frying

Kitchen Stuff

Dry measuring cups

Food processor

Measuring spoons

Mixing bowl

Sauté pan or cookie sheet

In the bowl of food processor fitted with the metal chopping blade, place the bread slices. Process with on/off pulses until the bread has been chopped into coarse crumbs, 1 to 2 minutes. Transfer to a small bowl and set aside.

Place the garlic cloves in the processor and pulse until finely chopped, about 6 times. Add the parsley and onion and pulse until minced. Add the carrot and continue pulsing until finely chopped. Add the mushrooms and pulse until finely chopped. Add the bread crumbs and all of the remaining ingredients except for the vegetable oil. Stir up the mixture as much as you can in the food processor bowl to distribute the chopped vegetables among the chickpeas.

Process the entire mixture with on/off pulses until the chickpeas are chopped and the mixture has the consistency of a stiff spread. Open the lid once or twice to stir up the whole mess with a spoon while you are pulsing it.

Depending on the size of your food processor, you may need to process the mixture in 2 batches, splitting up the chopped vegetables between each batch and combining the whole thing afterwards in a large mixing bowl.

When you are finished processing everything, transfer to a mixing bowl. Stir 2 to 3 times to be sure the mixture is well blended, and shape into 10 thin patties. If the mixture is too loose to hold its shape, add more crumbs to stiffen it.

To cook the hamburgers, heat about $^1/_8$ inch vegetable oil in a large frying pan set over medium-high heat. Fry the burgers on both sides until brown and crisp. Alternately, you can bake the burgers on a cookie sheet in a 350°F oven for 30 minutes, turning once.

Links: Aioli (page 53), Lemon Tahini Dressing (page 155), Rémoulade (page 197).

Five-Minute Flounder Fillets

Makes 2 servings

³/₄ pound skinless and boneless flounder fillets

Drop of vegetable oil

1 to 2 tablespoons unsalted butter

Dash powdered sage

Dash paprika

Lemon wedges (optional)

Kitchen Stuff

Aluminum foil

Broiler

Cookie sheet

My friend Alexandra Leaf gave me this recipe because, in her words, "This is probably the world's easiest fish recipe and perhaps the fastest, too." How could I refuse it? The only variable here is the quality of the fish. Choose the freshest possible. You can substitute any mild fish with white flesh. Figure about three-fourths pound of fish for every two people, depending on the how much other food will be served.

Required Reading: Grilling, Barbecuing, and Broiling (page 13), Selecting Ingredients (page 11), Testing for Doneness (page 20).

Preheat the broiler. Rinse the fillets with cold water and pat dry with paper towels. Line a cookie sheet with aluminum foil. Rub the underside of the fillets with a drop of vegetable oil to prevent sticking and set on the pan. Cut the butter into small pieces and place a piece on top of each fillet. Sprinkle with sage and paprika. Broil the fish until the flesh is white and it separates into tender flakes, about 5 minutes. (Cooking time depends on the thickness of the fillets.) Serve with lemon wedges, if desired.

Links: Any of the side dishes in this book.

Flavored Oils

Flavored oils became wildly popular a few years back as chefs learned how to infuse different flavors into oils to make surprising new flavor combinations and zany colors. Flavored oils are also practical for the home cook because they are simple to make, they keep a long time, they are pretty, and they add a little zing to a dish that might otherwise be drab.

My friend Leslie Brenner even co-wrote a whole book on the subject called <u>Essential Flavors</u> (Viking, 1994). I've experimented with Leslie's technique for a couple of years. All you need is a food processor or blender, a coffee filter, and a funnel. Use an oil that has very little flavor of its own, such as safflower oil. Stay away from stronger flavored oils such as corn oil and peanut oil. Extra-virgin olive oil is good for Mediterranean-flavored oils, such as rosemary and garlic. But otherwise the olive taste overpowers most flavors.

Use flavored oils as the base for dressings such as French Vinaigrette (page 125) or to garnish meats and vegetables such as Leg of Lamb (page 152) or Grilled Vegetables (page 137). Get creative. A drop of curry oil in the Curried Chicken Salad (page 113) or in the Yogurt Curried Chicken marinade (page 240) will make a strong statement. Required Reading: Patience (page 16).

Herb-Infused Oils

For these oils, make sure your herbs are very well cleaned and totally dried before beginning. Bruise the herbs by smashing them with a mallet, rolling pin, or heavy frying pan, in order to release some of their essential oils.

In a saucepan place the oil and the bruised herbs and heat very gently over a low flame until you perceive a strong herb scent, about 10 minutes. Don't let the oil get so hot that it fries the herbs.

Transfer the warm oil to a blender or food processor and process with 2 to 3 on/off pulses until the herbs have been broken up into small particles. Alternately, you can use a hand-held blender to break up the herbs. Place the oil with chopped herbs in a jar, cool, and seal. Let steep in the refrigerator for 1 or 2 days to infuse the oil with a strong flavor.

To clarify the oil, if you don't want things floating around in it, you have to filter it through a coffee filter. Be forewarned, this is a tedious process that I sometimes like to skip. Line a funnel with a coffee filter and set it over a clean bottle. Pour the oil into the filter and let it sit until the oil has passed through the filter. Depending on the density of the herbs, this can take some time (an hour or more). I usually loose patience at about 35 minutes. Then I transfer the oil to a clean filter.

Makes about 1 1/2 cups

Herb-Infused Oils
1 large bunch fresh herbs (such as rosemary, basil, chive, tarragon)

1 1/2 cups safflower oil

Spice-Infused Oils
3 tablespoons ground spice (such as curry powder, ground cumin, ground coriander, or a combination), or one 3- to 4-inch piece fresh ginger, chopped, or 3 heads garlic, roasted (see page 207)

1 1/2 cups olive or safflower oil

Citrus-Infused Oils
2 oranges, or 3 lemons, or 1 grapefruit, or a combination

1 1/2 cups safflower oil

Kitchen Stuff

Coffee filter

Food processor or blender (for Herb-Infused Oils)

Funnel (large enough to hold the coffee filter)

Mallet, rolling pin, or heavy frying pan

Measuring spoons

Oil is fat in its most liquid form, prized by some for frying fish and by others for seasoning salad, but by the Greeks of Homeric times for clothing, since, long underwear not yet having been invented, they coated their bodies with it in winter to keep warm.

—WAVERLY ROOT, *FOOD* (SIMON AND SCHUSTER, 1980)

After waiting about another 15 minutes, I start to bunch up the top of the filter, in order to contain the oil, and apply pressure to make the oil go through faster. Just be careful that none of the oil flows out of the top of the filter or it will contaminate the already filtered oil and you'll have to start over again.

When all of the oil has passed through the filter, or at least enough so that you don't care if you throw away the rest, close the jar tightly and store in the refrigerator until ready to use. The herb oil will last over a month.

Spice-Infused Oils

To prepare these oils, if using dry, ground spices, place them in a small saucepan and gently heat over a low flame until the spice has a strong, toasted smell, 4 to 5 minutes. Swirl the pan around every once in a while so that the spice doesn't burn. Pour in the oil and continue heating over the low flame for 10 minutes.

If using roasted garlic, squeeze out the cloves, combine with olive oil, and gently heat over a low flame for 10 minutes. For ginger, combine the ginger and oil in a small saucepan and gently heat for 15 minutes. Transfer to a clean container and allow the oil to steep in the refrigerator for 1 or 2 days.

Line a funnel with a coffee filter and set over a clean bottle. Pour the oil into the filter and let it sit until the oil has passed through the filter. Depending on the density of the spices, this can take some time—see commentary in Herb-Infused Oil directions, page 121. When all of the oil is clarified, close the jar tightly and store in the refrigerator until ready to use. Oils infused with dry spices will last up to 3 months; those made with fresh garlic or ginger will keep about 1 month.

Citrus-Infused Oils

To prepare these oils, using a carrot peeler or zester, peel away the orange, lemon, and/or grapefruit rinds (see Zesting, page 23), being careful not to

pick up any of the white pith. In a small saucepan, combine the rind with the oil and gently heat for 10 minutes over a low flame. Transfer to a clean container and allow the oil to steep in the refrigerator for 1 or 2 days.

Line a funnel with a coffee filter and set over a clean bottle. Pour the oil into the filter and let it sit until the oil has passed through the filter—see commentary in Herb-Infused Oil directions, page 121. When all of the oil is clarified, close the jar tightly and store in the refrigerator until ready to use. Oils infused with citrus will last about 1 month.

Links: Any recipe that could use a little zing.

French Toast

Despite the name, no one is sure where French toast originated. Nothing in France compares, although some people liken it to <u>pain perdu</u> ("lost bread"), which is more like bread pudding than anything else. In his <u>Dictionary of American Food and Drink</u> (Hearst, 1994), food and dining authority John Mariani writes that at different times in America, French toast has been called "Spanish," "German," or "nun's toast."

No matter what you call it or where it's from, it is almost impossible to find a decent piece of French toast at a restaurant these days.

What's odd is that a buttery, crisp piece of French toast with a custardy center is probably one of the easiest things to make on a lazy morning. Any stale bread will do, but a piece of rich challah or a crusty and dense sourdough country bread makes an ordinary French toast into an other-worldly experience. Be sure the bread is stale. Fresh bread will not absorb the egg mixture and the end result will be too bready.

You can flavor either the egg mixture or the finished French toast to your taste. Being the purist that I am, I prefer basic French toast with a hint of vanilla and cinnamon and a lightly caramelized sugar crust. The first time I made it this way for my friend Judy, she became a believer.
Required Reading: Reheating (page 16), Sautéing, Frying, and Stir-Frying (page 19), Selecting Ingredients (page 11), Testing for Doneness (page 20), Using Leftovers (page 21).

Makes 3 servings

1 large egg

1 cup half-and-half or whole milk

1 tablespoon pure vanilla extract

1/2 teaspoon ground cinnamon

1/4 cup (1/2 stick) unsalted butter

6 slices stale bread, preferably cut 1 inch thick (see headnote)

3 teaspoons granulated sugar (optional)

Kitchen Stuff

Fork

Large shallow bowl

Large skillet

Measuring cups

Measuring spoons

Spatula

Into a medium-sized bowl, wide enough to lay a piece of bread flat in it, crack the egg and beat it with a fork to break up the yolk. Slowly add the half-and-half or milk while continuing to beat with a fork until well mixed. The mixture should be an even, pale yellow color with air bubbles around the edges. Add the vanilla and ground cinnamon and beat again until well mixed. Some of the cinnamon may clump and float to the top. Don't worry about it. The clumps will break up when you dip the bread.

In a heavy skillet (cast iron works best), melt one or two tablespoons of the butter over medium-high heat. If the butter starts to brown, turn down the flame. Stir up the egg mixture. With the fork in one hand and a piece of bread in the other, dunk the bread in the egg mixture on one side and quickly turn it over with the fork. The bread will soak up the egg mixture at varying rates, depending on how dense and/or stale it is. The more stale the bread, the quicker the egg will be soaked up; the more dense, the less it will absorb. The idea here is not to let the bread soak up so much mix that it becomes sopping wet or falls apart. Too little liquid is not good either because the center of the bread will not become custardy when it's finished cooking. Transfer the soaked bread to the hot skillet and repeat with the remaining bread until the pan is full. Be sure to stir up the egg mixture before each slice is dunked. If you run out, add another egg, some more half-and-half or milk, vanilla, and cinnamon.

Meanwhile, keep your eye on the French toast in the pan. When the edges appear to be brown, peek under a slice with a spatula to see if it is evenly cooked. If not, turn the slices around in the pan to even out the heat. Once evenly browned, flip the French toast. If all of the butter has been absorbed, add more. While the second side is cooking, sprinkle the French toast evenly with the granulated sugar. Try not to get sugar in the pan, just on the bread, or the sugar will burn.

If your toast is particularly thick, and/or your stove runs hot, the French toast might brown before it has cooked through. You'll know this is the case because when you press the center of a slice or cut one open, liquid will ooze out. In this case, turn down the heat or finish cooking the French toast in a preheated 350°F oven. Be sure the handle of your skillet is oven-safe (made out of metal, not plastic or wood) before you do this, or you'll have a real mess. Even if your French toast is finished on top of the stove, you may want to pop it in the oven to ensure the sugar coating is nicely caramelized.

The finished French toast should be golden brown and buttery on the outside and custardy on the inside. If you are making a lot of French toast, you can keep the first pieces warm in a 250°F oven while you finish cooking the rest.

Variations
Bourbon French Toast
Instead of vanilla, add a shot or two of bourbon to the egg mixture and eliminate the cinnamon. Serve with sliced fresh peaches and toasted pecans and a dollop of whipped cream for a real Southern-style French toast.

Chocolate French Toast
You'll be surprised how good this is. Omit the vanilla and cinnamon and substitute 1 cup chocolate milk plus $^1/_4$ cup chocolate syrup (I prefer to use Hershey's). Because the chocolate mixture is sweetened, you won't need to add the sugar at the end.

French Toast on a Diet
For a lighter French toast with less fat, substitute skim milk or 1% milk for the half-and-half. Use a nonstick skillet and add only enough butter to flavor the French toast and give it a nice golden brown color, about 1 teaspoon.

No Ordinary Loaf
One of the easiest ways to vary the flavor of your French toast is to change the bread. A raisin walnut bread will make a hearty French toast. Rye bread

and pumpernickel French toast has an unusual flavor, but I think it's delicious. For a sweeter French toast use slices of stale pound cake or angel food cake. Be careful when dipping the cake in the egg mixture, however, because it becomes very delicate. Use a wide spatula to transfer it to the skillet. I've even used old croissants and bagels with varying degrees of success.

Whenever possible, buy your bread unsliced. Thick slices make a more impressive French toast that tastes better.

PB&J French Toast
Using two pieces of sandwich bread, make a standard peanut butter and jelly sandwich. Dip in the egg mixture and fry as for regular French toast.

Links: Bread Pudding—like a big, baked french toast (page 75), Home Fries— why not? as long as you're cooking (page 143), Pancakes (page 175), Whipped Cream (page 239).

French Vinaigrette

In France, this is practically the only salad dressing you will ever see—if you ever see a salad, that is. If you want something easier, you are pretty lazy and you should use the Italian stand-by: toss your salad with balsamic vinegar, extra-virgin olive oil, salt, and pepper. If you prefer your dressing less vinegary, substitute two tablespoons boiling water for two tablespoons of vinegar. Required Reading: Emulsifying Demystified (page 13), Saucing (page 17), Selecting Ingredients (page 11).

In a small bowl, place the mustard, add the vinegar, and beat together with a fork until combined. While beating with a fork—using the same motion you would use to beat an egg—slowly drizzle in the olive oil, stopping now and then to make sure the olive oil is being incorporated. You are trying to make a smooth emulsion. If you add the oil too quickly, and don't beat it into the mustard mixture, it will break. When all of the oil is incorporated, add the pepper, mix, and serve. The dressing will keep in an airtight jar at room temperature indefinitely. Just shake before serving.

Links: Chicken Salad (page 91), Warm Potato Salad (page 235), any salad.

Makes 1 cup

2 tablespoons Dijon mustard

$^1/_4$ cup vinegar (cider, balsamic, sherry, tarragon; anything except plain white vinegar)

$^3/_4$ cup extra-virgin olive oil

Freshly ground black pepper to taste

Kitchen Stuff

Small bowl

Fresh Tomato Sauce

No, this isn't a tomato sauce that talks back. Unlike the familiar marinara or red sauces, which are staples in suburban American Italian restaurants and which are simmered for longer than most Italian governments stay in power, fresh tomato sauce only takes a few minutes to prepare. Any tomato will do, but plum or roma tomatoes are generally preferred. Depending on your level of commitment, you can peel and seed the tomatoes before you begin for a more sophisticated sauce. Otherwise, like my friends Amy and Jon do, you can leave it chunky, seedy, and rustic. For more sauce, just double or triple the recipe. If ripe tomatoes aren't available, prepare a Spaghetti Sauce instead (see page 227). Required Reading: Peeling and Seeding Tomatoes (page 16), Saucing (page 17), Sautéing, Frying, and Stir-Frying (page 19), Seasoning to Taste (page 19), Selecting Ingredients (page 11), Straining (page 20).

In a large skillet, heat the olive oil over medium-high heat. Add the onion and sauté until translucent, 2 to 3 minutes. Add the garlic and continue sautéing for another couple of minutes, stirring constantly to be sure the garlic doesn't color or burn.

Add the chopped tomatoes, red wine, if using, chopped herbs, and bay leaf. Turn down the heat and simmer until the tomatoes have "melted" and the sauce has become more liquid, 8 to 12 minutes. Taste and adjust the seasoning with salt and pepper. Remove the bay leaf and serve.

Variations

A More Refined Tomato Sauce
The advantage of this variation is that you don't have to peel and seed the tomatoes. To make a more refined sauce, transfer the hot tomato mixture to a blender, food processor, or vegetable mill after it has finished simmering. Puree until smooth and strain through a fine sieve, using a wooden spoon to push the mixture through. Be sure to get out all the juice.

Golden Tomato Sauce
More and more readily available, yellow tomatoes are a fun alternative to your basic red tomato. Follow the recipe exactly as for red tomatoes, but add 2 teaspoons of balsamic vinegar to the sauce to compensate for the yellow tomato's low acidity.

Pasta Primavera
Just after the tomato sauce has finished simmering, add 1 1/2 cups chopped, cooked vegetables (broccoli, cauliflower, carrots, peas, zucchini, eggplant). Continue simmering until the vegetables are hot. Toss with pasta and cheese.

Links: Pasta Primer (page 177), Spaghetti Sauce (page 227).

Makes 2 servings

3 tablespoons extra-virgin olive oil

1 medium onion, finely chopped

1 clove garlic, minced

4 to 8 ripe tomatoes, depending on their size, chopped (if you are feeling industrious, you should peel and seed the tomatoes; see page 16)

1/4 cup red wine (optional)

1 teaspoon chopped fresh herbs (thyme, rosemary, oregano, marjoram)

1 bay leaf

Salt and freshly ground black pepper to taste

Kitchen Stuff

Food processor, blender, or vegetable mill (optional)

Measuring cups

Measuring spoons

Sieve (optional)

Skillet

Fried Eggplant, Middle-Eastern Style

Makes 12 to 15 slices,
enough for about 4 people

1 large eggplant

Salt

1 cup olive oil
(preferably not extra-virgin)

Juice of 2 lemons

Freshly ground black pepper

Kitchen Stuff

Large skillet

Paper towel or brown paper bag

Great as an appetizer or on sandwiches, fried eggplant is one of my favorite foods. Stick it in a pita with cucumbers, tomatoes, sprouts, and the Lemon Tahini Dressing on page 155 and you have a great lunch. If you would prefer something lighter (with less oil) you can grill the eggplant using the technique on page 137. Required Reading: Cutting Up Things (page 13), Making a Sandwich (page 15), Patience (page 16), Sautéing, Frying, and Stir-Frying (page 19), Selecting Ingredients (page 11), Squeezing Lemons (page 20).

Wash the eggplant thoroughly and pat dry with a paper towel. With a sharp knife, thinly slice the eggplant either crosswise or lengthwise, no more than 1/4 inch thick. The way I am going to use the eggplant determines how I choose to slice it—for a hero sandwich I slice it lengthwise into long pieces, for a pita I slice it crosswise into rounds.

Lay the slices out on a plate. Generously sprinkle both sides with salt and let sit for at least 30 minutes. The salt helps to draw out some of the bitter juices, which will bead up on the surface. When you are ready to use the eggplant, wipe down the slices with paper towel to remove the moisture and some of the salt.

In a large sauté pan, heat about 1/4 cup of the oil. When the oil is hot, lay a single layer of eggplant in the pan. Fry until deep brown, but not burned. Turn over the slices with a fork and brown on the other side. When the eggplant is done, it should be golden brown, soft, and limp. Remove from the oil and drain on paper towel or on a clean brown paper bag. Repeat with the remaining slices until all of the eggplant is fried. Pat off any excess oil with paper towel and transfer to a clean plate. Squeeze the lemon over the fried eggplant and season with freshly ground black pepper. Serve either warm or at room temperature.

Links: Aioli (page 53), Eggplant Parmesan (page 116), Grilled Vegetables (page 137), Lemon Tahini Dressing (page 155).

Fried Green Tomatoes

This dish was popular in the South long before the tear-jerker movie of the same name was made. Equally good for breakfast, as a side dish for dinner, or as the main ingredient for a special vegetarian sandwich, fried green tomatoes are about as good as home cookin' gets. Green tomatoes in this case are unripened red tomatoes (in the case of the Green Tomato Salsa, page 134, they are Mexican tomatillos), and they are available at farmers' markets and local fruit and vegetable stands all summer long.

Required Reading: Breading (page 12), Making a Sandwich (page 15), Sauteing, Frying, and Stir-Frying (page 19), Selecting Ingredients (page 11).

Remove the stems and cut out the core of the tomatoes. Slice them crosswise into ¹/₄-inch-thick slices. In a wide, shallow bowl, beat the eggs with a fork until frothy. Add the milk and continue beating until combined. In another bowl or on a plate with a deep rim, combine the cornmeal, salt, and black pepper. Place some paper towel or a clean brown paper bag on another plate to drain the fried green tomatoes when they are done.

Dip the tomato slices in the egg mixture and dredge in the seasoned cornmeal mixture to coat well on all sides. Set aside on a clean plate or baking sheet. Repeat until all of the slices are breaded in the cornmeal.

Meanwhile, heat about ¹/₈ inch of vegetable oil in a frying pan set over medium-high heat. Place the cornmeal-breaded tomato slices in the hot oil and fry until golden brown, 4 to 6 minutes on each side. Remove to the paper towel or brown paper bag to drain. Repeat with the remaining slices until all of the tomatoes are fried. Keep warm in a low oven (about 250°F) until ready to serve.

Links: Green Tomato Salsa (page 134).

Makes 6 to 8 servings

5 green tomatoes (see headnote)

2 large eggs

¹/₂ cup whole milk

1¹/₂ cups yellow cornmeal

¹/₂ teaspoon salt

15 grinds black pepper

Vegetable oil for frying

Kitchen Stuff

Cookie sheet

Large skillet

Measuring cups

Measuring spoons

Paper towel or brown paper bag

Fried Rice

Another good vegetarian entrée and a great way to use leftover rice from take-out Chinese food, fried rice will welcome anything you have to put in it. If you have other leftover Chinese food, such as a stir-fried chicken and vegetable dish, chop it up and add it to the rice. Otherwise, you can add fresh vegetables, such as carrots and celery, or meat, such as chicken or pork seasoned with soy sauce. Required Reading: Cutting Up Things (page 13), Sauteing, Frying, and Stir-Frying (page 19), Selecting Ingredients (page 11), Convenience Foods (page 11), Using Leftovers (page 21), Working with Meat (page 21).

In a small bowl, beat together the eggs, sherry or stock, soy sauce, and chile sauce, if using. Heat a wok or large frying pan over high heat until hot. Add the peanut oil, spread around with a large spoon or spatula, and add the garlic and ginger. Sauté for 1 to 2 minutes, being careful not to let them burn. Add the chopped vegetables. If using raw vegetables, sauté for 2 to 3 minutes until wilted. If using cooked, just heat through. If using raw chicken or pork, add them now and sauté until cooked through.

Add the leftover rice and break it up with your spoon or spatula so that it begins to heat up. Mix with the other ingredients. Pour in the egg mixture and mix well so that the rice soaks it all up. This mixture will turn the rice the dark color of fried rice. As the egg begins to cook, the rice will also separate into grains. The whole process takes about 20 minutes. Cook until the rice is very hot. Adjust the seasoning with more soy sauce, garnish with chopped scallions, and serve.

Links: Stir-Fried Watercress or Bok Choy (page 228), Scrambled Tofu—it goes well on the side (page 221).

Makes 2 to 4 main course servings, depending on how much stuff you put in it

2 large eggs

$1/4$ cup dry sherry or chicken stock or leftover wonton soup

2 tablespoons soy sauce, tamari, or shoyu, or more to taste

$1/2$ to 1 teaspoon hot chile sauce (optional)

2 tablespoons peanut oil

1 clove garlic, minced

1 tablespoon minced fresh ginger

1 cup chopped raw or cooked vegetables or roughly chopped meat such as chicken or pork

2 cups leftover white or brown steamed rice, or a combination of both

3 scallions, finely chopped

Kitchen Stuff

Large sauté pan or wok

Measuring cups

Measuring spoons

Small mixing bowl

Fried Tofu Sandwiches

Makes 2 sandwiches

1 block extra-firm tofu,
about 6 to 8 ounces

$1/4$ cup unbleached all-purpose
flour

1 teaspoon salt

15 grinds black pepper

Vegetable oil for frying
(preferably peanut)

3 to 4 drops soy sauce, tamari,
or shoyu

4 slices toasted bread (sourdough,
challah, rye, whatever you like)

Lettuce, tomato, cucumber,
sprouts, and mayonnaise for
garnish

Kitchen Stuff

Measuring spoons

Small plate

Small skillet

Call me crazy, but I think tofu is a wonder food (see also Miso Mania, page 163). It takes on almost any flavor you give it, changes texture depending on what you do to it, and is very high in protein. This is one of my favorite sandwiches because I like the contrast of the hot tofu and the cold accompaniments, and because it tastes like a fried egg sandwich without the fried egg. Use any combination of veggies you like. Required Reading: Breading (page 12), Making a Sandwich (page 15), Sautéing, Frying, and Stir-Frying (page 19), Selecting Ingredients (page 11).

Rinse the tofu under cold water and drain. Slice into rectangular pieces about $1/4$ inch thick. Place the flour on a small plate and season heavily with salt and freshly ground pepper. Mix well. Dredge the tofu slices in the seasoned flour to coat on all sides. Tap the slices with your finger to remove any excess flour.

In the bottom of a frying pan, heat about $1/8$ inch of peanut oil over medium-high heat. When the oil is hot, place a layer of tofu slices in the pan and fry until the tofu is a deep golden brown, 4 to 6 minutes. Turn over the slices and fry the other side until brown. Drain on paper towels. Place a drop or 2 of soy sauce, tamari, or shoyu on each slice and assemble the sandwich on toasted bread with your favorite garnishes.

Links: Aioli (page 53), Lemon Tahini Dressing (page 155), Rémoulade (page 197).

Gazpacho

The Spanish drink this chilled soup in glasses for a snack on hot afternoons. Poured over garlic croutons (page 81), it's a perfect starter for a summer gathering because it does not require you to turn on the stove.

There are several ways to prepare gazpacho. The most authentic is to chop all of the ingredients by hand separately and combine them in a large bowl to season. To speed up the preparation time, however, the easiest thing is to put all of the ingredients in a blender or food processor and process until smooth. Depending on the size of your blender or food processor, and how much soup you are preparing, you may have to process the ingredients in batches and combine the soup in a large bowl to season.

When you are preparing your gazpacho, keep in mind that flavors become less pronounced when chilled. Taste the soup just before serving to adjust the seasoning. Of course there is nothing like using fresh, ripe tomatoes. Red tomatoes are traditional, but yellow tomatoes make an attractive and flavorful gazpacho. Unfortunately fresh tomatoes aren't in season very long and they need to be peeled and seeded (see page 16) before they are pureed. They also have a low per-pound yield. Instead, you can use canned tomatoes and tomato juice. Adding some fresh tomato along with the canned tomatoes will improve the flavor. Required Reading: Convenience Foods (page 11), Peeling and Seeding Tomatoes (page 16), Resting (page 17), Seasoning to Taste (page 19), Selecting Ingredients (page 11), Using the Food Processor (page 21).

In a blender or food processor, place the garlic and process with quick on/off pulses until minced. Add the onion and repeat. Add the cucumber and peppers and continue pulsing until finely chopped. If the vegetables are too dry to chop finely, add some of the olive oil. Keep scraping them down from the sides of the bowl as you work.

Add the tomatoes and tomato juice and process until smooth. Transfer to a large bowl. Add the olive oil, vinegar, salt, and pepper and stir well. Taste and adjust the seasoning. Remember that when the soup is chilled, the flavors will be less pronounced. Cover and chill for at least 4 hours. Readjust the seasoning—more olive oil and/or vinegar may be necessary—and serve in chilled bowls or glasses.

My friend Mildred garnishes her gazpacho with garlic croutons (see Caesar Salad recipe on page 81), diced cucumber, diced yellow tomato, cooked shrimp, and fresh cilantro.

Links: Caesar Salad—for the croutons (page 81).

Makes 6 to 8 servings

2 cloves garlic, peeled

1/2 red onion, peeled and roughly chopped

1 cucumber, peeled, seeded, and cut into pieces

1 green pepper, seeded

1 red pepper, seeded

1 jalapeño pepper, seeded

5 large ripe tomatoes, peeled, seeded, and chopped (see page 16), or 1 large can or box (28 ounces) Italian-style crushed tomatoes

3/4 cup (one 6-ounce can) tomato juice

1/2 cup extra-virgin olive oil

1/3 cup vinegar (red wine, sherry, or balsamic are best)

2 teaspoons salt

1 teaspoon freshly ground black pepper

Kitchen Stuff

Can opener

Food processor or blender

Liquid measuring cups

Measuring spoons

Green Tomato Salsa

Makes about 1 cup

One 10-ounce can Mexican green tomatoes, or $1/2$ pound fresh tomatillos

1 to 2 fresh hot red or green peppers, seeded

1 clove garlic, crushed

3 tablespoons vinegar (white, white wine, red wine, sherry, or what have you)

$1/8$ teaspoon dried oregano

$1/8$ teaspoon ground allspice

Salt and freshly ground black pepper to taste

Kitchen Stuff

Food processor or blender

Measuring spoons

Though you might think this is another use for unripened, green tomatoes (like the Fried Green Tomatoes recipe on page 129), the truth is that so-called Mexican green tomatoes are actually tomatillos, a relative of the tomato, but a distinctly different fruit. This is a Guatemalan recipe from my friend Chris. Though it is traditionally used as a sauce for meats, fish, or shellfish, it's also good on corn chips.

Look for canned Mexican green tomatoes in Mexican bodegas or in the Mexican foods section of your local grocery store. If fresh tomatillos are available—they come wrapped in a protective and decorative leafy encasing that has to be removed—they work well too. Required Reading: Convenience Foods (page 11), Saucing (page 17), Seasoning to Taste (page 19), Selecting Ingredients (page 11), Using the Food Processor (page 21).

Drain the canned tomatoes, or remove the dry outer husks of the fresh tomatillos and wash them well. Roughly chop. In a blender or food processor, place all of the ingredients and pulse on and off until pureed. Store in a tightly covered container in the refrigerator. The salsa will keep for about 2 to 3 weeks.

Links: Fried Green Tomatoes (page 129).

Grilled Cheese Sandwich

It's gotten harder and harder to find a good grilled cheese sandwich these days, so I thought I would include this recipe just in case you ever get the hankering. There are two schools of thought when it comes to the application of the butter. Some people prefer to butter both sides of the bread, sandwich the cheese in the middle, and fry the whole thing in a dry, hot pan. Since I find it difficult to handle a piece of bread that has been buttered on both sides, and since I usually don't have soft butter around and I hate when the butter tears up the bread, I like to sandwich the cheese between the bread, heat the butter in the pan, and fry the sandwich that way. Come to think of it, the name of this sandwich is a little odd, since it isn't actually grilled, but fried or "griddled" in most diners. Who cares? It's a classic. Add the bacon and tomato for a little variation. Required Reading: Making a Sandwich (page 15), Sautéing, Frying, and Stir-Frying (page 19), Selecting Ingredients (page 11).

Divide the sliced cheese between the two sandwiches. If using bacon and/or tomato, sandwich them between slices of cheese and then between the bread. In a frying pan large enough to fit the two sandwiches side by side, heat half of the butter over medium-high heat. When the butter is frothy and hot, add the sandwiches.

With a spatula, press down on each sandwich to be sure the bread soaks up the butter and to encourage the cheese to melt. Keep pressing down periodically as the sandwiches cook. When the bread is a glistening golden brown on the bottom, turn over and cook the other side, adding the remaining butter to the pan and pressing down the sandwich again. Cook until the bread is crispy and golden brown. Serve immediately.

Variations

Croque Monsieur

A simulation of this classic French bistro sandwich can be made by spreading the bread with Dijon mustard, substituting Swiss cheese for the cheddar, and sandwiching 1 or 2 slices of cooked ham in the middle. Follow the directions above.

Reuben

What is a Reuben sandwich, except a grilled cheese on rye bread with Swiss cheese, corned beef, and sauerkraut? Be sure to drain the sauerkraut well before you assemble the sandwich. Follow the directions for a regular Grilled Cheese (left).

Links: Potato Salad—goes well on the side (page 191).

Makes 2 sandwiches

1/4 pound cheddar cheese, sliced thinly, or, if you must, 4 slices American cheese

4 slices fresh bread (challah or fresh bakery sandwich bread work very well)

6 slices cooked bacon (optional)

4 slices ripe tomato (optional)

4 to 6 tablespoons butter, depending on your constitution

Kitchen Stuff

Large skillet

Metal spatula

Grilled Vegetables

Perhaps one of the most delicious things to come out of the Mediterranean health craze of late has been a preponderance of grilled vegetables on menus and salad bars throughout the country. Grilled vegetables are versatile: they are good in sandwiches, on salads, with pasta, or alone as an informal antipasto. They are nutritious. And they are just about the only thing you can do with that stove-top grill you got as a house-warming gift last year. If you don't have a grill or access to a barbecue, you can roast the vegetables with equally yummy results (see page 209).

You can grill almost any vegetable, but my favorites are peppers, fennel, radicchio, red onions, eggplant, scallions, zucchini, yellow squash, and the inimitable portobello mushroom. Be sure to cut the vegetables in uniform pieces of equal thickness so that grilling times remain constant. And grill similar vegetables at the same time so that they cook evenly.

Required Reading: Grilling, Barbecuing, and Broiling (page 13), Making a Sandwich (page 15), Preheating (page 16), Seasoning to Taste (page 19), Selecting Ingredients (page 11), Testing for Doneness (page 20).

Makes more than enough vegetables for a few sandwiches, an antipasto, and a couple of small salads

1 small head radicchio

1 bulb fennel, tops removed

1 red pepper

1 yellow pepper

1 bunch scallions

1 small eggplant

1 small zucchini

1 red onion

4 portobello mushrooms

1 bunch asparagus

$1/2$ to $3/4$ cup olive oil

Salt and freshly ground black pepper to taste

3 to 4 tablespoons balsamic vinegar

Kitchen Stuff

Pastry brush

Stove-top grill or barbecue

Tongs (to help with the turning)

To prepare the radicchio and the fennel, trim a thin layer off the bottom of the central white core. Slice the heads in half through the core, being sure to keep the leaves attached to the core. Slice each half into uniform-sized wedges, first in half, then in half again, each time cutting through the core so that you keep the leaves attached. Set aside.

To prepare the red and yellow peppers, cut out the central stem and slice the peppers in half through the middle. Remove the seeds and the white ribs. Cut each half into diamonds or rhomboid-shaped pieces. You should get 3 to 4 per half, depending on the size of the peppers.

For the scallions, cut off the root end and trim about 1 to 2 inches off the

greens. Pull off any dark or dried-out outer layers. To prepare the eggplant and the zucchini, slice the vegetables into $1/4$-inch thick disks on a slight angle to produce an almost oval slice. Peel the red onion and slice into rings.

To prepare the portobello mushrooms, remove the stems. Trim the dirty end of the stems and slice in half lengthwise. Keep the mushroom caps intact. If the asparagus spears are more than about $1/2$ inch in diameter, lightly peel the lower portion of the spears with a carrot peeler.

Once all of the vegetables are cut and ready to cook, preheat the grill. If using a cast-iron grill, set over medium-low flame to heat for 2 to 3 minutes, then increase the heat to medium-high. If

> I have always considered vegetable cookery the most interesting part of cuisine. Vegetables provide an incredible depth and complexity in both flavor and texture, not to mention an extraordinary range of colors and shapes... The act of preparing vegetables is an especially life-giving exercise, primarily because it leads to serving and eating foods that are inherently good for you.
>
> —CHARLIE TROTTER, *CHARLIE TROTTER'S VEGETABLES*
> (TEN SPEED, 1996)

using a grill that requires a pan of water underneath, fill the pan with water, set over medium-high heat, place the grill top over the water, and heat until hot. To test if the grill is hot, sprinkle a couple of drops of water on it. It should sizzle and evaporate almost instantly if the grill is sufficiently preheated. If using a barbecue, wait until the flames die down and the charcoal becomes red hot before beginning to grill.

Using a pastry brush, generously brush all sides of the prepared vegetables with olive oil and sprinkle with salt and freshly ground black pepper. Grill the vegetables one at a time, until all sides have nice grill marks and the vegetables are tender. The peppers, radicchio, zucchini, and scallions will take less time than the eggplant and fennel. There is nothing worse than undercooked eggplant, so be sure it is tender throughout.

The less you handle the vegetables while they are grilling, the prettier they will look when done. If the vegetables begin to burn before they are cooked through, lower the heat. As the vegetables are cooked, remove to a serving plate. When all of the vegetables are done, toss with a little of the left over olive oil and the balsamic vinegar. Serve at room temperature.

Variation

Grilled Vegetable Sandwich

Just in case you couldn't come up with a version of this sandwich on your own, I thought I would give you some guidelines. You can use any bread and condiment you like. I prefer toasted seven-grain bread because the texture of the bread and the smoky flavor of the vegetables makes me think I'm eating a BLT. Grilled portobello mushrooms make this sandwich fit for a king. Spread the Rémoulade (page 197) on one side of all 4 pieces of toasted seven-grain bread. Lay the grilled vegetables on the bread. Top with the lettuce, tomato, and sprouts. Top each sandwich with the second piece of bread. Spear each sandwich with two toothpicks and slice into halves.

Links: Aioli—great for dipping the veggies in (page 53), French Vinaigrette—to toss the vegetables, if you like (page 125), Roasted Vegetables (page 209).

Guacamole

Of all the recipes for guacamole I've tried, I enjoy this one best. It's similar to a recipe given to me by my friend Pac, and it's so simple to make. There are two secrets to great guacamole. First, the avocados must be perfectly ripe—firm, but soft, sweet, and rich. If yours are hard as rocks, let them sit on the counter for a couple of days before you prepare the Guacamole. Then you have to be sure not to mash the avocado too much, but to leave it lumpy. The amount of the other ingredients can vary to taste, although one of my pet peeves is underseasoned guacamole— I've even been served bland, unsalted guacamole in Mexico. Don't make the same mistake. Required Reading: Making a Sandwich (page 15), Seasoning to Taste (page 19), Selecting Ingredients (page 11), Squeezing Lemons (page 20).

Cut the avocados in half around the pit and separate into 2 pieces. Scoop out the flesh into a bowl and roughly mash with a fork. Add the remaining ingredients and mix well, being careful not to overmix or the texture will become too smooth. Taste the guacamole and adjust the seasoning with more lemon or lime juice and/or salt and pepper. Serve with corn chips or fresh corn tortillas.

Links: Avocado Sandwich (page 59).

Makes 4 to 6 servings

3 ripe Haas avocados
(the small, black, nubby ones, which have the best flavor)

Juice of 1 to 2 lemons, or 3 to 4 limes

1 medium tomato, cored and diced

1 small handful fresh cilantro, finely chopped

1/2 red onion, finely chopped

1 tablespoon olive oil

1 teaspoon salt

6 to 8 grinds black pepper

1 dash hot sauce

Kitchen Stuff

Fork (you better have one)

Measuring spoons

Hamburgers

Makes 6 large hamburgers

2 pounds medium ground beef

1 large egg

1 tablespoon Dijon mustard

2 tablespoons ketchup

3 tablespoons ice water

$^1/_2$ small onion, grated or minced

2 tablespoons unflavored bread crumbs

Dash hot sauce (optional)

1 teaspoon salt

10 grinds black pepper, or to taste

Kitchen Stuff

Barbecue, grill, cast-iron pan, or broiler

Measuring spoons

Mixing bowl

There are those who like to make hamburgers by taking freshly ground beef, shaping it into patties, and cooking it without adding anything to flavor or otherwise enhance the meat. Unless your ground beef is made from the highest quality aged beef, which is almost impossible to find, I think you get better results if you doctor it up a little.

Never use extra-lean ground beef for hamburgers. The results are just too dry and flavorless. Instead, if fat is an issue, try ground turkey. There's nothing better than a charcoal barbecue to cook the burgers. But a stove-top grill, cast-iron pan, or broiler produces acceptable results. Experiment with your own ingredients to produce different types of hamburgers. Required Reading: Grilling, Barbecuing, and Broiling (page 13), Sautéing, Frying, and Stir-Frying (page 19), Seasoning to Taste (page 19), Selecting Ingredients (page 11), Testing for Doneness (page 20), Working with Meat (page 21).

Combine all of the ingredients in a mixing bowl and mix with a wooden spoon until blended. Rinse your hands in cold water and shape the meat mixture in your wet palms into six uniform patties, no more than $^3/_4$ to 1 inch thick. Keep wetting your hands so that the meat doesn't stick. Layer the burgers on a plate with plastic wrap between the layers and refrigerate until ready to serve.

Preheat the barbecue, stove-top grill, cast-iron pan, or broiler. Cook the burgers to desired doneness, about 8 minutes on each side for medium rare. Try to turn the burgers only once during cooking so that you don't risk letting out any of their natural juices. To be sure they are cooked, cut into the center of one to check the color. Serve the cut one to yourself.

Variations

Bacon Cheeseburgers

Just before the burgers have finished cooking, top each with a slice of cheddar cheese and 2 or 3 slices of cooked bacon. If using a cast-iron pan or grill, drop a couple of tablespoons of cold water in the pan and cover immediately with a lid. The steam helps melt the cheese and warm the bacon.

Gorgonzola and Sun-Dried Tomato Burgers

Add about $^1/_2$ cup of chopped sun-dried tomatoes (the soft ones that have been soaking in olive oil) to the meat mixture before forming burgers. Just before the burgers have finished cooking, top each with a handful of crumbled Gorgonzola or other blue cheese. If using a cast-iron pan or grill, drop a couple of tablespoons of cold water in the pan and cover immediately with a lid. The steam helps melt the cheese.

The hamburger cook-out is another favorite with the teen-agers. It's just like the wiener roast except that hamburgers are cooked on a grate or in a skillet, and the buns are round... For a change, have the ground beef formed in the shape of hot dogs and wrapped in bacon. You'll then need the long rolls, of course.

—JAMES BEARD AND HELEN EVANS BROWN,
THE COMPLETE BOOK OF OUTDOOR COOKERY (DOUBLEDAY, 1955)

Mushroom and Onion Burger
Smother the hamburgers with sautéed Mom's Mushrooms and Onions (see page 166) just before serving.

Turkey Burgers
Substitute 2$\frac{1}{2}$ pounds ground turkey for the ground beef. Proceed with the recipe as directed. The water keeps the burgers moist. (A friend of mine who finds even the idea of turkey burgers sacrilegious thought these were delicious.)

Links: Mom's Mushrooms and Onions—for the Mushroom and Onion Burger (page 166), Potato Salad (page 191), Warm Potato Salad (page 235).

Home Fries

In the best diners across America, piles of home fries crispen in butter and bacon and sausage fat all morning long on the griddle. This is the best recipe I know for home fries made without the benefit of cooking all morning in bacon and sausage fat. It takes a little time because you have to blanch the potatoes first, but the effort is worth it. I used to have a regular Sunday brunch in my apartment, and although the menu changed from week to week, I could never not make these home fries for fear of disappointing my friends. Required Reading: Salting Water (page 17), Sautéing, Frying, and Stir-Frying (page 19), Seasoning to Taste (page 19), Selecting Ingredients (page 11).

Set a large pot of salted water on the stove to boil. Meanwhile, wash the potatoes thoroughly under cold water. Remove any eyes or other blemishes. Cut the potatoes into chunks with the skins on. The chunks should be about $1/2$ inch square and $1/4$ to $1/2$ inch thick. When the water comes to a full boil, add the potatoes and cook until they just begin to soften ever so slightly, 4 to 5 minutes. Drain.

Preheat the oven to 425°F. In a large sauté pan that can go in the oven (meaning it doesn't have plastic or wood handles), heat the butter and/or bacon fat over medium-high heat. Add the sliced onion and sauté until translucent, 5 to 8 minutes. Add the blanched potatoes and mix well. If it looks like you need more fat—home fries can always use a little more fat—add it. Add the salt and freshly ground black pepper.

Continue to cook the potatoes, stirring frequently to prevent burning, until they begin to brown, 15 to 20 minutes. The potatoes should be tender but still hold their shape somewhat. Flatten the potatoes out so that they are an even thickness in the pan. Set the pan in the preheated oven and roast for about 10 minutes until the top is golden brown. Remove from the oven and serve. You can keep the potatoes warm in a 250°F oven until the rest of the meal is ready.

Links: French Toast (page 123), Pancakes (page 175), Scrambled Eggs (page 220).

Makes 4 to 6 servings

4 large red-skinned potatoes

4 to 6 tablespoons butter or bacon fat or any combination of the two

1 large onion, thinly sliced

About 2 teaspoons salt, or to taste

10 to 15 grinds black pepper, or to taste

Kitchen Stuff

Large oven-proof skillet

Large saucepan or stock pot

Measuring cups

Measuring spoons

Honey-Buttermilk Cornbread

Makes 6 to 8 servings

Butter for pan

1 cup yellow cornmeal

1 cup unbleached all-purpose flour

$^1/_2$ teaspoon salt

1 teaspoon baking powder

1 teaspoon baking soda

$^1/_4$ cup honey

1 large egg, beaten

2 cups buttermilk

Kitchen Stuff

8-inch cake pan or
$8^1/_2$ x $4^1/_2$ x $2^1/_2$-inch loaf pan

Measuring cups

Measuring spoons

Mixing bowl

Somewhere between a cake, a muffin, and a quick bread, this cornbread is delicious for breakfast or brunch or as a side to a bowl of soup. As when making Bran Muffins (page 73) or Banana Bread (page 63), it is important not to overmix the batter. For a Southwestern spin, add chopped ham and jalapeño. Required Reading: Buttering and Flouring (page 23), Preheating (page 16), Mixing versus Overmixing (page 25), Selecting Ingredients (page 11).

Preheat the oven to 375°F. Butter an 8-inch square cake pan or an $8^1/_2$ x $4^1/_2$ x $2^1/_2$-inch loaf pan. In a large mixing bowl, combine the cornmeal, flour, salt, baking powder, and baking soda. Make a well in the center and pour in the honey, beaten egg, and buttermilk. Stir with a fork just until the ingredients are combined.

Pour into the prepared pan and bake in the middle of the preheated oven. If using a square cake pan, bake for approximately 35 minutes, or until the bread is brown and has pulled away from the sides. Insert a skewer or a small knife in the center to double check. If it comes out clean, the cornbread is done. If using a loaf pan, the cornbread may take closer to 50 minutes to bake.

Links: Any brunch dishes, Mushroom Barley Soup—it goes well on the side (page 169).

Honey-Citrus Asian Salad Dressing

This recipe was given to me by my sister Carrie. It is a great dressing for any salad. I love the sweet-and-sour flavor and the fact that there are only two tablespoons of oil in the whole thing. Be sure to include something sweet in the salad, such as orange sections or litchi; something crunchy, like blanched snow peas, bean sprouts, daikon, or chopped peanuts; and something spicy, such as fresh chiles, arugula, or sliced red onion. Actually, why not put them all in? Required Reading: Mixing in a Jar (page 16), Selecting Ingredients (page 11).

In a glass jar with a tightly fitting lid, combine all of the ingredients and shake until the sugar is dissolved and the dressing is well blended.

Links: French Vinaigrette (page 125).

Makes ³/₄ cup

2 tablespoons rice wine vinegar

2 tablespoons vegetable oil (preferably peanut)

2 tablespoons freshly squeezed orange juice

2 tablespoons white sugar, brown sugar, or honey

2 tablespoons soy sauce, tamari, or shoyu

2 tablespoons Dijon or grainy mustard

¹/₄ teaspoon toasted sesame oil

3 to 4 grinds black pepper, or to taste

Kitchen Stuff

Jar with a tightly fitting lid

Measuring spoons

Honey-Garlic Chicken Wings

Here's a great recipe for a snack, hors d'oeuvre, or light dinner. A little different from your classic honey-garlic chicken wings, this version has an Asian flavor provided by the soy sauce and browned garlic. If you have the time, it's best to roast the wings in the morning and let them sit in the sauce all day before you broil them to their sweet, crispy glory.

Required Reading: Grilling, Barbecuing, and Broiling (page 13), Marinating (page 15), Roasting, Braising, and Steaming (page 17), Selecting Ingredients (page 11), Working with Meat (page 21).

Preheat the oven to 425°F. Line a cookie sheet (with sides) or roasting pan with aluminum foil (so it will be easier to clean). Or better yet, buy a disposable aluminum cookie sheet. Arrange the chicken wings in the pan in a single layer; they should not be touching. Season liberally with the salt, freshly ground black pepper, and garlic powder.

Set in the oven and roast for 15 minutes, until the skin begins to brown slightly. Turn over the wings and roast for another 10 to 15 minutes, until the second side is also lightly browned.

While the wings are roasting, prepare the sauce. In a small saucepan, heat the oil over medium-high heat. Add the minced garlic and sauté until it turns a golden brown, about 5 minutes. Be sure it doesn't burn. If it turns black, throw it out and start again. When the garlic is golden brown, add the remaining ingredients to the pan. Bring to a boil, turn down the heat, and simmer for 10 minutes.

Pour off any excess fat that has rendered off the wings. Pour the sauce over the wings in the pan and move the wings around to coat. The sauce will be thin, but it will thicken during the final baking. If you have the time, leave the wings sitting in the sauce for 8 to 10 hours, turning them once in a while to coat with the sauce.

Preheat the broiler. Broil the wings until they become dark brown and crispy, 5 to 8 minutes. Turn them over and broil the second side. The sauce will thicken and become tacky. If you don't have a broiler, bake the wings in a preheated 450°F oven for about 15 minutes on each side.

You may be alarmed by the mess the sauce has made in your pan. But don't worry, it is water soluble. Just soak the pan in hot, soapy water and it will wipe clean.

Links: These stand alone.

Makes 4 main course servings, 10 hors d'oeuvres or snack servings

3 pounds chicken wings, tips cut off and separated in half (ask your butcher to do it or separate them yourself at the joints, discarding the pointed tips)

2 teaspoons salt

10 to 15 grinds black pepper

2 teaspoons garlic powder

3 tablespoons vegetable oil

2 large cloves garlic, minced

3/4 cup honey

1/2 cup water

1/2 cup soy sauce

1 tablespoon molasses

Kitchen Stuff

Aluminum foil or better yet a disposable aluminum cookie sheet

Cookie sheet

Liquid measuring cups

Measuring spoons

Small saucepan

Hummus

Whether you pronounce it HOO-moos or HUH-muhs, you can't deny this Middle-Eastern chickpea spread has become an American staple. Spread in pita sandwiches or used as a dip, hummus is a satisfying, nutritious food that is always good to have on hand. If you keep a can or two of chickpeas in the cupboard, you can whip up a batch in minutes. A food processor works best, but you can use a hand-held blender or a counter-top one if you thin down the hummus with some of the liquid from the canned chickpeas.

When you are feeling particularly industrious, you can soak and cook your own chickpeas (see Mister Bean, page 164), which will give you a more authentic, more flavorful result. Serve with a drizzle of olive oil and Lemon Tahini Dressing (see page 155). Required Reading: Convenience Foods (page 11), Seasoning to Taste (page 19), Selecting Ingredients (page 11), Smashing Garlic (page 19), Squeezing Lemons (page 20), Using the Food Processor (page 21).

Makes 3 cups

Two 16-ounce cans chickpeas, or 3 cups cooked chickpeas and $^1/_2$ cup cooking liquid

2 cloves garlic, peeled

$^1/_4$ cup tahini, or to taste

$^1/_4$ cup extra-virgin olive oil

Juice of 2 to 3 lemons, to taste

$^1/_2$ teaspoon paprika

$^1/_2$ teaspoon salt

10 to 15 grinds black pepper, or to taste

Additional extra-virgin olive oil for garnish

Kitchen Stuff

Food processor, blender, or hand-held blender

Liquid measuring cups

Measuring spoons

Drain the chickpeas, reserving about 2 tablespoons of the liquid, which you will use to thin down the hummus later. (If using a blender, you will need more liquid.) In the bowl of a food processor fitted with the metal chopping blade, place the drained chickpeas, reserved liquid, and all of the other ingredients. Using on/off pulses, puree the hummus until smooth, making sure there are no large lumps of garlic hiding. If using a blender, start with $^1/_4$ cup of the reserved liquid and add more only if the mixture will not puree properly. Once the mixture is pureed, let the food processor or blender run for about a minute to ensure smoothness. Serve in a bowl or spread on plates with a drizzle of olive oil and Lemon Tahini Dressing.

Links: Chickpea Salad (page 94), Lemon Tahini Dressing (page 155), Mister Bean (page 164).

Just-Between-You-and-Me Mashed Potatoes

In my mom's vocabulary, **good means butter, and lots of it.** Long before **Joël Robuchon in Paris shocked the world with his artery-clogging proportion of butter to potatoes in his famous potato puree, Mrs. Sondra Davis was satisfying us with her smooth and buttery mashed potatoes.**

Every once in a while for added richness she would throw in an egg and some sour cream and bake the mashed potatoes in the oven before serving them. One time, at a dinner for my sisters, she used so much butter that she called me in New York to confess. "Just between you and me," she began, **"I used a lot of butter." I can't begin to think how much. Anyway, now we have a new name for the mashed potatoes. I've given you a few lower-fat variations, just in case these mashed potatoes are too rich—but I would recommend you just eat less.** Required Reading: Cutting Up Things (page 13), Salting Water (page 17), Selecting Ingredients (page 11), Using Leftovers (page 21).

If you like skin-on mashed potatoes (I don't), cut the potatoes into equal-sized chunks, about 1 1/2- to 2-inch pieces. Otherwise, peel the potatoes first and then cut them into chunks. It is important that the potato pieces are of uniform size so that they cook evenly. Rinse the potato pieces, place in a saucepan with enough room to allow an inch of water at the top, and fill with cold water. Add about 2 teaspoons of the salt to the water, set over high heat and boil until the potatoes are very tender when pricked with a fork, 20 to 25 minutes, depending on how large you've cut them.

Drain the potatoes. Mash with a potato masher or a ricer if you have one. Whatever you do, don't put them in a food processor or blender. The result is more like wallpaper paste than mashed

potatoes. Add the butter and stir to melt. Add the sour cream, if using, and adjust the consistency with the milk or cream. Season with about 2 teaspoons of salt and freshly ground black pepper to taste. Serve immediately.

Variations

Flavored Mashed Potatoes

Lately I've been adding all sorts of things to my mashed potatoes with terrific results. Chopped, Sautéed Greens (page 214) and Stir-Fried Watercress or Bok Choy (page 228) are terrific mashed potato additions. Heat them first and stir in just before serving. Roasted red peppers and roasted garlic add a Mediterranean twist (see Mediterranean Potato Dip on page 162 for guidelines). A handful of chopped basil and some olive oil gives a summery flavor. If you boil a peeled parsnip and/or turnips

---

Makes 1 to 6 servings

2 pounds Yukon Gold or red-skinned potatoes (about 4 large potatoes or 6 medium)

About 4 teaspoons salt

1 stick unsalted butter

2 tablespoons sour cream (optional)

2 to 3 tablespoons milk or heavy cream (if you're feeling really indulgent)

Freshly ground black pepper to taste

Kitchen Stuff

Large saucepan

Measuring spoons

Potato masher or ricer

Man, it is said, could live on potatoes alone, with just a bit of fat now and then to keep the motor running smoothly... Boxed dehydrated mashed potatoes can be remarkably good when properly buttered up. But a dish of homemade mashed potatoes, freshly cooked and rich with milk and butter, smelling and tasting like real potato, is a soul-warming treat.

—JULIA CHILD, THE WAY TO COOK (KNOPF, 1989)

with the potatoes and mash them together, you will have a slightly different flavor. Adding 2 tablespoons of prepared white horseradish makes a terrific accompaniment to Beef Stew (page 68) or Osso Buco (page 172).

Mashed Potatoes on a Diet
You can get away with using only 3 or 4 tablespoons of butter if you increase the amount of milk. Substitute nonfat yogurt or sour cream for the regular sour cream.

Mashed Potato Cakes
To use up leftover mashed potatoes, stir 1 egg into 2 cups cold mashed potatoes, along with 3 to 4 tablespoons of unflavored bread crumbs and $1/4$ cup freshly grated imported Parmesan cheese. Mix well. Pat the mixture into hamburger-like cakes and fry in butter, of course, until golden brown on all sides.

Links: Beef Stew (page 68), Mediterranean Potato Dip (page 162), Osso Buco (page 172), Sautéed Greens (page 214), Stir-Fried Watercress or Bok Choy (page 228).

Latkes

My mother's traditional potato latke recipe earned me top honors in the amateur category of the First Annual James Beard Foundation Latke Cookoff in December 1995. Her secret ratio is one onion for every two potatoes. Although they are traditionally eaten at Hannukah, latkes are a great side dish for any roasted or braised meat. They make a good brunch entrée, too. Latkes are always best eaten right out of the pan with fresh applesauce and sour cream. Required Reading: Reheating (page 16), Sautéing, Frying, and Stir-Frying (page 19), Seasoning to Taste (page 19), Selecting Ingredients (page 11), Using the Food Processor (page 21).

Makes 8 to 10 side dish servings

4 medium to large russet potatoes (about 2 pounds), peeled

2 large onions, peeled

2 large eggs

1/3 cup matzo meal or plain bread crumbs

1 tablespoon salt

10 to 15 grinds black pepper

Vegetable oil for frying

Kitchen Stuff

Clean dish towel

Dry measuring cups

Hand-held grater or food processor fitted with shredding disk

Large skillet

Measuring Spoons

Paper towel or brown paper bag

Using the coarse holes of a hand grater or the large shredding blade of a food processor, grate the potatoes into long strands. Grate the onions on top of the potatoes—note that the onions will become mush—which helps keep the potatoes from browning. Transfer the grated mixture into the center of a clean dish towel. Roll up the towel lengthwise like a sausage and wring out as much liquid as possible. Discard the liquid and transfer the mixture to a mixing bowl. (Rinse the dish towel under cold running water and hang to dry so it doesn't mold.) Add the eggs, matzo meal or bread crumbs, salt, and pepper, and mix well. This mixture must be used as soon as possible, as the potatoes will start to turn brown almost immediately.

In a large skillet (cast iron works best), heat about 1/8 inch of oil over a medium-high flame. To test the seasoning, pinch about a tablespoon of latke mixture and form a little pancake in the pan. Fry until golden brown on both sides. When the second side is golden brown, taste. Adjust the seasoning.

In your hands, form the latkes by patting them into pancakes, squeezing out any excess liquid as you work. A lot of liquid will begin to accumulate in the bowl, so be sure to keep squeezing out the excess. Fry the latkes until they are deep golden brown in color. If the potato shreds around the edges and darkens very quickly, turn down the heat.

To avoid excess oil absorption, it is best to flip the latkes only once. If you're not sure, leave them a little longer. "Better they should be overcooked," my mother would say. Flip and fry until golden brown on the other side. Add oil as necessary, making sure to bring it back up to temperature before you add another batch. Drain the latkes on paper towels or a clean brown paper bag. Serve immediately. To reheat the latkes, place them on a rack in a roasting pan and set in a preheated 300°F oven for 10 to 15 minutes until crisp and warmed through.

Links: Applesauce (page 57), Brisket (page 76).

Leg of Lamb

**Makes 4 to 8 servings,
with leftovers, depending on
the size of the leg**

1 trimmed leg of lamb, boned,
rolled, and tied (3 to 6 pounds)

1 to 2 tablespoons salt

15 to 20 grinds black pepper

1 head garlic, separated into
cloves and smashed

3 sprigs fresh rosemary, chopped

1/4 cup extra-virgin olive oil

1 cup dry red wine

Kitchen Stuff

Instant-read thermometer
(if you want to be sure it is done)

Large roasting pan with a
roasting rack

Liquid measuring cups

Measuring spoons

If you like lamb, this is one of the easiest, most delicious ways to prepare it. The size of a leg can vary considerably. Unless you are familiar with the anatomy of the lamb, and can therefore easily carve it off the bone, I would recommend buying a leg that has been trimmed, boned, rolled, and tied. Most butchers will sell you as much of a boned, tied leg as you want. Figure about two to three servings per pound.

Serve a roasted leg of lamb with Chickpea Salad (page 94) and/or Grilled Vegetables (page 137) for a great Mediterranean-inspired meal. Make terrific sandwiches with leftovers and Lemon Tahini Dressing (page 155) or Rémoulade (page 197). Required Reading: Cutting Up Things (page 13), Making a Sandwich (page 15), Preheating (page 16), Resting (page 17), Roasting, Braising, and Steaming (page 17), Saucing (page 17), Selecting Ingredients (page 11), Testing for Doneness (page 20), Using Leftovers (page 21), Working with Meat (page 21).

Preheat the oven to 425°F. On a rack set in a roasting pan, place the lamb. Season generously with salt and freshly ground black pepper. Rub the smashed garlic over the lamb and leave it in the pan. With your hands, rub the chopped rosemary into the meat. Drizzle the olive oil over the meat and rub into the flesh with your hands.

Set the roast in the middle of the preheated oven and roast for anywhere between 1 and 2 hours depending on the size and the desired doneness. A 3-pound roast will be medium-rare in about 1 hour. A 6-pound roast will take about 35 minutes more. (Roasts with the bone in will take less time because the bone conducts the heat to the center of the meat.)

If you're not sure if the roast is done, remove it from the oven and cut into the center of it with a sharp knife. If it

looks too rare, set it back in the oven. The only surefire way to know if it's done is to insert an instant-read thermometer in the center of the roast. It should read 125°F for rare, 130°F for medium-rare, and 140°F for medium.

Remove from the oven and let sit at room temperature for about 20 minutes. Transfer the roast to a cutting board or serving platter and snip off the strings. Using a soup spoon or a small ladle, skim off any excess fat from the pan juices. Set the pan over a burner on the stove, add the red wine, and bring to a rapid boil. Allow the liquid to reduce by half. Strain through a fine sieve. Slice the lamb about 1/4 inch thick and serve with the pan juices.

Links: Chickpea Salad (page 94), Grilled Vegetables (page 137), Lemon Tahini Dressing (page 155), Rémoulade (page 197).

Lemon Curd

The precursor to lemon meringue pie filling, lemon curd is a staple of English cookery. In England they spread it on toast, use it to fill tarts and layer cakes (see the Victoria Sandwich Cake on page 234), or enjoy it with fresh fruit for dessert. If you put it in a pretty jar, it makes a nice gift, too. The secret is to cook the lemon curd slowly (some people insist it should be done in the top of a double boiler over gently simmering water) so that the eggs don't curdle. Once you master the technique, you can try some other variations such as lime curd, just by substituting lime juice for the lemon juice. Required Reading: Selecting Ingredients (page 11), Squeezing Lemons (page 20), Zesting (page 23).

Grate the zest of one of the three lemons, juice them all, and remove the pits. If you don't have about $^1/_2$ cup of juice, add some more fresh juice until you do. Place the juice and zest in a small heavy-bottomed saucepan. Add the sugar and stir to dissolve. Add the egg yolks and beat until blended. Set the saucepan over a very low flame and cook, stirring constantly with a wooden spoon, until the sauce thickens enough to coat the back of the spoon, about 15 minutes. If the flame is too high, you run the risk of cooking the egg yolks, so it's better to err on the low side and just cook the whole thing a little longer. Avoid the temptation to turn up the heat if you feel like it's taking too long.

Just when the mixture has thickened, remove the pan from the heat and beat in the butter, a couple of chunks at a time. Once all of the butter is incorporated, pass the whole mess through a fine mesh strainer and transfer to a clean bowl or jar. Chill in the refrigerator until set.

Links: Victoria Sandwich Cake (page 234).

Makes about 2 cups

3 large lemons

1$^1/_2$ cups sugar

6 egg yolks

$^1/_4$ pound (1 stick) unsalted butter, cut into chunks and chilled

Kitchen Stuff

Heavy-bottomed saucepan

Liquid and dry measuring cups

Strainer

Zester, box grater, or carrot peeler

Lemon Parmesan Dip

Makes 2 cups

1¹/₂ cups crème fraîche,
or 1 cup sour cream and
¹/₂ cup plain yogurt

Juice of 2 lemons

³/₄ cup freshly grated imported
Parmesan cheese

1 large head garlic, roasted

Salt and freshly ground
black pepper to taste

Kitchen Stuff

Liquid and dry measuring cups

Mixing bowl

Plastic knife, coffee cup,
and microwave (if preparing
the dip in your office)

My friend Karen brought this dip to my prebook party in a beautiful basket surrounded by cooked and chilled tortellini that she had skewered individually on bamboo skewers. So I was surprised that she gave specific directions on how to prepare the dip in your office (if you're in a party pinch), using a plastic knife, a coffee cup, plastic serving pieces left over from catered lunches, and a microwave designed only to heat water for tea. I figured it must be pretty easy if that's how she did it. And, in fact, it is. (And pretty good to eat, too.) Required Reading: Presenting and Serving (page 16), Roasting, Braising, and Steaming (page 17), Squeezing Lemons (page 20), Seasoning to Taste (page 19), Selecting Ingredients (page 11).

In a small mixing bowl, combine the crème fraîche, lemon juice, and Parmesan cheese. Squeeze the cloves of roasted garlic one at a time into the mixture, stir, and adjust the seasoning with salt and freshly ground black pepper. Serve with vegetables, tortellini, bread, or other yummy things to dip.

Links: Pasta Primer—if you want to dip tortellini in it (page 177), Roasted Garlic (page 207), Roasted Vegetables (page 209).

Lemon Tahini Dressing

This is one of the most versatile dressings you'll ever make. Depending on how much liquid you add, you can use it as a salad dressing, a sauce for Hummus (see page 148) or Fried Eggplant, Middle-Eastern Style (see page 128), a dip for Sesame Chicken Fingers (see page 223), or a base for dishes like Sesame Noodles (see page 224).

    If you find that your tahini is bitter, you can add the optional mayonnaise or vegetable oil to tone down the flavor. One famous dive in New York City adds a lot of carrot juice to thin down the tahini instead of water. The result is delicious. For a more sesame taste, add a couple of drops of toasted sesame oil. Required Reading: Mixing in a Jar (page 16), Saucing (page 17), Selecting Ingredients (page 11), Squeezing Lemons (page 20), Using the Food Processor (page 21).

In a glass jar with a tight-fitting lid, combine all of the ingredients. Cover tightly and shake until smooth. The tahini will clump at first, but it will dissolve while you continue shaking. Alternately, place all of the ingredients in a food processor and process until smooth. For a thinner dressing, add more water and/or lemon juice.

Links: Falafel Vegetable Burgers (page 119), Fried Eggplant, Middle-Eastern Style (page 128), Hummus (page 148), Sesame Chicken Fingers (page 223), Sesame Noodles (page 224).

Makes 1 cup

¹/₂ cup tahini

³/₄ cup water

Juice of 2 lemons

2 teaspoons honey

2 tablespoons mayonnaise or vegetable oil (optional)

¹/₂ teaspoon salt

Freshly ground black pepper to taste

¹/₂ teaspoon toasted sesame oil to taste (optional)

Kitchen Stuff

Glass jar with a tightly fitting lid

Liquid measuring cups

Measuring spoons

Light and Flaky Pie Crust

If you have a food processor and the ingredients on hand, this is simply the best pie crust you can make. It is a little more complicated than the Simple Pie Crust on page 226, but once you do it a couple of times, you can make it in a snap. You can even make a few batches in advance and keep it in the freezer. It is important to have all of the ingredients measured and ready to go before you start. The recipe and technique were originally developed by Julia Child, and perfected by my sister Carrie. Use it for pies, tarts, or other pastry-wrapped goodies. Required Reading: Cutting in Butter (page 24), Resting (page 17), Shortening (page 27), Using the Food Processor (page 21), Working with Pastry (page 27).

In the bowl of a food processor fitted with the metal chopping blade, place the flours and salt. Pulse on and off a couple of times to blend. Add the chilled butter and pulse 5 to 6 more times until the mixture resembles coarse crumbs. Add the vegetable shortening, turn on the processor and quickly pour the ice water down the feed tube. Stop the machine. Pulse once or twice until the dough begins to bunch up. Remove the lid and feel the dough. It should hold together if you squeeze it between your fingers.

Turn the whole thing out onto a lightly floured counter and gently mush it together with the palm of your hand to form a smooth, soft dough. Do not overwork it or you will develop the gluten too much and melt the butter, which will result in a tough, less flaky dough. Form the dough into two equal circles, wrap in plastic and chill for about 1 hour before using. (If you don't have the time, you can work with the dough very gently and with a lot of excess flour while rolling it out, but the result won't be as good.) At this point the dough can be kept in the refrigerator for up to 2 days or frozen for 2 to 3 months. Roll out the dough according to the recipe for the pie, tart or quiche, or whatever you are making.

Links: Apple Pie (page 55), Clafoutis (page 100), Pecan Pie (page 182), Real Man's Quiche (page 195), Rhubarb or Nectarine Tart (page 199), Simple Pie Crust (page 226).

Makes two 9-inch pie crusts

$1^1/2$ cups unbleached all-purpose flour

$1/2$ cup cake flour (available in the baking section of the grocery store; it usually comes in a box)

$1/2$ teaspoon salt

$3/4$ cup ($1^1/2$ sticks) unsalted butter, chilled and diced

$1/4$ cup vegetable shortening, chilled

$1/2$ cup ice water

Kitchen Stuff

Food processor

Liquid measuring cups

Measuring spoons

Plastic wrap

Rolling pin

Macaroons

Makes 12 to 20 cookies,
depending on the size

2 large egg whites

$^1/_3$ cup sugar

1 teaspoon vanilla

Pinch salt

$2^1/_2$ cups sweetened shredded
coconut

Kitchen Stuff

Dry measuring cups

Cookie sheet

Measuring spoons

Small mixing bowl

These are the easiest cookies you'll ever make. And just in case you're worried that there aren't enough ingredients to make them taste good, the last time I made them, one of my friends asked how much butter I used. As you can see from the recipe, there is none. To make them a little fancier, dip the macaroons into, or drizzle them with, melted chocolate.
Required Reading: Cooling (page 24), Preheating (page 16), Selecting Ingredients (page 11), Separating Eggs (page 25).

Preheat the oven to 350°F. In a medium-sized mixing bowl, combine all of the ingredients and stir until well mixed. To shape the cookies, dip your fingertips in a bowl of cold water. Grab about 2 to 3 tablespoons of the coconut mixture and shape into mounds. Place the mounds evenly spaced on a baking sheet. The cookies won't spread, but they should not be so close so that they can't brown evenly.

Bake for about 15 minutes, until the coconut has begun to brown and the bottoms are an even, golden brown. Remove from the oven and cool for 5 minutes on the pan before removing with a spatula to finish cooling on a wire rack or a clean plate. Store in an airtight container.

Links: Brown Sugar Shortbread (page 77).

Marinated Mozzarella alla Anna Teresa

My friend Anna Teresa, an expert on regional Italian cuisine, brought this dish to my prebook party because she just "refuses to serve cold pasta." Bocconcini are little, fresh balls of mozzarella in brine available in cheese shops or Italian gourmet stores. They are often available already marinated, but you never know what's in the marinade if you haven't made it yourself.

Anna Teresa recommends these flavorful cheese balls as a savory antipasto, either for a buffet or in individual portions garnished with sun-dried tomatoes, black olives, or radicchio. You can adjust the proportions for more or fewer people, as you need to. Required Reading: Marinating (page 15), Patience (page 16), Presenting and Serving (page 16), Seasoning to Taste (page 19), Selecting Ingredients (page 11).

In a large mixing bowl or container with a lid, combine all of the ingredients except the mozzarella and the garnish. Mix well. If the bocconcini are too big to pop in your mouth, cut them in half. Toss mozzarella in the mixing bowl and mix to coat with the marinade. Set in a serving bowl and garnish with sun-dried tomatoes and black olives, if desired. The mozzarella will keep for up to 5 days covered in the refrigerator.

Links: Tomato Salad with Mozzarella and Basil (page 233).

Makes 8 to 10 antipasto servings, depending on what else you are serving with it

$^1/_2$ tablespoon anchovy paste, or 2 anchovies, minced (optional, but much better with it)

2 tablespoons ketchup

1 tablespoon balsamic vinegar

2 tablespoons chopped chives

1 tablespoon minced Italian parsley

1 tablespoon chopped fresh basil

2 to 3 pounds fresh mozzarella bocconcini, "little balls" (available in most cheese departments or specialty stores)

Sun-dried tomatoes in olive oil and/or black olives for garnish (optional)

Kitchen Stuff

Large mixing bowl or container with a lid

Measuring spoons

Marinated Shrimp

Makes 8 appetizer servings

2 pounds medium shrimp, uncooked

1 lemon, very thinly sliced

1 red onion, thinly sliced

$^1/_2$ cup pitted black olives

2 tablespoons chopped pimiento

1 cup fresh lemon juice, about 6 to 8 lemons

$^1/_2$ cup olive oil

2 tablespoons red wine vinegar

2 cloves garlic, crushed or minced

1 bay leaf, crushed in the palm of your hand

2 tablespoons dry mustard, or 3 tablespoons Dijon

$^1/_2$ teaspoon hot sauce (more if you like things fiery)

2 teaspoons salt

Freshly ground black pepper to taste

Kitchen Stuff

Large container with a tightly fitting lid or a resealable plastic bag

Measuring cups

Measuring spoons

Mixing bowls

A relative of the Pickled Shrimp on page 185, this dish was brought to my prebook party by my friend Julia. It was one of the first things to disappear. It's her mother's recipe, and in Julia's words, "If I can do it, so can you." If you don't have one or two of the ingredients, don't worry, as long as you have the shrimp. Experiment with other combinations, if you like. Required Reading: Marinating (page 15), Salting Water (page 17), Seasoning to Taste (page 19), Selecting Ingredients (page 11). Squeezing Lemons (page 20).

If your shrimp have the shells on, peel them and remove the tails. Run a small, sharp paring knife down the backs of the shrimp and remove the dark vein (called "deveining"). Bring a quart of salted water to a boil. Add the shrimp and cook just until the flesh turns white, for a scant 3 minutes. Drain at once and transfer to a large container with a tightly fitting lid. Add the lemon slices, onion slices, olives, and chopped pimientos.

In another bowl, combine the remaining ingredients and mix well. Pour this mixture over the shrimp and stir to coat. Place the lid on the container and refrigerate for at least 2 hours—overnight is better. Flip or shake the container once or twice as it chills to make sure all the shrimp are coated in the marinade. Serve chilled.

Links: Pickled Shrimp (page 185).

Meat Loaf to Be Proud Of

In another language, maybe meat loaf would sound more dignified. <u>Pâté de boeuf</u>, or <u>bûche de viande</u>, perhaps? However you slice it, everybody loves meat loaf—hot out of the oven with mashed potatoes (page 149) and gravy, or cold on rye bread with spicy mustard and coleslaw.

This talisman of 1950s homemakerdom is now featured on menus of trendy restaurants. Here is my mother's simple, classic version. It's important not to use ground beef that is too lean or the resulting loaf will be dry and less flavorful. You can wrap the meat loaf in bacon for extra flavor (and fat). Placing two or three potatoes cut into chunks in the pan will give you a great side dish without having to dirty another pot.

Required Reading: Making a Sandwich (page 15), Preheating (page 16), Selecting Ingredients (page 11), Testing for Doneness (page 20), Using Leftovers (page 21), Working with Meat (page 21).

Preheat the oven to 375°F. In a large mixing bowl, combine all of the ingredients except the potatoes and bacon, if using. Stir with a wooden spoon until everything is well mixed. This will take some strength. My mother used to use an old-fashioned wooden bowl with a meat chopper to make the mixing easier and to obtain a finer texture, but I've never been able to find one.

Transfer the mixture to a roasting pan or similar oven-proof dish and shape into a log, about 2^1/$_2$ inches wide and 6 inches long. If roasting potatoes along with the meat loaf, scatter them around the sides. Lay the strips of bacon on top of the loaf, if using. Bake for about 1 to 1^1/$_2$ hours, until the outside is dark brown and the loaf feels very solid to the touch. An instant-read thermometer should register 170°F. While baking, some of the juices will ooze out of the sides. Don't worry if it looks weird, the juices will settle in the pan and make the potatoes taste good. If you are not sure if the meat loaf is done, cut it in half—you're going to slice it to serve it anyway—to see if it's cooked through. Remove from the oven, cool for 10 minutes, slice, and serve.

Links: Just-Between-You-and-Me Mashed Potatoes (page 149), Roasted Vegetables (page 209), Sautéed Greens (page 214).

Makes 4 servings

2 pounds ground beef, not too lean

1 large egg

1 tablespoon Dijon mustard

2 teaspoons salt

^{1}/$_4$ cup ketchup

^{1}/$_2$ teaspoon garlic powder

10 to 15 grinds black pepper, or to taste

^{1}/$_4$ cup unflavored bread crumbs or matzo meal

3 potatoes, cut into ^{1}/$_2$-inch pieces (optional)

4 strips bacon (optional)

Kitchen Stuff

Large mixing bowl

Measuring cups

Measuring spoons

Roasting pan

Mediterranean Potato Dip

Makes 8 to 10 hors d'oeuvre servings (as long as you have something else to go along with it)

2 red bell peppers

1 head garlic

1½ pounds red-skinned potatoes (about 3 large potatoes)

¼ cup extra-virgin olive oil

¼ cup white wine vinegar (red wine, sherry, or balsamic will work, too)

1 tablespoon salt

Freshly ground black pepper

Kitchen Stuff

Potato masher or ricer

The potatoes in this dip aren't exactly of Mediterranean origin, but the flavorings are definitely from that sunny part of Europe. Actually, this dip is not exactly a dip, either. It's more like seasoned mashed potatoes that turn out to be delicious spread on bread. My friends Jaimee and Matt brought it to my prebook party in a round, hollowed-out loaf of sourdough bread. "Mom made it, we loved it," Matt said. If you prefer, serve it as a side dish to something like Leg of Lamb, page 152. Required Reading: Roasting, Braising, and Steaming (page 17), Seasoning to Taste (page 19), Selecting Ingredients (page 11).

Preheat the oven to 450°F. On a baking sheet, put the peppers and the head of garlic and place in the oven for about 40 minutes while you prepare the rest of the dip.

Cut the unpeeled potatoes into equal-sized chunks, place them in a large saucepan, cover with water, and set over a high heat to boil. Boil until the potatoes are tender when poked with a knife or fork, 20 to 25 minutes, depending on how large the chunks are. When they are cooked, drain the potatoes thoroughly. Mash in the pot with a potato masher or rice them with a ricer.

Meanwhile, keep your eyes on the peppers and garlic in the oven. When the peppers are blackened on all sides, remove the tray from the oven and cool. As soon as they are cool enough to handle, peel off the skin. Remove the seeds and chop. Add this to the mashed potatoes. Separate the roasted garlic head into cloves and squeeze the cloves between your thumb and your finger into the mashed potatoes. Add the remaining ingredients. Mix well and adjust the seasoning to taste. Serve at room temperature with bread or crackers.

Links: Just-Between-You-and-Me Mashed Potatoes (page 149), Roasted Vegetables (page 209).

Miso Mania

There are a few things that I feel like I could live on if I had to. Miso is one of them. (See also Fried Tofu Sandwiches, page 132.) If you have miso in the fridge—I don't think it ever goes bad if you store it in an airtight container—you are always just a few minutes away from a soul-satisfying bowl of soup.

Miso is also good to cook with, especially if you will be doing a lot of vegetarian cooking. The Japanese use miso in sauces, marinades, dips, main dishes, salad dressings, and as a condiment on the table. A shot of miso in a vegetarian dish (like a soup) also adds body and richness that you would normally attain with meat. Some of my friends think miso is an acquired taste. Feel free to experiment.

Miso is a fermented soy bean paste with the consistency of peanut butter. It comes in several varieties (barley, rice, and soybean). It also comes in a variety of colors (white, red, brown) and ages (six months to three years). Generally, the older and darker misos are stronger in flavor. The only way to know which one you prefer is to try them all. You are never supposed to boil miso, just simmer it, although sometimes when I use it in a vegetarian soup I can't help but jack up the heat. Required Reading: Presenting and Serving (page 16), Selecting Ingredients (page 11), Simmering versus Boiling (page 19).

In a small saucepan, bring the water to a boil. Reduce the heat to a simmer and stir in the miso until dissolved. Add the tofu and straw mushrooms and gently simmer until heated. Serve in bowls garnished with chopped scallions.

Links: Honey-Citrus Asian Salad Dressing (page 145), Scrambled Tofu (page 221).

Makes 2 bowls of soup

3 cups water

2 tablespoons miso (any variety), or to taste

4 ounces ($1/4$ pound) soft tofu, cut into small cubes

8 straw mushrooms (available canned in Chinese markets), optional

2 scallions, chopped, white and green parts

Kitchen Stuff

Measuring spoons

Small saucepan

Mister Bean

Makes about 3 cups cooked beans

1 cup dried beans

1 stalk celery, chopped

1 carrot, peeled and chopped

Assorted herbs

Kitchen Stuff

Saucepan with a lid

Didn't everybody skip around the school yard at recess chanting, "Beans, beans, they're good for your heart. The more you eat them the more you…" They're also delicious. Freshly cooked dry beans have an even better flavor and texture than canned beans. Although I've indicated in some recipes in this book when it's possible to substitute canned beans, the results will almost always be less than optimal. Most people don't bother cooking their own beans, not because it's difficult, but because it's time consuming. If you plan properly, however, it really doesn't take that much more effort.

Almost all beans, except lentils and split peas, need to be soaked overnight before being cooked. (An exception to this rule is beans used in slow-cooked recipes such as the Baked Beans While You Sleep on page 62. The slow cooking softens the beans enough while they cook.) Soaking partially rehydrates the beans, which makes them cook more quickly. It also helps break down some of the chemical components that cause the end of that dirty school yard rhyme. Required Reading: Patience (page 16), Salting Water (page 17), Selecting Ingredients (page 11).

Picking

Before using any beans, you must pick them over to remove any stones, twigs, broken or blemished beans, or any other foreign objects. You'll be surprised at the things you might find. To pick through them, it's easiest to spread the beans out over half a cookie sheet and pass them from one half to the other as you scrutinize what's going by. Remove anything that looks questionable.

Soaking

To soak the beans, place them in a bowl and cover with cold water about 2 to 3 inches higher than the beans themselves (about 4 times the volume of water to beans). Let sit on the counter overnight. If the water level ever goes down below the beans, add more.

When you go to cook the beans the next day, drain them (never use the soaking water). They should be plump. The beans should never be allowed to soak for more than 18 hours because they start to sprout, which changes the chemical composition of the bean and alters their flavor and texture.

If you haven't planned ahead, there is a quicker method that produces pretty good results. Place the beans in a saucepan and cover with 2 to 3 inches of water. Bring to a boil, cook for 2 minutes, turn off the burner, cover, and let sit for about 1 hour. Drain the beans and they are ready to cook. The heat speeds up the softening of the beans, but some cooks find the texture better with the traditional method.

Then there's the battle between the beaners and the nonbeaners, a battle that will be waged for as long as we eat chili. Beaners believe that chili must be cooked with kidney beans or pinto beans, as well as the meat. I do not subscribe to this. I think beans are marvelous *with* chili. I like refried beans...and I like red kidney beans or pinto beans, but they must be cooked separately and served with chili, along with rice.

—JAMES BEARD, *JAMES BEARD'S SIMPLE FOODS*
(MACMILLAN, 1993)

Cooking

To cook beans on top of the stove, just cover them with water or unsalted stock, add some aromatic vegetables, such as onions, carrots, and celery, throw in a few herbs, and bring to a boil. Turn down the heat to a simmer and set the lid ajar. Never add any salt or anything acidic (lemon juice, wine, vinegar) while the beans are cooking because the reaction of salt and acid to the beans causes them to toughen, which increases the cooking time considerably.

If a scum forms on top as the beans cook, skim it off with a large spoon or ladle. If the water boils down below the level of the beans, just add more. The beans are done when they are tender, but not mushy. The only way to tell is to taste one. Most beans cook in about 45 minutes to an hour. Split peas and lentils, which do not require soaking, are cooked in the same way.

If you are using the beans in a soup, after soaking, the beans are ready to use in the recipe. A simple bean soup can be made by adding carrots, onions, celery, herbs, and root vegetables to the beans. Cover with ample water and simmer until tender. Season with salt and pepper. You can add pasta if you like, too.

Serving

The cooked beans can be seasoned and served plain as a side dish, or chilled and mixed with vinaigrette and vegetables for a cold salad (such as the Chickpea Salad on page 94).

Links: Baked Beans While You Sleep (page 62), Beans from the Girl from Ipanema (page 119), Chickpea Salad (page 94), Falafel Vegetable Burgers (page 119), Hummus (page 148).

Mom's Mushrooms and Onions

Makes about 1 quart

1/4 pound (1 stick) unsalted butter

3 large onions, chopped

2 pounds fresh mushrooms, sliced

About 2 teaspoons salt,
or to taste

10 to 15 grinds black pepper,
or to taste

Kitchen Stuff

Sauté pan, saucepan,
or large skillet

There are some combinations of ingredients that are so fundamental to good cooking that the combinations have become ingredients themselves—peanut butter and jelly or ham and cheese, for example. In my mother's home, mushrooms and onions sautéed in butter and heavily seasoned with salt and pepper was a combination that found its way into many dishes. Stirred into rice, stuffing, kasha, egg barley, mashed potatoes, you name it, they provide a delicious flavor.

Mushrooms and onions over broiled flank steak are divine. My mother even serves mushrooms and onions plain over toast as an appetizer. You can use any combination of fresh mushrooms—button, portobello, cremini, shiitake—and adjust the amounts to suit your needs. If you want to eyeball the quantities, figure about 2 1/2 times more sliced mushrooms than chopped onions. Required Reading: Cutting Up Things (page 13), Increasing or Decreasing Recipes (page 15), Peeling Onions (page 16), Seasoning to Taste (page 19), Selecting Ingredients (page 11).

In a large sauté pan or saucepan, heat the butter until frothy. Add the chopped onion and sauté until translucent, 8 to 10 minutes. Add the mushrooms and continue sautéing until the mushrooms have given off their juice and are cooked through, about another 10 minutes. The mushrooms will lose a lot of their volume as they cook. Season with salt and a generous amount of freshly ground black pepper.

Links: Cream Puffs (page 109), Hamburgers (page 140), Scrambled Eggs (page 220), Toast.

Moroccan-Style Couscous Salad

My friend (and roommate) Izabela learned a lot of things while she was an intern in the kitchens of New York City's famed Chanterelle restaurant. But as far as I'm concerned, the grueling three months she spent there were worth it, if only because she learned how to make chef David Waltuck's couscous salad. Here is Izabela's version. It can be served hot, cold, or at room temperature. I prefer it at room temperature over a bed of greens for a main course salad. Required Reading: Cutting Up Things (page 13), Resting (page 17), Seasoning to Taste (page 19), Selecting Ingredients (page 11), Squeezing Lemons (page 20).

In a small saucepan, combine the water, turmeric, coriander, cumin, and salt and bring to a boil. Place the couscous in a large mixing bowl. Slowly pour in the hot liquid spice mixture while mixing the couscous with a fork. Cover and let stand for 15 minutes. All of the liquid should be absorbed. Uncover and stir in the lemon juice and olive oil. The mixture should hold its shape when molded, like wet sand.

Add the diced vegetables, currants, parsley, and lemon zest and mix well. Season with salt and, if you have the time, let rest for a couple of hours to allow the flavors to come together. The salad will keep covered in the refrigerator for up to 5 days.

Links: Leg of Lamb—goes well on the side (page 152), Waves of Grain (page 236).

Makes 4 cups; serves 8 as a side dish, 4 as a main course

1 cup water

1 teaspoon turmeric

2 teaspoons ground coriander

2 teaspoons ground cumin

1 teaspoon salt

1 cup uncooked couscous

Juice and zest of 2 to 3 lemons

1/3 cup extra-virgin olive oil

Skin of 1 medium zucchini, finely diced (use a carrot peeler to remove the skin)

2 bell peppers, 1 green and 1 red, seeded and finely diced

1/2 medium red onion, finely diced

1/2 cup currants, soaked for 10 minutes in hot water and drained

2 tablespoons chopped Italian parsley

Salt to taste

Kitchen Stuff

Measuring cups

Measuring spoons

Small bowl

Small saucepan

Mushroom Barley Soup

This is a hearty vegetarian soup that seems almost meaty. Just put all of the ingredients in a pot and simmer until it's done. What could be easier?

Required Reading: Cutting Up Things (page 13), Reheating (page 16), Seasoning to Taste (page 19), Selecting Ingredients (page 11), Simmering versus Boiling (page 19).

In a small bowl, place the dried porcini mushrooms and cover with boiling water. Let soak until softened, about 25 minutes. Meanwhile, heat the oil and butter in a large saucepan. Add the chopped onion and sauté until translucent, about 5 minutes. Add all of the remaining ingredients and the drained porcini. Add a couple of tablespoons of the flavorful porcini soaking liquid, being careful not to stir up the sand on the bottom.

Bring the soup to a boil. Turn down the heat and simmer, with the cover ajar, until the barley is soft, about 45 minutes. If the water level falls below the vegetables, add boiling water to cover. Adjust the seasoning with salt and pepper. Serve hot. The soup is even better reheated the next day.

Links: Waves of Grain (page 236).

Makes 4 to 6 servings

1 to 2 ounces dried porcini mushrooms

1 cup boiling water

2 tablespoons vegetable oil

2 tablespoons butter

1 large onion, chopped

3 large carrots, peeled and diced

3 stalks celery, chopped

$^1/_2$ pound mushrooms, cut into quarters

1 bay leaf

$^3/_4$ cup pearl barley

6 cups water or chicken stock

Salt and freshly ground black pepper to taste

Kitchen Stuff

Large saucepan

Liquid measuring cups

Measuring spoons

Small bowl

One-Pot Brownies

There are more complicated, maybe fudgier recipes for brownies, but this one only takes a few minutes to prepare. Best of all, you only dirty one pot (not even a bowl). They are one of my mother's sweet standbys.

Required Reading: Cooling (page 24), Melting (page 25), Mixing versus Overmixing (page 25), Preheating (page 16), Selecting Ingredients (page 11), Testing for Doneness (page 20).

Preheat the oven to 350°F. In a small saucepan, melt the butter and chocolate over low heat. When melted, remove from the heat and stir in the sugar with a wooden spoon until the sugar is dissolved and the mixture has cooled. Add the eggs and vanilla—the mixture will tighten up a little. Stir in the flour and nuts.

Pour the batter into an ungreased 8 x 8-inch baking pan and set in the middle of the preheated oven. Bake for 20 to 25 minutes, just until the sides of the brownies begin to pull away from the pan and the middle has barely set. They should be just slightly underbaked so they retain a fudgy consistency. Remove from the oven, cool, and cut into squares.

Links: Cheesecake Brownies (page 85), You Gotta Try These Blondies (page 241).

Makes 9 brownies

¹/₄ pound (1 stick) unsalted butter

¹/₂ cup walnuts or pecans (see Chopping Nuts, page 23)

2 ounces unsweetened baking chocolate

1 cup sugar

2 large eggs

1 teaspoon vanilla

³/₄ cup unbleached all-purpose flour

Kitchen Stuff

8-inch square baking pan

Dry measuring cups

Measuring spoons

Small saucepan

Osso Buco

Makes 4 servings

4 ossi buchi, cross-section slices
cut from the veal shank
(one is osso, two or more is ossi)

Salt and freshly ground
black pepper

$1/4$ cup virgin olive oil

1 large onion, chopped

2 cloves garlic

2 carrots, chopped

One 28-ounce can Italian-style
plum tomatoes, drained and
chopped

1 bay leaf

One 2-inch sprig fresh rosemary

1 bottle dry white wine,
or 3 cups chicken stock

Gremolata (see headnote)

Kitchen Stuff

A large pot or casserole with a lid
that can go both on top of the
stove and in the oven

Liquid measuring cups

Oven bags (if you want to cheat
a little)

A trendy main course, osso buco is easy to prepare and it can be done in advance and reheated, which as you know by now is true of most of my favorite recipes. Traditionally made with cross-sectioned slices of veal shank, now you see osso buco of everything, including monkfish.

My friend Mildred skips the initial browning stage by putting everything in a casserole, placing the whole thing, uncovered, in an oven bag (available in the paper goods section of the grocery store), and baking at 350°F for about two hours. By substituting whole lamb shanks, you get Braised Lamb Shanks (see Variation). In Italy, osso buco is almost always served with gremolata—a garnish of chopped lemon zest, chopped parsley, and chopped garlic that is sprinkled on top just before serving—and saffron-flavored Risotto (page 200). Required Reading: Cutting Up Things (page 13), Preheating (page 16), Reheating (page 16), Roasting, Braising, and Steaming (page 17), Selecting Ingredients (page 11), Working with Meat (page 21).

Preheat the oven to 350°F. Generously season the ossi buchi with salt and pepper. In a large, deep casserole or saucepan that has a cover and that can go in the oven (meaning it doesn't have plastic or wood handles), heat the oil. Place the seasoned shanks in the hot oil and sear on all sides to brown, about 10 minutes. Remove from the pan and set aside.

Add the onion, whole garlic cloves, and carrots to the hot pan and sauté until wilted, about 5 minutes. Return the seared veal shanks to the pan along with the chopped tomato, bay leaf, and rosemary. Add enough wine or stock to cover. Bring to a boil.

Cover the pan and set in the preheated oven for about $1^1/2$ hours. Remove the cover and continue baking for another 20 to 30 minutes, until the sauce has reduced and thickened and the veal has nicely browned. Sprinkle the gremolata on top and serve. The osso buco can be reheated on top of the stove or in the oven.

Variation
Braised Lamb Shanks
Follow the same recipe for Osso Buco, but substitute 4 lamb shanks for the ossi buchi and use dry red wine instead of white.

Links: Braised Red Cabbage (page 72), Just-Between-You-and-Me Mashed Potatoes (page 149), Risotto (page 200).

Oven-Roasted Tomatoes

Here's a simple side dish that everybody loves. (I even taught this one to my mother!) This is a good way to use underripe tomatoes because they sweeten and become more flavorful as they bake. Any combination of herbs you have on hand will work, but my favorite is rosemary and thyme. Required Reading: Cutting Up Things (page 13), Patience (page 16), Roasting, Braising, and Steaming (page 17), Selecting Ingredients (page 11), Smashing Garlic (page 19).

Preheat the oven to 300°F. On a cookie sheet with sides (a jelly roll pan) or in a large baking dish, arrange the tomato halves. Distribute the smashed garlic (with the peel on) and fresh herbs around the cookie sheet. Season generously with salt and freshly ground black pepper. Drizzle the olive oil over the whole mixture (use more if you need it).

Toss the tomatoes with your hands to coat with the olive oil and the seasonings. Return them all to the upright position (cut side up) and set in the middle of the preheated oven. Roast for about 1¹/₂ hours, until the tomatoes have plumped and begun to brown. If you don't have that much time, turn up the heat to 375°F and roast for 45 minutes to 1 hour, keeping a close eye on the tomatoes to be sure they do not burn. Some of the herbs will burn, but don't worry, the smoky flavor is welcome.

If you have more time, lower the temperature to 250°F and roast the tomatoes for 3 to 4 hours. The longer the roasting time, the sweeter and more concentrated the tomato flavor will be. Remove from the oven, cool to room temperature, and serve. If you like, drizzle some extra-virgin olive oil on top before serving. The tomatoes can be made 2 or 3 days in advance, and gently reheated to room temperature before serving.

Links: **Anything they might go well with Leg of Lamb—good on the side (page 152), Osso Buco—ditto (page 172).**

Makes 4 to 6 side dish servings

12 plum tomatoes, cored and cut in half, lengthwise

6 cloves garlic, smashed

6 to 8 sprigs fresh herbs (rosemary, thyme, oregano, marjoram, etc.)

Salt and freshly ground black pepper

¹/₃ cup extra-virgin olive oil

Kitchen Stuff

Cookie sheet with sides (jelly roll pan) or large baking dish

Liquid measuring cups

Pancakes

I first came upon this recipe in the February 1996 issue of <u>Cook's Illustrated</u> magazine. After much experimentation, writers Pam Anderson and Karen Tack determined that this was the perfect recipe for buttermilk pancakes. After I made them almost every Sunday for a year, my roommates Izabela and Jennifer agreed.

I have made a couple of changes to the basic recipe, but the idea is the same. These pancakes are infallible. You can add anything you like to make flavored pancakes—blueberries, sautéed apples, bananas, chocolate chips, you name it. It's best to have a cast-iron pan, but any large frying pan will do. Take out the ingredients before you get in the shower so they will be at room temperature before you begin. The pancakes are best if they are served hot out of the pan, but if you need to make them in advance, <u>Cook's</u> recommends wrapping them in a clean dish towel and setting them on a cookie sheet in a 250°F oven to keep warm. Required Reading: Bringing to Room Temperature (page 12), Mixing versus Overmixing (page 25), Selecting Ingredients (page 11), Testing for Doneness (page 27).

Makes about eight 3-inch pancakes

1 cup unbleached all-purpose flour

2 teaspoons sugar

$1/2$ teaspoon salt

$1/2$ teaspoon baking powder

$1/4$ teaspoon baking soda

$3/4$ cup buttermilk, at room temperature

$1/4$ cup milk, at room temperature

1 large egg, at room temperature

2 tablespoons unsalted butter, melted and cooled

Additional butter for frying

Kitchen Stuff

Cast-iron pan, if you have one

Large mixing bowl

Measuring cups

Measuring spoons

In a large mixing bowl, mix the dry ingredients (flour, sugar, salt, baking powder, and baking soda). In another bowl, beat together the remaining ingredients except for the additional butter for frying. Pour the wet ingredients into the dry ingredients all at once and stir with a fork just until mixed.

In a large frying pan (cast iron works best), heat a tablespoon or two of butter over medium-high heat. When the butter sizzles, pour in the batter about $1/4$ cup at a time, making sure not to overcrowd the pan so that the edges do not run together. When the edges are golden brown and bubbles begin to appear on the surface of the pancakes, flip and cook until the second side is brown.

Serve the pancakes at once. Remove the pan from the stove for 3 to 4 minutes to cool slightly. Add more butter and repeat the process until all of the batter is used up. Serve with warmed maple syrup.

Variations
No Buttermilk?
Combine $3/4$ cup milk with 1 tablespoon of lemon juice and allow the mixture to sit for 5 minutes. Substitute this sour milk for the $3/4$ cup buttermilk and $1/4$ cup regular milk in the recipe.

Apple Pancakes
Before you begin to prepare the batter, peel, core, and dice 2 apples. Sauté in about 2 tablespoons of butter with $1/4$ teaspoon of cinnamon and 1 tablespoon of sugar until tender.

We stopped at Mac's with a hillbilly friend from Kentucky, a string-bean-shaped guy who could eat more than a hungry wrestler. We started with oatmeal and thick-sliced toast, mugs of pulpy orange juice squeezed to order, then dug into giant-size platters of sourdough French toast sprinkled with confectioner's sugar, and a stack of out-of-this-world banana nut pancakes. The pancakes, steamy hot and dripping butter, contained bits of nut and mashed bananas in the batter, plus the stack (about a dozen four-inchers) was loaded with nuts and sliced bananas between the cakes.

—JANE AND MICHAEL STERN,

REAL AMERICAN FOOD (KNOPF, 1986)

Prepare the batter and immediately after you have poured it into the hot pan, scatter 1 to 2 tablespoons of the sautéed apple on top of each pancake. Gently push the apple into the batter with the back of a spoon. Cook as directed above.

Banana Chocolate Chip Pancakes
Immediately after you have poured the batter into the hot pan, sprinkle the top of each pancake with chocolate chips and slices of ripe banana. Push the chips and banana slices gently down into the batter with the back of a spoon and cook as directed above.

Blueberry Pancakes
Immediately after you have poured the batter into the hot pan, scatter about 10 to 12 blueberries on the top of each pancake and gently push them into the batter. Cook as directed above.

Peach and Pecan Pancakes
Before you begin to prepare the batter, sauté 3 thinly sliced peaches in about 2 tablespoons of butter with $1/4$ teaspoon cinnamon, 1 tablespoon of sugar, and 3 tablespoons of bourbon. Just when the peaches are soft, add about $1/4$ cup chopped pecans. Serve this mixture on top of the cooked pancakes.

Links: French Toast (page 123), Home Fries (page 143), Scrambled Eggs (page 220).

Pasta Primer

It used to be we ate macaroni or noodles, and maybe the occasional dish of spaghetti. Now everything is called pasta. There is dried pasta, fresh pasta, imported pasta made with 100 percent durum semolina. It comes in hundreds of shapes and flavors. How do you know what to buy? And then what do you do with it, besides pouring on a ladleful of Ragu? Required Reading: Reheating (page 16), Salting Water (page 17), Selecting Ingredients (page 11), Testing for Doneness (page 20).

Fresh versus Dried

Forget store-bought fresh pasta. It's overpriced and overrated. True, there is nothing like fresh, homemade pasta. But the key to it is that it is homemade. The overpriced doughy strips of mush sold in the refrigerated section of almost every grocery store these days are made with industrial machines that require the dough to be so stiff, the final product looses all of the desirable finesse of homemade fresh pasta. Dry pasta is the staple of Italy. Commercially made fresh pasta is like those odd curls of lemon rind served with espresso in this country: the Italians find our interest in them fascinating, but they stay clear.

Just about the only exception to this rule is stuffed pasta. Not that most fresh stuffed pasta is any better, but if you have a hankering for ravioli, and you don't have an entire day to make it yourself, you don't have a choice.

Selection

Since I don't think anyone reading this book is about to make fresh pasta— even though it's really simple—let's talk about buying and cooking dried pasta.

Begin by only buying pasta made from 100 percent durum semolina. Durum wheat is also known as hard wheat because it is high in gluten, a tough, elastic protein that provides the resilience and bite you want in a good pasta. Whether you want to splurge on imported pasta is a matter of taste. Some dried pastas imported from Italy can be very expensive, but the elevated price doesn't mean they taste any better.

Believe it or not, choosing a pasta shape depends on what you are going to do with it. Long, thin pasta like spaghetti, linguine, and fettuccine are best with thin, smooth sauces like the pureed version of Fresh Tomato Sauce on page 127, or the Spaghetti Sauce on page 227. Smaller pasta, such as penne, shells, or rotelle, are better with chunky sauces like the Pasta with Wild Mushrooms on page 181. Flat pasta like parpardelle or farfalle (bow ties) work well with thick, smooth sauces such as the Pesto on page 183.

Cooking

Figure on about 4 ounces ($^1/_4$ pound) of uncooked pasta per person for a main course, or 2 to 3 ounces as a first

Makes 4 to 6 servings

1 pound dried pasta, any shape

5 quarts water

2 tablespoons salt

Kitchen Stuff

Colander

Large saucepan or stock pot

> When I first came to this country, I was astounded by some of the meals I was served at dinner parties. The menus frequently consisted of spaghetti and salad, followed by a splashy dessert of garnished ice cream. The spaghetti sauce was all too often a runny mess and the salad made of raw, wilted spinach. "Mamma mia!" I would say to myself. "This is how they eat in America?"
>
> —ANNA TERESA CALLEN, *ANNA TERESA CALLEN'S MENUS FOR PASTA* (CROWN, 1985)

course. Pasta needs to be cooked in a lot of water to prevent sticking and to assure it is cooked evenly. About 5 quarts of water per pound is a good ratio. This will seem like a lot of water, but it really is necessary. Add a lot of salt, about 2 to 3 tablespoons per 5 quarts. Adding oil to the water does nothing to prevent sticking.

Once you dump the pasta into the boiling salted water, you must stir it up so that it doesn't settle on the bottom and stick together. Stir the pasta now and then throughout the cooking process to prevent clumping.

To test if the pasta is done, you can throw the noodles against the wall to see if they stick, pinch them between your fingers, or closely examine the color, but the only way to be sure is to put them in your mouth. Perfectly cooked pasta is a relative concept. Some people prefer it more cooked than others. Some recipes require it to be more cooked than others. Generally, it should retain only a slight resistance when you bite into it—*al dente*. Properly cooked pasta should be firm enough to hold its shape, but not so firm that it crunches or sticks to your teeth. If the pasta is going to be used in other dishes (such as the Cheese Thing on page 87), you have a little more leeway because you are going to continue cooking it in the oven.

Once the pasta is cooked, strain it, reserving some of the cooking water for the sauce. If you are going to be using it right away, toss the cooled pasta hot into the sauce and proceed with the recipe.

Almost every pasta in Italy is "finished" or "mounted" (*montecato*) with a shot of butter or olive oil and freshly grated Parmesan cheese. If fat doesn't concern you, do the same. (The exception is seafood pasta, with which the Italians never serve cheese.)

Storing

If you are not going to use all of the pasta right away, make sure it is drained well and toss it with some olive oil to prevent it from clumping as it cools. Cover it tightly and keep it in the refrigerator. Just before you go to use the cold pasta, bring a large pot of water to a boil. Drop in the cold pasta for a minute or two to refresh it and heat it through. Then proceed with your recipe.

Links: Cheese Thing (page 87), Chop Suey, Korean-Style (page 99), Pasta with Seafood (page 179), Pasta with Smoked Salmon and Capers (page 180), Pasta with Wild Mushrooms (page 181), Sesame Noodles (page 224).

Pasta with Seafood

A classic Italian combination, different versions of pasta and seafood are served along the entire length of Italy's coastline. You can use any combination of seafood and shellfish you like. Shrimp and scallops are easy to handle. But if you would like to add clams or mussels, feel free. Just be sure all of the shells are tightly closed (throw away any that aren't). A tight seal indicates the bivalve is still alive. Soak the clams for about an hour in salted water so they give up some of their sand, and pull the beards (those hairy strings that stick out from the flat side) out of the mussels. To be truly authentic, don't offer any Parmesan cheese with this dish. In Italy, you will never be offered Parmesan with seafood pasta. Instead, try toasting some bread crumbs in butter in a frying pan and sprinkling them on top. Required Reading: Cutting Up Things (page 13), Saucing (page 17), Sautéing, Frying, and Stir-Frying (page 19), Seasoning to Taste (page 19), Selecting Ingredients (page 11).

In a large sauté pan, heat the olive oil over medium-high heat. Add the anchovies and garlic and sauté until the anchovies have disintegrated and the garlic has turned translucent. Don't be alarmed by the strong anchovy smell—this will dissipate, leaving a mild flavor.

Add the seafood, the mussels and clams, if using, and the white wine, cover, and cook until the flesh has just barely turned white and the shells have begun to open, 3 to 4 minutes.

Add the parsley, red pepper flakes, salt, pepper, and pasta and toss to mix. If there doesn't appear to be enough sauce to coat, add 3 to 4 tablespoons of the reserved pasta cooking water. Adjust the seasoning with more salt and pepper and serve immediately, making sure to distribute the seafood evenly among all the portions.

Links: Clam Dip (page 101), Pasta Primer (page 177), Pasta with Wild Mushrooms (page 181), Pasta with Smoked Salmon and Capers (page 180).

Makes 4 servings

$^1/_2$ cup extra-virgin olive oil

4 anchovies, or 1 tablespoon anchovy paste (optional, but it's better with it)

2 cloves garlic, minced

1 pound assorted seafood (peeled shrimp, scallops, lobster and/or crabmeat)

12 to 16 mussels and/or clams (optional; see headnote)

$^1/_2$ cup dry white wine

1 handful Italian parsley, chopped

$^1/_2$ teaspoon dried red pepper flakes

Salt and freshly ground black pepper to taste

1 pound dried pasta, cooked al dente, drained (reserving about $^1/_4$ cup of the cooking water), and tossed with olive oil

Kitchen Stuff

Large frying pan

Liquid measuring cups

Measuring spoons

Pasta with Smoked Salmon and Capers

Makes 4 servings

1/4 cup extra-virgin olive oil

1 small onion, chopped

1/4 pound smoked salmon, chopped

1 cup heavy cream (aka whipping cream)

3 tablespoons capers, drained

Salt and freshly ground black pepper to taste

1 pound pasta, cooked al dente, drained (reserving about 1/4 cup of the cooking water), and tossed with olive oil

Freshly grated imported Parmesan cheese

Kitchen Stuff

Large frying pan

Liquid measuring cups

Measuring spoons

Another classic combination, this dish makes people think you went to a lot of trouble. Actually it's quite simple. It's an adaptation of a dish my friends Ed and Katie brought to my prebook party. Any shape of pasta works, but I prefer a small noodle such as shells or bowties. Despite what an Italian might otherwise recommend, I like to serve this dish with freshly grated Parmesan cheese. Required Reading: Cutting Up Things (page 13), Saucing (page 17), Sautéing, Frying, and Stir-Frying (page 19), Seasoning to Taste (page 19), Selecting Ingredients (page 11).

In a large skillet, heat the olive oil over medium-high heat. Add the onion and sauté until translucent, but not browned. Add the smoked salmon and continue cooking just until the salmon turns opaque, 1 to 2 minutes. Pour in the cream and add the capers. Taste and adjust seasoning with salt and pepper. Be careful how much salt you add because the smoked salmon and capers are both salty. Add the pasta and toss to coat. If there doesn't appear to be enough sauce, add a couple of tablespoons of the pasta cooking water to thin it down. Serve with freshly grated Parmesan cheese.

Links: Pasta Primer (page 177), Pasta with Seafood (page 179), Pasta with Wild Mushrooms (page 181).

Pasta with Wild Mushrooms

These days, grocery stores have begun to offer a pretty good selection of mushrooms, some wild, some cultivated. A new gourmet store in my neighborhood always stocks more than twelve varieties of fresh mushrooms and about five different dried ones. One of the reasons I love to use mushrooms is that they give a rich, meaty taste to things without the addition of fat. For this dish, use any selection you can find. I always like to include some rehydrated porcini because they have such a strong flavor. They are expensive, but a little goes a long way. Required Reading: Cutting Up Things (page 13), Saucing (page 17), Sautéing, Frying, and Stir-Frying (page 19), Seasoning to Taste (page 19), Selecting Ingredients (page 11).

In a small bowl, place the porcini, cover with boiling water, and let stand for 20 to 30 minutes until soft. Meanwhile, heat the olive oil in a large frying pan. Add the garlic and onion and sauté until translucent, 5 to 8 minutes. Add the fresh mushrooms and continue cooking until they begin to wilt and give off some of their water.

Add the heavy cream and season heavily with salt and black pepper. Add the cooked pasta and a couple of tablespoons of the porcini soaking liquid (be careful not to pick up any of the sand that has sunk to the bottom) or the pasta cooking water and toss until the pasta is coated. Cook just until the noodles are heated through. Add the butter and Parmesan cheese, toss, and serve immediately.

Links: Pasta Primer (page 177), Pasta with Seafood (page 179), Pasta with Smoked Salmon and Capers (page 180).

Makes 2 servings

1 ounce dried porcini

1 cup boiling water

2 tablespoons olive oil

1 small clove garlic, minced

1/2 small onion, minced

1/2 pound assorted fresh mushrooms (use oyster, shiitake, or portobello), cleaned, stems removed, and cut into small pieces

1/2 cup heavy cream (aka whipping cream)

Salt and freshly ground black pepper to taste

1/2 pound dried pasta, such as farfalle (bow ties) or shells, cooked al dente, drained (reserving about 1/4 cup of the cooking water), and tossed with olive oil

2 tablespoons unsalted butter

2 tablespoons imported Parmesan cheese

Kitchen Stuff

Measuring cups

Measuring spoons

Large frying pan

Small bowl

Pecan Pie

Makes one 9-inch pie, serves 8

$^1/_2$ recipe Light and Flaky Pie Crust (page 157) or Simple Pie Crust (page 226), or one store-bought 9-inch pie crust

1 cup sugar

1 cup light or dark corn syrup

$^1/_3$ cup unsalted butter, at room temperature

4 large eggs, slightly beaten

$^1/_4$ cup unbleached all-purpose flour (optional, see headnote)

1 teaspoon pure vanilla extract

$1^1/_2$ cups pecan halves

Kitchen Stuff

Measuring cups

Measuring spoons

Mixing bowl

9-inch pie plate

Rolling pin

Small saucepan

As American as pecan pie? Where else would you find anything so sweet, so rich, and so delicious. It also happens to be so easy, you'll never settle for another over-nuked stale piece of pecan pie again. How you like your pecan pie is a matter of taste. If you prefer a softer filling that sort of oozes out of the crust, omit the flour. Otherwise, the resulting pie will be firm and yummy, especially served warm with a scoop of vanilla ice cream. Required Reading: Cooling (page 24), Preheating (page 16), Resting (page 17), Selecting Ingredients (page 11), Testing for Doneness (page 20), Working with Pastry (page 27).

Preheat the oven to 375°F. If you are using a homemade pie crust, roll it out to an 11-inch circle to line a 9-inch pie plate. Lift the crust onto the rolling pin and lay in the center of the pie plate, with the excess dough hanging over the edge. Fold the overhang underneath the edge of the dough to make an even edge. Crimp the edges and chill.

In a saucepan, combine the sugar, corn syrup, and butter and set over medium heat. Cook until the sugar has dissolved and the butter has melted. Remove from the heat and cool. Pour the eggs into the syrupy mixture while beating constantly. Beat in the flour, if using, and stir in the vanilla and the pecans.

Pour this mixture into the pie crust and bake for 45 minutes, until the center has set and the crust has browned. The center will puff up and crack slightly when the pie is done. Remove from the oven and cool. (The center will sink back down when the pie is cooled.)

Variation

Chocolate Pecan Pie
Scatter 4 ounces of semisweet chocolate pieces (1 large bar broken up into bits) on the bottom of the pie crust before pouring in the filling. Bake as directed.

Links: Buttermilk Biscuits (page 78), Light and Flaky Pie Crust (page 157), Simple Pie Crust (page 226).

Pesto

With the increase in interest in Italian food over the past few years, once-obscure pesto has almost become an American staple. If you keep some in your freezer (it will last for up to four months), you will always be able to have a delicious meal in the time it takes to boil some pasta. Make a double batch in late summer, when large bunches of locally grown basil are everywhere, and you'll have it deep into winter.

Traditionally made with a mortar and pestle in its native Genova, pesto is no longer a chore since the advent of the food processor. I leave the grated imported Parmesan cheese out of my pesto until I serve it.

Required Reading: Freezing (page 13), Reheating (page 16), Saucing (page 17), Seasoning to Taste (page 19), Selecting Ingredients (page 11), Smashing Garlic (page 19), Using the Food Processor (page 21).

In the bowl of a food processor fitted with the metal chopping blade, place all of the ingredients except the cheese if you are going to be storing your pesto for future use. Using quick on/off pulses, process the pesto until smooth. Store in the refrigerator until ready to use or freeze in small portions so you always have it on hand.

When you go to use the pesto, heat about 1/4 to 1/2 cup of the pesto in a large frying pan. Toss with the cooked pasta (see Pasta Primer on page 177), 1/2 cup freshly grated imported Parmesan cheese, freshly ground black pepper, and 3 to 4 tablespoons of the pasta cooking water.

Links: Pasta Primer (page 177).

Makes 1 1/2 cups

1 large bunch basil, about 12 to 15 stems, washed thoroughly and dried

2 cloves garlic, peeled

1 cup pine nuts

3/4 cup extra-virgin olive oil

1 teaspoon salt

1/2 cup freshly grated imported Parmesan cheese (to use when serving)

Kitchen Stuff

Food processor

Measuring cups

Measuring spoons

Pickled Shrimp

Another recipe of my friend Evelynne's (see the Thrifty Lemon Pound Cake on page 231), these pickled shrimp are a great hors d'oeuvre for a party because they can be made well in advance. In fact, they get better with age. Required Reading: Marinating (page 15), Peeling Onions (page 16), Selecting Ingredients (page 11).

In a large pot with enough water to cover the shrimp, combine the pickling spices and celery stalks. Cover and bring to a boil. Add the shrimp and cook just until pink, 5 to 8 minutes. Drain the shrimp and cool to room temperature. Peel off the shells, leaving the tails attached, and with a small, sharp paring knife remove the dark vein that runs down the back (called "deveining"). Layer the shrimp in a glass serving dish or bowl, alternating layers with the sliced onion and bay leaves.

In a separate bowl, mix together the oils, celery seed, and salt. Pour over the shrimp. Tightly cover the serving dish with plastic wrap and refrigerate for at least 24 hours before serving. Alternately, you can combine the shrimp, onions, bay leaves, and dressing in a resealable plastic bag and transfer to a serving dish before serving. The shrimp will keep covered at least a week in the refrigerator. Serve with Tabasco sauce.

Links: Marinated Shrimp (page 160).

Makes 8 to 10 appetizer servings

$1/4$ cup pickling spices (available in the spice section of the grocery store)

---

4 ribs celery, with the leaves

$2^1/2$ pounds medium-sized shrimp in their shells

---

2 medium onions, thinly sliced

---

10 bay leaves

$3/4$ cup extra-virgin olive oil

$3/4$ cup vegetable oil

$2^1/2$ teaspoons celery seed

---

2 teaspoons salt

Tabasco sauce

Kitchen Stuff

Glass serving dish or bowl

Large pot

Large resealable plastic bag

Measuring cups

Measuring spoons

Pizzabilities

If you are like me, then the quickest thing you can think of to eat is a slice of pizza. Pizza can also be one of the quickest things to make. When it comes to topping, anything's game: barbecued chicken, Thai curry, bacon, lettuce, and tomato, you name it. Use leftovers or prepare a topping from scratch. I've listed some suggestions, but the sky's the limit.

Now all you need is the dough. Pizza dough is a basic yeast dough like any ordinary bread. The difference is that you only have to let it rise once because you want the end product to be flat, anyway. You can keep fresh pizza dough in the refrigerator for about a week. Or you can freeze it and keep it several months. Some grocery stores and bakeries even sell pizza dough ready for you to use. Here is a recipe from my friend Felice, who has been a professional baker in New York City for many years. Make enough so that you can throw a pizza in the oven two or three times during the week. You can also use the dough to make calzones, garlic knots, and focaccia. Required Reading: Cutting Up Things (page 13), Patience (page 16), Preheating (page 16), Selecting Ingredients (page 11).

In a small bowl, combine the yeast and lukewarm water and set aside. The yeast should dissolve and begin to froth. If it doesn't, throw it away and buy new. (Sorry, you'll have to order pizza.) In a large mixing bowl, combine the flour, salt, and sugar, and mix well. Make a well in the center of the dry ingredients and pour in the yeast mixture and the olive oil. Using a wooden spoon, stir to form a soft dough.

Transfer the dough onto a lightly floured surface, a clean counter top works well. Knead with your hands until the dough becomes smooth and elastic. The most effective way to knead is to fold the dough over on top of itself (the way they fold sweaters at the Gap) and push it out in front of you with both hands. If after the first few minutes the dough is still very sticky, add a little more flour. Continue kneading for about 10 minutes.

Place the dough in a large, clean bowl. Cover with a dish towel and set in a warm place to rise (inside an oven that is turned off is a good place). When the dough has doubled in volume, about 1 hour, punch it down with your fist. Let the dough rest for 15 minutes. Now you are ready to make pizza.

If you are not going to use the dough immediately, place it in a plastic bag, close the bag tightly, and set it in the refrigerator. The dough will rise periodically, so just keep punching it down inside the plastic bag until you are ready to use it. It will keep for about 3 to 4 days.

Makes enough for three 10-inch pizzas

For the pizza dough

1 1/2 teaspoons (1/2 package) dry active yeast (available in the baking section or refrigerator case of the grocery store)

1 1/3 cups lukewarm water

4 cups unbleached all-purpose flour

2 teaspoons salt

1/4 teaspoon sugar

1/3 cup extra-virgin olive oil

Kitchen Stuff

Large baking sheet or, better yet, a pizza stone

Measuring cups

Measuring spoons

Ruler

Small and large mixing bowls

To be sure you always have pizza dough on hand, you can divide it into 3 equal portions, wrap them individually in plastic wrap, and freeze them for up to two months. The day before you want to make a pizza, just place one of the frozen balls of dough in the refrigerator. It will be ready to use the next day.

When you are ready to prepare a pizza, preheat your oven to 500°F. If you have a pizza stone (available in gourmet shops, and probably a good investment if you expect to make pizza often, or if you find yourself reheating take-out pizza a lot), set it in the oven before you turn it on. The stone ensures you will have a crisp crust because it heats up hotter than the oven and you bake the pizza right on top of it. Follow the manufacturers' instructions. Alternately, you can bake the pizza on a cookie sheet or any number of specially designed pizza pans. Some have holes in the bottom to allow the crust to breath, others have ridges to help it crispen. Lightly oil the pan with olive oil and dust with cornmeal or semolina so the crust does not stick.

Lightly oil your hands with olive oil. Grab off a piece of pizza dough about the size of a small baseball. Shape the dough into a ball in your hands. While you are shaping the dough into a ball, begin to pinch it in the center with your thumb and forefinger and flatten the dough into a disk. Lay the dough on a lightly floured surface and press

with your fingertips until you have a 10-inch disk.

Alternately, you can roll out the dough with a rolling pin on a lightly floured surface. If the dough won't cooperate because it is too elastic, let it rest for 15 to 20 minutes before you continue to roll it out. The finished pizza should be about 10 inches in diameter.

If you want to use a sauce, start with that, place the vegetables or meats on top, and cover with a blanket of cheese. If you are using meats like sausage or bacon, fry them first and drain the fat on a paper towel. For the cheese, I find a combination of fresh mozzarella and grated Parmesan works well. Finish off with a drizzle of olive oil, a sprinkle of salt, and a grind or two of black pepper.

Bake the pizza for about 15 to 20 minutes, until the cheese has melted and the crust is golden brown and crisp. Remove from the oven, slice, and serve immediately.

Suggested Toppings
- For sauce, use Fresh Tomato Sauce (page 127), Spaghetti Sauce (page 227), or a top-quality bottled sauce.
- Oven-Roasted Tomatoes (page 173), fresh basil, and fresh mozzarella
- Artichoke hearts, black olives, and mozzarella
- Smoked salmon, capers, and brie (no sauce)
- Garlic, olive oil, ricotta, and Parmesan

- Sautéed sausage, roasted red peppers, arugula, and grated Parmesan
- Grilled eggplant (page 137), toasted pine nuts, fresh thyme, and grated Asiago
- Crumbled meat loaf (page 161), blue cheese, and sautéed onions (no sauce)
- Pesto (page 183) and Parmesan cheese (no sauce)

Variation
A Simpler Version
As my friend Lara will attest, you can easily substitute frozen bread dough for homemade pizza dough.

Cold-Cut Loaf
Like a giant calzone without the sauce, Cold-Cut Loaf is a dish first made for me by my L.A. friend Jen. It is made by flattening out pizza or bread dough (use about 1/2 recipe of Pizza Dough or 2 loaves' worth of frozen bread dough) and layering Genoa salami, prosciutto, pepperoni, and mozzarella slices, about 1/4 pound of each, on top. The whole thing up is rolled and baked in a 400°F oven for 45 to 50 minutes, until the loaf has risen and browned. Slice it thinly on the diagonal to serve. Yummy.

Links: Fresh Tomato Sauce (page 127), Grilled Vegetables (page 137), Meat Loaf to Be Proud Of (page 161), Oven-Roasted Tomatoes (page 173), Pesto (page 183), Roasted Vegetables (page 209), Spaghetti Sauce (page 227).

Potato and Leek Soup

One of the easiest and quickest soups to make, Potato and Leek Soup always tastes good, no matter what you do to it. With a loaf of French bread and a salad, it also makes a cheap, satisfying meal. If you want a richer soup, substitute milk or chicken stock (see Chicken Soup, page 92) for the water and/or add half a cup of heavy cream to the soup just before it has finished cooking. Required Reading: Cutting Up Things (page 13), Seasoning to Taste (page 19), Selecting Ingredients (page 11), Simmering versus Boiling (page 19).

To clean the leeks, cut off the tough green tops and the roots and slice the leeks in half lengthwise. Separate the layers and rinse under plenty of cold, running water to remove any imbedded sand. Drain. Slice the leeks lengthwise into strips and then crosswise to dice.

In a large saucepan, heat the butter. Add the leeks and sauté until tender and translucent, 8 to 10 minutes. Add the cubed potatoes and water, milk, or broth and bring to a boil. Turn down the heat and simmer until the potatoes fall apart when poked with a fork, 20 to 25 minutes. If using cream, add it now and bring the soup back up to the boil. For a thicker soup, mash some of the potatoes against the side of the pot with a fork. Adjust the seasoning with salt and pepper. The soup will keep for 3 to 4 days in the refrigerator. Do not freeze because the potatoes become watery.

Links: **Just-Between-You-and-Me Mashed Potatoes—like soup but with less water (page 149), Scalloped Potatoes—ditto (page 216),**

Makes 4 to 6 servings

3 leeks

$^1/_4$ cup butter

3 medium-size red-skinned potatoes, peeled and diced into $^1/_2$-inch cubes

$4^1/_2$ cups water, milk, or chicken broth

$^1/_2$ cup heavy cream (aka whipping cream; optional)

About 1 tablespoon salt

Freshly ground black pepper

Kitchen Stuff

Large saucepan

Liquid measuring cups

Measuring spoons

Potato Salad

There are as many variations of potato salad as there are summer picnics. This is a pretty classic version that would be at home alongside **Hamburgers (page 140), Roasted Chicken (page 203),** or even a **Fried Tofu Sandwich (page 132).** Don't be afraid to throw in other things you have in your fridge, except that bag of coffee beans and your rolls of film.

Required Reading: Cooking Eggs (page 12), Cutting Up Things (page 13), Salting Water (page 17), Seasoning to Taste (page 19), Selecting Ingredients (page 11), Testing for Doneness (page 20).

Clean the potatoes under cold running water, but do not peel them. Place them in a medium-sized saucepan, and add 1$\frac{1}{2}$ teaspoons of the salt and the whole eggs and cover with cold water. Set the pot over high heat, and bring to a boil. Boil for about 10 minutes and remove the eggs. Continue boiling until the potatoes are soft when pricked with a fork, but not so soft that they fall apart, about another 20 minutes. The skin should have loosened noticeably.

Remove from the heat, drain, and cool. If you have the time, refrigerate the potatoes and eggs until chilled. Peel the potatoes and remove the shells from the hard-cooked eggs under cold, running water. Cut the potatoes into $\frac{1}{2}$-inch cubes and set in a large mixing bowl. In a separate bowl, mash the eggs with the tines of a fork and add to the potatoes. Add the remaining ingredients, mix well, and adjust the seasoning with salt and pepper to taste.

Variation

Potato Salad on a Diet
Substitute $\frac{1}{3}$ cup plain nonfat yogurt and 2 tablespoons mayonnaise for the mayonnaise in the recipe. Proceed as directed.

Links: Chicken Salad (page 91), Classic Tuna Salad (page 103), Fried Tofu Sandwiches (page 132), Hamburgers (page 140), Roasted Chicken (page 203).

Makes 6 to 8 side dish servings

3 large red-skinned potatoes of uniform size (about 1$\frac{1}{2}$ to 2 pounds)

2 teaspoons salt

2 large eggs, kept in their shells

2 ribs celery, diced

1 small onion, or 3 scallions, chopped

5 sweet gherkin pickles (that's a small, sweet pickle), chopped

2 tablespoons gherkin pickle juice

1 teaspoon Dijon mustard

$\frac{1}{2}$ to $\frac{3}{4}$ cup mayonnaise, to taste

5 to 6 grinds black pepper, or to taste

Kitchen Stuff

Large and small mixing bowls

Liquid measuring cups

Measuring spoons

Medium saucepan

Ratatouille

Another dish that hails from France's sunny Provence region (see Aioli on page 53), Ratatouille can be served as a side dish or baked with a crust of cheese as a hearty vegetarian meal. The traditional technique is to sauté each vegetable in olive oil separately and assemble the whole dish at the end. A speedier option (which I think works well enough) is to add the vegetables in stages to the same pot. Either way, I think you'll be pleased with the results. Required Reading: Cutting Up Things (page 13), Sautéing, Frying, and Stir-Frying (page 19), Seasoning to Taste (page 19), Selecting Ingredients (page 11).

Makes 4 to 6 side dish servings with leftovers for lunch the next day, or 2 main course servings

$^1/_2$ cup olive oil

1 clove garlic, minced

1 onion, chopped

Salt and freshly ground black pepper to taste

1 small eggplant, diced (with the peel)

1 red pepper, seeded and diced

1 small zucchini, diced

$^1/_4$ pound white mushrooms, cut into quarters

4 to 5 canned plum tomatoes, drained and chopped

$^1/_2$ teaspoon dried oregano or thyme

1 sprig fresh rosemary (optional)

1 bay leaf

1 cup grated cheese, such as fresh mozzarella, Swiss, or raclette (optional)

Kitchen Stuff

Baking dish

Grater (for optional cheese)

Large saucepan

If you are planning to use the traditional technique of sautéing all of the vegetables separately, begin by heating 2 tablespoons of the olive oil in a large sauté pan set over medium-high heat. When the oil is hot, add the garlic and onion, season with salt and pepper, and sauté until tender and translucent, 5 to 8 minutes. Remove to a large baking dish and spread the mixture out in an even layer. Heat another 2 tablespoons of olive oil, add the diced eggplant, season with salt and pepper, and sauté until tender, adding more oil if necessary. Transfer to the baking dish and layer on top of the onions. Repeat with the remaining vegetables (except the tomatoes) until they are all layered in the baking dish.

To prepare the Ratatouille in a hurry, heat about $^1/_4$ cup of olive oil in a medium to large saucepan (you'll need less than for the other version). Add the garlic and onion and sauté until translucent. Season with a pinch of salt and a grind or two of pepper. Add the eggplant and continue cooking until almost tender. Season. Add the red pepper and continue cooking until tender. Add the zucchini and the mushrooms and cook until the mushrooms begin to give up some of their water, an additional 5 minutes. Add the remaining ingredients except for the cheese, season with salt and pepper, and continue cooking until all of the vegetables are tender. Serve as is or transfer to a baking dish.

Preheat the oven to 350°F. If you used the traditional method, top the layered sautéed vegetables with the chopped tomatoes, sprinkle with oregano, add the rosemary and bay leaf, and top with the optional grated cheese. If you used the quicker method, just top with the grated cheese. Set the dish in the preheated oven and bake 20 to 25 minutes, until bubbly and the cheese is browned. If the top begins to brown too much, cover with aluminum foil and continue baking until heated through.

Links: Hamburgers (page 140), Leg of Lamb—great on the side (page 152), Scrambled Eggs (page 220).

Real Man's Quiche

Despite the kitsch factor, quiche is still a great dish for lunch or brunch. You can put almost anything you have available lying around in it, such as cheese, bacon, onions, smoked salmon, or peppers. You don't even need to make a crust if you don't want to bother. To vary the amount of fat, use anything from heavy cream to skim milk for the base. If you use a glass or ceramic pie plate, you can even present the quiche in the same dish it was baked in. I've given the recipe for the quiche base and some suggestions for fillings. But use your imagination. Required Reading: Cooling (page 24), Cutting Up Things (page 13), Resting (page 17), Selecting Ingredients (page 11), Testing for Doneness (page 20), Working with Pastry (page 27).

Preheat the oven to 425°F. Roll out the pie crust to a circle of about 11 inches in diameter to line a 9-inch pie plate. Lift the crust up on the rolling pin and transfer to the center of the pie plate. Let the crust hang over the edge. Fold the overhang under to form a uniform edge. Decorate the edge by pinching between your thumb and forefinger or by pressing with the floured tines of a fork. Press a piece of aluminum foil over the dough, fill the center with dried beans or raw rice to press down the foil and bake in the preheated oven for 15 to 20 minutes, until the dough has set and the edges have begun to brown. Remove from the oven, remove the foil and beans or rice, being careful not to spill any, and let cool. Turn the oven down to 400°F.

Meanwhile, prepare the filling of your choice (see Variations). To prepare the quiche base, whisk the eggs until light and frothy. Beat in the milk, salt, nutmeg, and freshly ground black pepper. Place the filling in the partially baked pie crust and pour the quiche base over top. Be careful not to allow the base to flow over the edge of the crust.

Transfer the quiche to the middle rack of the preheated oven and bake at 400°F until the top begins to puff and brown. Turn down the oven to 350°F and continue baking for another 20 minutes, until the filling has completely set and the crust has browned. Remove from the oven and cool. Serve warm or at room temperature.

Variations

Broccoli Cheddar Quiche
Line the bottom of the partially baked crust with about 1 cup chopped, cooked broccoli. Season with salt and pepper. Sprinkle on 1 cup (about 1/3 pound) grated cheddar cheese. Pour the quiche base over and bake as directed for the basic quiche.

Crustless Quiche
If you don't have the time or energy to

Makes 6 to 8 servings

1/2 recipe Light and Flaky Pie Crust (page 157) or Simple Pie Crust (page 226) or 1 store-bought pie crust

4 large eggs

1 1/2 cups milk

Pinch salt

Pinch nutmeg

8 to 10 grinds black pepper, or to taste

1 cup grated cheese (about 1/3 pound; see Variations)

1 cup filling (see Variations)

Kitchen Stuff

Large skillet or sauté pan

Measuring cups

Measuring spoons

Mixing bowl

9-inch pie plate

Rolling pin

Ruler

> Quiche's enduring popularity into the Seventies had a great deal to do with the scope it allowed creative cooks...By the early Eighties Americans had been served too many quiches—at bad restaurants, at every catered event, even at the corner deli—and the dish took a nose dive in popularity...Of late, however, quiche has been making a slight comeback. Considering how simple and elegant a dish it is—when well made—it's not surprising. And don't forget quiche's seemingly infinite capacity to absorb the creative cook's fillips.
>
> —SYLVIA LOVEGREN, *FASHIONABLE FOOD* (MACMILLAN, 1995)

make a crust, you can try this easy quiche, which is sort of like a baked omelet. Choose a filling as you would for any other quiche. In a medium bowl, whisk 5 eggs until light and frothy. Beat in 2 cups milk, 3 tablespoons unbleached all-purpose flour, pinch salt, nutmeg, and freshly ground black pepper. Place the filling in a buttered 9-inch pie plate and pour in the quiche base. Bake as for the regular quiche above.

Mushroom and Onion Quiche
Use about 1 cup of Mom's Mushroom and Onions (see page 166), drained. Place in the bottom of the partially baked crust. Sprinkle on 1 cup (about $1/3$ pound) grated Monterey Jack cheese. Pour the quiche base over and bake as directed for the basic quiche.

Quiche Lorraine
In a large skillet, sauté 2 diced leeks (see Potato and Leek Soup on page 189 for cleaning instructions) in 2 tablespoons butter until tender, about 10 minutes, and season with salt and pepper. Place the leeks in the bottom of the partially baked crust. Add 5 slices cooked and crumbled bacon or ham and 1 cup (about $1/3$ pound) grated Swiss cheese. Pour the quiche base over and bake as directed for the basic quiche.

Smoked Salmon and Onion Quiche
In a large skillet, sauté 1 large, thinly sliced onion in 2 tablespoons unsalted butter. Season with salt and pepper. Place the sautéed onion in the partially baked crust. Add 2 to 3 ounces of chopped smoked salmon and 1 cup (about $1/3$ pound) grated Swiss cheese. Pour the quiche base over and bake as directed for the basic quiche.

Links: Light and Flaky Pie Crust (page 157), Simple Pie Crust (page 226).

Rémoulade

This is a quick version of the classic French sauce that traditionally begins with a homemade mayonnaise. I use prepared mayonnaise to make it faster. (You can even use light mayonnaise to make it lighter.) I like to keep rémoulade in the fridge (it lasts about a month) to add a little zing to sandwiches. It is a good sauce for Leg of Lamb (page 152) or roast beef, and if you use it in salads—such as Chicken Salad (page 91) or Classic Tuna Salad (page 103)—instead of mayonnaise, you get a zippier result. Required Reading: Saucing (page 17), Seasoning to Taste (page 19), Selecting Ingredients (page 11), Using the Food Processor (page 21).

In a small mixing bowl or the bowl of a food processor, combine all of the ingredients. Mix well and season to taste. Store refrigerated in an airtight container.

Links: Avocado Sandwich (page 59), Chicken Salad (page 91), Classic Tuna Salad (page 103), Fried Tofu Sandwich (page 132), Leg of Lamb (page 152).

Makes 1 1/2 cups

1 1/4 cups mayonnaise

1 tablespoon Dijon mustard

Juice of 1/2 lemon

4 cornichons (little French pickles), finely chopped

3 tablespoons capers, drained and finely chopped

1 tablespoon chopped fresh tarragon

1 tablespoon chopped fresh Italian parsley

1/2 teaspoon salt

8 to 10 grinds freshly ground black pepper

Dash Tabasco

Kitchen Stuff

Liquid measuring cups

Measuring spoons

Small mixing bowl

Rhubarb or Nectarine Tart

A simple, free-form tart, this "galette" technique, which I first made using a recipe by Jacques Pépin, can be prepared quickly with a variety of fillings. Let the amount of dough and/or filling you have on hand determine the size of the tart you make. Required Reading: Cutting Up Things (page 13), Preheating (page 16), Resting (page 16), Selecting Ingredients (page 11), Using the Food Processor (page 21), Working with Pastry (page 27).

Preheat the oven to 425°F. Roll out the pie crust on a lightly floured work surface until it is about 1/8 inch thick. You should have a rough circle about 15 inches in diameter. Transfer the dough to a baking sheet and set in the refrigerator. Meanwhile, cut the rhubarb into 2-inch pieces, splitting the ribs in half if they are particularly wide, or slice the nectarines off the stone into 1/4-inch thick slices, leaving the skin in tact.

In the bowl of a food processor, combine 2 tablespoons of the sugar with the flour and ground nuts. Process with 8 to 10 on/off pulses until the nuts are ground to a fine meal. Do not over-process or the nuts will release their oil and turn the mixture into a paste.

Remove the dough from the refrigerator. Sprinkle the sugar and nut mixture on the dough. Arrange the cut rhubarb or nectarines in an attractive pattern in the center of the circle, leaving a 2-inch border of dough around the circumference of the circle. Fold up the border of dough to encase the fruit and create a 1 1/2-inch lip around the tart. Sprinkle the fruit with the remaining sugar and dot with small teaspoon-sized pieces of butter.

Set in the preheated oven and bake, about 1 hour, until the crust is dark brown and the rhubarb or nectarines are tender. Remove from the oven and cool for 5 to 10 minutes on the pan. Slide a knife underneath to loosen the tart and transfer to a wire rack or serving plate to finish cooling. Cut into wedges to serve (with vanilla ice cream, if you have it).

Variations

Any Fruit Tart

You can use this technique with any fresh fruit as long as you adjust the amount of flour sprinkled on the base to compensate for the varying juice content of the fruit. For example, berries need a little more flour, figs a little less. Add some orange juice. Use your imagination.

Links: Apple Pie (page 55), Light and Flaky Pie Crust (page 157), Simple Pie Crust (page 226).

Makes 8 to 10 servings

1/2 recipe Light and Flaky Pie Crust (page 157), Simple Pie Crust (page 226), or 1 store-bought pie crust

2 1/2 pounds fresh rhubarb or 8 ripe nectarines

1/2 cup sugar

3 tablespoons unbleached all-purpose flour

3 tablespoons almonds or hazelnuts

3 tablespoons butter

Kitchen Stuff

Cookie sheet

Dry measuring cups

Food Processor

Measuring spoons

Rolling pin

Ruler

Risotto

Here is a simple dish that, oddly enough, is only good in two places: the finest, most expensive Italian restaurants, and at home. The reason is that the technique requires a watchful eye and a dedicated burner that most restaurant kitchens cannot provide. It is a creamy, rich dish that is infinitely adaptable to ingredients you have on hand.

The secret is to have the right rice (one of the Italian varieties such as arborio, vialone nano, or carnaroli) and enough stock on hand (about three times the volume of rice). A good shot of butter and freshly grated Parmesan cheese doesn't hurt, either. I've given a few flavor variations, but the possibilities are endless. The finished risotto should not be thick or gloppy, but creamy and rich. The rice should be slightly al dente. It must be served immediately. If you have leftovers, press the risotto into a pancake and fry it in butter for a truly authentic Italian breakfast or lunch the next day. Required Reading: Patience (page 16), Seasoning to Taste (page 19), Selecting Ingredients (page 11).

Makes 4 to 6 servings

$^1/_4$ cup extra-virgin olive oil

1 large onion, minced

$1^1/_2$ cups Italian rice
(see headnote)

$^1/_2$ cup dry white wine

$4^1/_2$ cups chicken stock (page 92)
or vegetable stock, or top-quality,
unsalted commercially made
stock, or better yet, order 2
quarts of broth from your local
Chinese restaurant, simmering

1 teaspoon salt

2 tablespoons unsalted butter

$^1/_2$ cup freshly grated
Parmesan cheese

Additional salt and freshly ground
black pepper to taste

Kitchen Stuff

Ladle

Large and small saucepans

Wooden spoon

In a heavy, medium saucepan, heat the olive oil over medium-high heat. Add the onion and sauté until translucent, about 5 minutes. Add the rice and stir just to coat with the oil. Add the wine, stir, add about $^1/_2$ a cup of the simmering stock (it's important that the stock is hot), and the teaspoon of salt. Stir until the liquid is absorbed.

Continue adding the hot stock in cupfuls, stirring between each addition until it is almost completely absorbed. When the rice is creamy and al dente, 15 to 20 minutes, remove from the heat. Beat in the butter and cheese, adjust the seasoning with salt and pepper to taste, and serve immediately.

Variations

Porcini Risotto
Add $^3/_4$ pound sliced fresh porcini or other meaty mushrooms to the sautéing onion and proceed with the recipe as directed. To use dried mushrooms, see the rehydrating technique in the recipe for Mushroom Barley Soup (page 169) and add with the first portion of stock.

Roasted Beet and Gorgonzola Risotto
Add 3 chopped roasted beets (see page 209) to the risotto when you add the first portion of stock. When the risotto is finished, stir in 3 ounces of Gorgonzola or other blue cheese along with the Parmesan and butter.

Asparagus Risotto
Add about $^1/_2$ pound of fresh asparagus that has been cleaned, peeled, and chopped, to the risotto 8 to 10 minutes into cooking. Proceed as directed.

Links: Chicken Soup—for stock (page 92), Mushroom Barley Soup (page 169).

Rita's Dinner Special

This recipe was given to me by a friend who wishes to remain anonymous. This friend's mother never liked cooking much, and like me and almost all of the people I know, this friend has a few "issues about food." Still, she has learned to enjoy cooking. But when I asked her to bring something to my prebook party, she was a little intimidated. Instead, she gave me this recipe from her mother's secret file, which I thought I would share with you. Required Reading: Selected prose of Woody Allen.

Remove the Lean Cuisine from the bottom of the freezer, carefully replacing the other boxes. Prime the microwave. Make 6 or 7 very important phone calls while eating leftover apple cake from last Friday's dinner—eat with your fingers so it doesn't count. Gather family members and inform them that you are "off-duty" for dinner tonight because the kitchen is a disgusting mess and you are very angry. Hover. Make comments about fat content of loved ones' dinner selections. Leave the Lean Cuisine on the counter to mellow while you lie down for an hour to counter exhaustion from picking up after everyone all day. Return to the kitchen, replace the Lean Cuisine carefully in the freezer. Remove the ice cream from the freezer. Standing at the counter, eat ice cream. Repeat, "I shouldn't have eaten that" several times.

Links: Scary Prefab Surprise (page 217)

Makes 1 serving

1 Stouffer's Lean Cuisine Chicken Oriental with Vegetables and Vermicelli (260 calories)

Some angst

1 pint Häagen-Dazs, flavor of choice

Kitchen Stuff

Microwave

Spoon

Various defense mechanisms

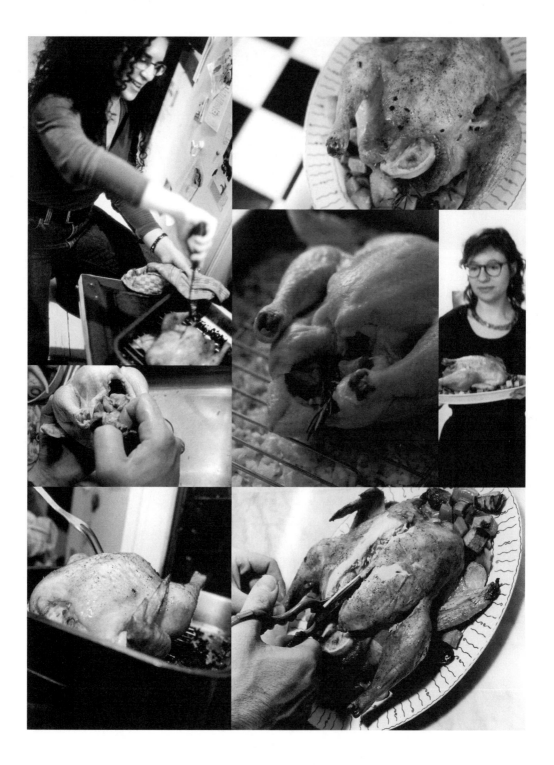

Roasted Chicken

Perhaps no other dish is so universally well received as a properly roasted chicken. Even the fast-food chains have caught on, what with KFC offering a rotisserie option and Boston Markets sprouting up across the country. Served at Jewish holidays and Italian family suppers, roasted chicken spans the cultural horizon. Parisian markets are perfumed with the smell of chickens roasting outside of butchers' stalls. Take-out shops in Portugal sell a spicy roasted chicken by the pound.

When I lived in Torino, Italy, there was a small shop that only sold roasted chicken and potatoes. Although the rotisserie had space for several more skewers, the owner would only put six chickens on at a time. If you came in and all the birds were claimed, you'd have to wait for the next batch of six. A trough of potatoes tossed with garlic and rosemary sat under the slowly roasting chickens, sopping up the fat as they roasted to a golden brown.

For a dinner party, roasted chicken is a perfect entrée because it is almost foolproof. You can be cooking it while you share a drink with your guests. And all the while that lovely Parisian market smell emanates from your kitchen.

When buying a chicken, look for a plump four- to five-pound roasting chicken, which will serve about four people. Don't be fooled by "yellow" chickens. The yellow color does not indicate a better quality chicken as some purveyors would have you believe. I happen to think the yellow color is unappetizing. Organically raised free-range chickens are the most flavorful, but they are $1 to $2 per pound more expensive than ordinary grocery store chickens. In general, organic meats cook faster than other meats. Deduct fifteen to twenty minutes off the cooking time of an organic bird. Required Reading: Cutting Up Things (page 13), Preheating (page 16), Roasting, Braising, and Steaming (page 17), Saucing (page 17), Testing for Doneness (page 20), Working with Meat (page 21).

Serves 4 to 6

One 4- to 5-pound roasting chicken (see headnote)

4 medium onions, peeled and diced

1/4 cup extra-virgin olive oil

1 to 2 tablespoons salt

10 to 15 grinds black pepper

1 whole head garlic split in half, plus 2 cloves peeled and finely chopped

1 sprig fresh rosemary, stems removed and finely chopped

1 lemon, cut in half

Kitchen Stuff

Kitchen shears or sharp knife

Large roasting pan with a roasting rack

Preheat the oven to 375°F. Remove the neck and innards from the central cavity (if they are there) and rinse the chicken under cold water. (If you have a cat, it will love the liver.) Pat the skin dry with paper towels. Place a wire roasting rack in the center of a roasting pan that is large enough to hold the bird with some space around the sides.

Set the chicken on the rack and scatter 3/4 of the diced onion on the bottom of the roasting pan around the sides of the chicken.

Using your hands, rub the bird with the olive oil to coat the skin. Be sure to rub the top and bottom. Liberally sprinkle the top, bottom, and cavity of the chicken with the salt and pepper. Place the remaining onion in the center cavity. Place the split head of garlic in the cavity. Rub the remaining chopped garlic and the rosemary on the skin. Squeeze the lemon halves over the top of the bird and place the squeezed halves (silly as it sounds) in the cavity of the chicken. As the bird roasts, the lemon will release a steam that perfumes and moistens the chicken.

Turn the chicken breast-side up on the rack and set the roasting pan in the center of the preheated oven and roast for about 1 hour, periodically basting with the pan juices and any leftover olive oil.

Turn up the heat to 425°F and continue roasting for an additional 15 minutes, checking to make sure the chicken is not browning too fast. Test for doneness by inserting a fork in the breast meat (it should easily slide in and out if it is cooked) and by pricking the thigh. The fork should go in easily, and the juices should run clear. If you are still not sure, pull away a piece of meat from inside the thigh and check that there is no pink color left near the bone. To be certain, use an instant-read thermometer. The correct temperature should be 170°F. Once the bird is an even golden brown color, remove from the oven. Let sit on the counter for 15 minutes before cutting into pieces.

To serve, cut the chicken into eight or ten pieces with kitchen shears or a sharp knife. Make one long cut down the center, between the two breasts,

and along the back bone to make two halves. Cut off the thighs and separate the legs at the joint. Remove the wings from the breast at the joint and cut the breasts into two equal pieces. Serve the pan juices on the side.

Variations

Asian Roasted Chicken

It seems like lemongrass finds its way into everything these days. And it's delicious with chicken. Create an Asian marinade for chicken (or any other meat) by combining $1/2$ cup soy sauce, 2 tablespoons peanut oil, 2 tablespoons honey, 2 cloves garlic that have been peeled and finely chopped, 1 knob of ginger that has been peeled and finely chopped, 1 tablespoon sesame oil, and a shot of Asian chile sauce. Stuff the cavity of the bird with half a bunch of cilantro, some pieces of ginger, two or three whole cloves of garlic, and if you can find it, three or four pieces of fresh lemongrass. Set the chicken over onions as for the classic roasted chicken and coat with the marinade (reserve the rest for basting). Roast as above.

Dijon Roasted Chicken

For a slightly different taste, omit the salt and combine the olive oil, chopped garlic, rosemary, and black pepper with $1/2$ cup Dijon mustard. Spread this mixture evenly over the chicken and roast as suggested. This mixture is also a terrific seasoning for Leg of Lamb (page 152).

Gorgonzola Roasted Chicken

This is an unusual chicken dish that my friend David brought to my prebook party and that everyone loved. Wash and pat dry the chicken. Gently lift the skin off the breast area by carefully sliding your hand between the breast meat and the skin. Try not to tear the skin as you move your hand around under the breast skin and the skin on the legs. Insert 6 ounces of softened Gorgonzola or other blue cheese under the skin. Season the chicken as for Classic Roasted Chicken, and roast as directed.

Jewish-Style Roasted Chicken

No matter what we do, none of my siblings nor I can recreate my mother's roasted chicken. My sister Carrie is convinced it is the roasting pan she uses—it was my grandfather's. What we do know is that instead of fresh garlic she uses granulated garlic powder, and lots of it. She salts the chicken inside and outside the cavity ("Like I'm salting the road," she says). And uses a lot of black pepper and paprika. The chickens start out upside down and covered. Then she opens the roaster, turns them over, turns up the heat, and roasts them until they are crispy brown and so overcooked the meat falls off the bone. Somehow, despite the overcooking, it is always moist and delicious.

Mosaic Roasted Chicken

For a more fun presentation, an assortment of herbs (parsley, sage, rosemary, and thyme, for example) and thin lemon slices can be inserted between the meat and the skin before

Why do I call roasting a "simple art"? Simplicity when it is good has to be artful, like the little black dress. There is no concealing flaws. What is seen and smelled is what is eaten. There is a method and there are rules; but they are easily mastered. The quality of ingredients is, if anything, more essential to good results in roasting.

—Barbara Kafka, *Roasting* (Morrow, 1995)

roasting. Insert your hand between the skin and the flesh and move it around to break the connective tissue that holds the skin to the meat. Be careful not to break the skin or it will shrink away while the chicken roasts, drying out the meat. Arrange the herbs and lemon slices under the skin in an attractive (or ugly, if you prefer) pattern. As the chicken cooks, the skin will become translucent so you can see the pattern underneath.

Portuguese Roasted Chicken
My sister Leslie lives in the Portuguese section of Toronto near what I would swear is one of the best take-out food places in the world. Their chicken has the traditional garlic, salt, and black pepper seasoning, but it is given a strong kick by a heavy dose of cayenne pepper. Season the chicken as for Roasted Chicken, above, adding as much cayenne as you can stand. If you don't have cayenne, use your favorite hot sauce or Tabasco to create a fiery version of your own.

Roasted Turkey
You can use virtually the same method to roast turkey, figuring about $3^1/_2$ to 4 hours for a 12- to 16-pound bird, $4^1/_2$ to 5 hours for a 16- to 20-pound one. If using a frozen turkey, be sure to plan ahead, allowing it to defrost for at least 2 days in the refrigerator before you intend to cook it.

Gravy
To make a gravy from the pan juices, remove the bird and the roasted vegetables and pour off any excess fat. Place the roasting pan over a low flame. Add about $3/_4$ cup water or stock to the pan and bring to a simmer. Using a wooden spoon or plastic spatula, scrape the bottom of the pan as the liquid simmers to loosen the flavorful bits. Add 2 tablespoons of butter and slowly whisk in 2 table-spoons flour, avoiding the formation of lumps if possible. When all of the flour is incorporated, simmer for about 5 to 8 minutes. Adjust the seasoning with salt and pepper. Strain and serve immediately.

Links: Chicken Salad (page 91), Chicken Soup—Chicken Soup from a Roasted Chicken Carcass variation (page 93), Leg of Lamb (page 152).

Roasted Eggplant Spread

Makes about 2 cups

2 pounds small Italian eggplant (better to have a couple of smaller ones than 1 big one)

5 cloves garlic

About ¹/₂ cup unflavored bread crumbs

1 tablespoon Worcestershire sauce

1 tablespoon red wine vinegar

Juice of 1 to 2 lemons, to taste

Fresh oregano or thyme to taste

Salt and freshly ground black pepper to taste

¹/₂ cup olive oil

Kitchen Stuff

Colander or strainer

Food processor

Measuring cups

Measuring spoons

My friend Karla serves this Greek version of baba ganoush as an hors d'oeuvre with toasted bread or crackers. She advises that it tastes better after it sits a day or two, but mine is never around that long. It can last up to a week or longer if is covered tightly and refrigerated. Depending on the qualities of your eggplant—moisture content, bitterness—you may have to adjust the seasoning to taste. Be sure your bread crumbs are fresh, or the spread will have an unpleasant, stale taste. Required Reading: Preheating (page 16), Roasting, Braising, and Steaming (page 17), Seasoning to Taste (page 19), Selecting Ingredients (page 11), Using the Food Processor (page 21).

Preheat the oven to 450°F. Cut about ³/₄ inch off each end of the eggplants, place them on a baking sheet, and set in the oven. Wrap the unpeeled garlic cloves in aluminum foil and place in the oven next to the eggplant. When the garlic is soft, about 20 minutes, remove it from the oven. Leave the eggplants in, turning them over once or twice with tongs, being careful not to break the skin, until they are completely soft and collapsed, 50 minutes to an hour, total.

Remove the eggplants to a colander or strainer in the sink and cut several slits in the skin, lengthwise, to allow the excess moisture to drain out while they cool. It's best to let them cool all the way to room temperature before proceeding. Peel off the purple skin—it should just lift off—and put the flesh in the bowl of a food processor fitted with the metal chopping blade.

Squeeze the garlic cloves out of their skin into the processor as well. Process until smooth. Mix in enough of the bread crumbs to make the mixture stiff and dry enough to cling to a spoon; the amount depends on the moisture left in the eggplant after cooking. Add the seasonings to taste. With the motor running, slowly drizzle in the olive oil through the tube to make a smooth and creamy spread. Chill. Adjust the seasoning and serve.

Links: Curried Carrot Spread—similar technique (page 112), Fried Eggplant, Middle-Eastern Style (page 128), Roasted Vegetables (page 209).

Roasted Garlic

Roasted garlic is one of those things that has taken the food world by storm. You can even buy specially made clay roasting dishes designed just for garlic. The truth is you don't need anything to make roasted garlic except garlic and an oven. Part of the reason for roasted garlic's popularity is that the roasting process takes away the bitter edge of raw garlic, making the flavor much milder.

You can use roasted garlic plain on fresh bread, or mixed into spreads like the Roasted Eggplant Spread (page 206) or the Mediterranean Potato Dip (page 162). At the "Nuevo Latino" restaurant Patria in New York City, the waiters mix roasted garlic into freshly churned butter at your table for you to spread on hot rolls. If you are serving the garlic as an hors d'oeuvre to spread on bread, you'll need a lot. Figure about two heads for every three people. Required Reading: Roasting, Braising, and Steaming (page 17), Selecting Ingredients (page 11).

Makes approximately ⅓ cup

2 whole, large heads garlic (or however much you need; see headnote)

Preheat the oven to 425°F. On the rack in the middle of the oven, place the whole heads of garlic and roast until tender, about 45 minutes. Don't worry if the edges of the garlic appear to burn, the smoky flavor this imparts to the garlic is desirable. Remove from the oven and cool to room temperature. To use, break the roasted heads up into cloves and squeeze the pointy side of each clove between your thumb and forefinger until the pulp pops out.

Links: Mediterranean Potato Dip (page 162), Roasted Eggplant Spread (page 206), Roasted Vegetables (page 209).

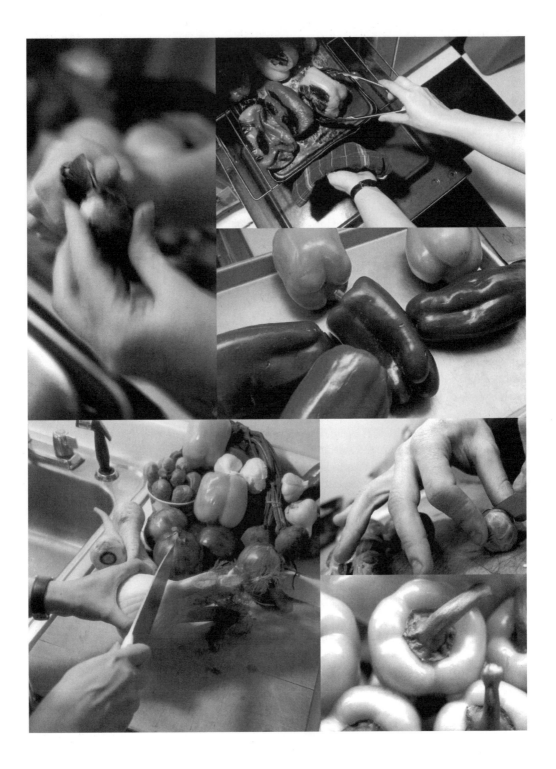

Roasted Vegetables

Roasting vegetables is one of my favorite ways to prepare them. I'm not alone. My friends Karla and Michael consider roasted veggies a staple in their home (see Roasted Eggplant Spread, page 206, too). All you need is some olive oil, salt, and freshly ground black pepper. If you have fresh herbs, garlic, or a squirt of fresh lemon juice around, all the better. Roasting enhances the natural sweetness of the vegetables. (Karla tells me that she only likes Brussels sprouts if they're roasted.) And it makes them look really good. Required Reading: Cutting Up Things (page 13), Preheating (page 16), Roasting, Braising, and Steaming (page 17), Seasoning to Taste (page 19), Selecting Ingredients (page 11), Testing for Doneness (page 20).

Makes approximately 4 side dish servings

1 pound assorted vegetables (see discussion in method)

Olive oil

Assorted fresh herbs

Salt and freshly ground black pepper to taste

Kitchen Stuff

Roasting pan

There are 2 methods to roast vegetables: either whole or cut up.

Whole Vegetables

You can roast whole vegetables separately—such as beets, peppers, potatoes, onions, eggplants (see page 206), or tomatoes (see page 173)—by setting them on the rack in the middle of a hot oven (about 450°F) and roasting until the skin has shriveled and browned and the flesh is tender. It usually takes 45 minutes to an hour, depending on the vegetable and the size. Whole-roasted vegetables are usually peeled after roasting. Cut them up, toss with olive oil, balsamic vinegar, salt, and freshly ground black pepper, and serve. You can also use them in other dishes such as Pizzabilities (page 187) and Roasted Beet and Gorgonzola Risotto (page 200).

Cut-Up Vegetables

You can also peel and cut up the vegetables and roast them together in a baking pan. To roast the vegetables this way, peel and cut them into uniform-size pieces. Stay away from particularly high moisture vegetables, such as tomatoes, when roasting several vegetables together because the extra moisture will prevent the vegetables from browning and crisping. Also avoid overcrowding the pan for the same reason. Toss with extra-virgin olive oil, salt, and freshly ground black pepper.

Set the pan in the middle of a hot oven (425°F) and roast, stirring once or twice, until tender, 30 to 40 minutes, depending on the vegetables and how big you've cut them. Try regular and sweet potatoes, asparagus, carrots, Brussels sprouts, broccoli, red onion, mushrooms, and fennel. You can even add apples or pears to sweeten the mix. Using bacon, chicken, or duck fat instead of all or some of the olive oil makes a yummy, cholesterol-rich treat.

Links: Curried Carrot Spread (page 112), Risotto (page 200), Roasted Eggplant Spread (page 206).

Salade Niçoise

Salade Niçoise falls into that ambiguous French category of <u>salades</u> <u>composées</u>, or "composed salads." For a composed salad you just have to put a lot of saladlike things together on a plate—compose them if you will. It's like a TV dinner or "meal-in-one." Should those things include potatoes, tuna, anchovies, green beans, black olives, and hard-boiled eggs, then your composed salad is a Salade Niçoise. Use the best ingredients you can find—real Niçoise olives will add authenticity. Using fresh tuna really makes a difference, but canned will work in a pinch, and it's more authentic. Required Reading: Cooking Eggs (page 12), Cooling (page 24), Cutting Up Things (page 13), Grilling, Barbecuing, and Broiling (page 13), Selecting Ingredients (page 11).

Begin by boiling the potatoes (if you have leftover baked potatoes or roasted potatoes, use them). In a small saucepan, place the whole potatoes with the eggs. Bring to a boil, lower the heat, and simmer. After about 10 minutes, remove the eggs and cool under cold running water. Continue simmering the potatoes until they are tender, but firm, 15 to 20 more minutes. Drain and chill. In a metal strainer set over a pot of simmering water, steam the string beans until they turn dark green and are tender, but still retain some of their crunch. Transfer to a small bowl or resealable bag and chill in the refrigerator.

Just before serving, prepare the fresh tuna, if using. Season the fillet(s) with salt and pepper and brush or rub with olive oil to coat. Heat a cast-iron or nonstick skillet over medium-high heat. Add the seasoned tuna and cook for 4 to 8 minutes on each side to desired doneness—some people prefer their tuna barely cooked, others like it well done. If you want, cut the tuna open to check the doneness (because you are going to slice it anyway, it doesn't matter if it's not whole). Remove the tuna from the heat, let cool for 5 minutes, and slice into thin strips.

Wash and spin dry the lettuce leaves and arrange to cover the base of 2 large plates. Slice the chilled potatoes and divide among the 2 plates. Peel the eggs, cut into quarters, and arrange 1 on each plate. Position the tuna, green beans, anchovies, and olives on top. Drizzle with vinaigrette and serve with a hearty French country bread, if you can find one.

Links: Classic Tuna Salad (page 103), French Vinaigrette (page 125), Potato Salad (page 91).

Makes 2 servings

2 small red-skinned potatoes, peeled

2 large eggs

1/4 pound fresh string beans

6 ounces fresh tuna, or one 7 1/2-ounce can, drained

Salt and freshly ground black pepper to taste

Olive oil

1 small head Boston or Bibb lettuce

6 anchovies (optional)

10 to 12 black olives (Niçoise if you can find them)

French Vinaigrette (page 125)

Kitchen Stuff

Can opener
(if using canned tuna)

Cast-iron or nonstick pan
(if using fresh tuna)

Salad spinner

Saucepan

Small bowl

Salmon Fillets with Mustard Sauce

Makes 4 servings

Four 6-ounce salmon fillets
(1½ pounds total)

Salt and freshly ground
black pepper

Flour for dredging

2 tablespoons vegetable oil

3 tablespoons unsalted butter

½ cup dry white wine

2 tablespoons Dijon mustard

½ cup fish or chicken stock

Juice of ½ lemon

¼ cup heavy cream
(aka whipping cream)

Kitchen Stuff

Large skillet

Measuring cups

Measuring spoons

This is a recipe that I used to make at a restaurant I worked at during college. It is another one of those very simple dishes that really impresses people. Use salmon fillets, not steaks, and be sure not to overcook them. Required Reading: Saucing (page 17), Sautéing, Frying, and Stir-Frying (page 19), Selecting Ingredients (page 11), Testing for Doneness (page 20).

Season the salmon fillets with salt and pepper and dredge in flour to lightly coat. In a large skillet, heat the vegetable oil over medium-high heat. Place the flour-coated salmon in the hot oil and sauté until golden, about 3 minutes. Turn over the fillets and sauté until the second side is nicely browned. Remove the salmon from the pan and discard the oil.

Add the butter to the pan with the wine and set over medium-high heat. When the mixture comes to a simmer, add the Dijon mustard, stock, and lemon juice. Continue cooking, always stirring, about 5 minutes. Slowly add the heavy cream, stirring constantly, and bring up to a simmer. Return the salmon to the pan and continue cooking until the sauce has thickened enough to coat the fillets, about 5 minutes. Adjust the seasoning with salt and pepper and serve immediately.

Links: Cabbage Sauté with Caraway— a good combination (page 79).

Salmon Mousse

This recipe comes from my friend Debbie, who makes a Salmon Mousse almost every New Year's Eve. "My mother makes it, now I make it. Tradition," she explains almost ironically. It looks really nice if you have a small mold shaped like a fish. The tricky part is to unmold the thing in one piece. Letting the mold sit in hot water for a minute or two before you try to get it out makes the process much easier. Required Reading: Cooling (page 24), Resting (page 17), Selecting Ingredients (page 11), Squeezing Lemons (page 20), Using the Food Processor (page 21).

Grease a 4- to 5-cup mold (fish-shaped if you've got it) with extra-virgin olive oil. In a blender or the bowl of a food processor, place the gelatin. Add the lemon juice, onion, and boiling water and blend or process until pureed, about 1 minute. Add the mayonnaise, paprika, dill, and salmon, and continue blending until the mixture is smooth. Blend in the heavy cream.

Pour this mixture into the oiled mold and refrigerate until set, about 6 hours. Unmold by running the tip of a knife around the rim of the mold, immersing the mold half way into hot water for 1 to 2 minutes and inverting it onto a serving plate. Chill further. Serve with Dill Sauce (page 115).

Links: Dill Sauce (page 115).

Makes 4 to 6 appetizer servings

1 envelope unflavored gelatin (available in the baking/spice section of the grocery store)

Juice of 1/2 lemon

1/2 small onion, coarsely chopped

1/2 cup boiling water

1/2 cup mayonnaise

1 teaspoon paprika

1 teaspoon dried dill

One 1-pound can salmon, drained, bones and skin removed

1 cup heavy cream (aka whipping cream)

Kitchen Stuff

Food processor or blender

4- to 5-cup gelatin mold

Sautéed Greens

Makes 4 side dish servings

1 large bunch greens
(kale, mustard greens, beet or
turnip tops, broccoli rabe,
or Swiss or red chard, or any
combination)

2 to 3 tablespoons olive oil

1 clove garlic, minced

Salt and freshly ground
black pepper to taste

Juice of $1/2$ lemon, or to taste

Kitchen Stuff

Colander

Large pot

Sauté pan

A great way to prepare bitter, green leafy things such as kale, mustard greens, beet or turnip tops, broccoli rabe, or Swiss or red chard is to boil them first and then sauté them in garlic and olive oil. The boiling removes the bitterness and makes them more digestible—despite the current North American trend to undercook all vegetables. You can use the sautéed greens as a side dish, toss them with pasta (see page 177), or stir them into mashed potatoes (page 149). For a different flavor, you can also stir-fry the boiled greens using the technique on page 228.
Required Reading: Cleaning Produce (page 12), Sautéing, Frying, and Stir-Frying (page 19), Seasoning to Taste (page 19), Selecting Ingredients (page 11).

Bring a large pot of salted water (about 4 quarts water with 1 tablespoon salt) to a boil. Clean the greens by removing any large, woody stems and/or bruised leaves, and by letting them soak in cold water. Be sure to lift them out of the cold water, rather than dumping them into a strainer, so you remove all the sand. Especially dirty greens should be soaked 2 or 3 times. Once the salted water is boiling, add the greens. Cook until the stems are tender, 10 to 15 minutes, depending on the age and toughness of the greens. Drain in a colander and rinse under cold running water. Chop the boiled greens into bite-sized pieces.

In a large skillet, heat the olive oil. Add the garlic and sauté until translucent, 2 to 3 minutes. Add the greens and sauté until they are hot and perfumed by the garlic, 5 to 6 minutes. Season with salt and pepper and a squirt or two of lemon juice. Serve immediately, or incorporate into other dishes as described above.

Links: Just-Between-You-and-Me Mashed Potatoes (page 149), Pasta Primer (page 177), Stir-Fried Watercress or Bok Choy (page 228).

Savory Bread Pudding

The first savory bread pudding I tried was made by my friends Lauren and Peter. Because I always have stale bread around the house (see Bread Pudding, page 75), I thought it was a great discovery. It's a good vegetarian entrée. Use any strong cheese you have lying around.

Required Reading: Preheating (page 16), Selecting Ingredients (page 11), Separating Eggs (page 25), Testing for Doneness (page 20), Using Leftovers (page 21).

Preheat the oven to 375°F. In a large mixing bowl, whisk together the eggs, egg yolks, milk, salt, and pepper until light and frothy. In a loaf pan or deep 2-quart baking dish (a soufflé dish works well), layer the bread cubes and cheeses ending with a layer of cheese. Pour the egg and milk mixture over and let sit for about 20 minutes for the bread to soak it up. Poke down the bread once or twice to be sure it all soaks up some of the egg mixture.

Set in the preheated oven and bake for about 1 to 1^1/$_2$ hours, until a knife or skewer inserted in the center comes out clean and the top is browned. (If the top begins to brown too much, cover it with aluminum foil.) The pudding will puff up like a soufflé just before it is done, which makes for a dramatic presentation if you serve it immediately. Otherwise, the pudding will deflate, but it tastes just as good.

Links: Bread Pudding (page 75).

Makes 4 main course servings

5 large eggs

2 large egg yolks

3 cups milk

1 teaspoon salt

7 to 8 grinds of black pepper

About ^{1}/$_2$ to ^{3}/$_4$ loaf (depending on size) stale bread, cut into ^{3}/$_4$-inch cubes to make 3^1/$_2$ cups

1 cup grated cheese (sharp cheddar, Swiss, raclette)

3 tablespoons freshly grated imported Parmesan cheese

Kitchen Stuff

Deep 2-quart baking dish or loaf pan

Large mixing bowl

Measuring cups

Measuring spoons

Whisk

Scalloped Potatoes

Makes 4 to 6 servings, but you can increase the ingredients ad infinitum

---

4 large Yukon Gold or red-skinned potatoes (about 2 pounds), peeled and thinly sliced

---

1 large onion, thinly sliced

---

2 heaping tablespoons unbleached all-purpose flour

---

2 teaspoons salt

---

10 to 15 grinds black pepper

About 1 cup (roughly ¹/₃ pound) grated Swiss cheese (optional)

---

2 tablespoons unsalted butter

---

2 cups chicken stock or milk

Kitchen Stuff

Large mixing bowl

Measuring cups

Measuring spoons

2-quart shallow baking dish

When I asked my high-school friend Judy for a recipe for my book, she said, "I know it's not exactly lark's tongues in aspic, but whenever I make scalloped potatoes, people always seem touched that someone went to the trouble to make them—and then they always ask me for the recipe." More of a technique than a recipe, it proves my point that cooking isn't like science. It's fun to play around. Judy notes that when she's feeling a little saucy, she adds a handful of chopped chives. Or she changes the type of cheese. Her only caveat is to make sure the potatoes are really well cooked. "The dish is terrible if the potatoes are hard," she warns, and I agree. Required Reading: Cutting Up Things (page 13), Selecting Ingredients (page 11), Testing for Doneness (page 20).

Preheat the oven to 350°F. Generously butter a shallow 2-quart baking dish. In a large mixing bowl, place the sliced potatoes and add the sliced onion, flour, and salt and pepper. Toss the potatoes around with your hands to be sure all of the ingredients are evenly distributed.

Dump half of the potatoes into the prepared pan and cover with a layer of the cheese, if using. Lay the remaining potatoes on top, top with more cheese, and dot with teaspoon-sized pieces of butter. Pour in the chicken stock or milk. It should come up almost to the top of the potatoes. Cover the baking dish with aluminum foil and bake for about 1 hour.

Remove the foil and continue baking for another 30 to 45 minutes, until the potatoes are tender when poked with a knife and the cheese begins to brown. Remove from the oven and serve. If you are not sure if the potatoes are done, put them back in the oven for 10 to 15 minutes more—remember Judy's warning.

Links: Chicken Soup—for stock (page 92).

Scary Prefab Surprise

In the same vein as Rita's Dinner Special (see page 201), my cousin Lloyd decided that he would bring a dish to my prebook party that he often enjoys—and I use the word enjoy loosely. I thought I would share it with you. Required Reading: <u>Macbeth</u>.

Remove the can from the cupboard, being careful not to disturb the layer of dust that has collected on top. Check for the expiration date. If the expiration date cannot be found, use the ruler to measure the depth of the dust coating on top of the can. If the dust exceeds $\frac{1}{16}$ inch, it is recommended that you locate the label and eat it instead.

Otherwise, open the can and empty contents into the microwave-safe bowl. Microwave on high for 4 minutes.

Remove from the microwave. Serve immediately in the same bowl, leaving covered until after you have recited a traditional premeal or prebattle prayer. Remove cover carefully, so as not to risk facial burns, which may mask more serious symptoms later. Serve with a long spoon, just in case. If serving guests, secure all sharp utensils away from dining area.

Links: Witches brew (see Shakespeare's <u>Macbeth</u>), Rita's Dinner Special (page 201).

Makes 1 to ? servings
(however many can stand it)

One 15- to 20-ounce generic can of food, peeled (no label)

Kitchen Stuff

Can opener

Dimly lit kitchen (to enhance the "surprise" aspect of the dish)

Even more dimly lit dining area (to prevent diners from getting a clear aim at the chef)

Microwave-safe bowl with cover (about 1 quart capacity)

Protective clothing

Ruler, $\frac{1}{16}$-inch calibration

Scones

Once you make your own scones, you'll never again eat those dry, tasteless wedges of dough they pass off at coffee bars across the nation. All you need to know is how to cut butter into flour (see page 24). The rest is easy. Put anything you like in them. I usually make two different types by dividing the dough in half before I add things like chocolate chips or currants. Required Reading: Cutting in Butter (page 24), Mixing versus Overmixing (page 25), Selecting Ingredients (page 11), Shortening (page 27), Testing for Doneness (page 20), Using the Food Processor (page 21), Working with Pastry (page 27).

Makes 16 large scones

$4^1/_2$ cups unbleached all-purpose flour

2 teaspoons baking powder

$^1/_2$ teaspoon baking soda

$^1/_3$ cup sugar

Pinch salt

2 sticks ($^1/_2$ pound) unsalted butter, cut into small cubes and chilled

1 cup heavy cream (aka whipping cream)

1 large egg

$^1/_4$ cup milk

Preheat the oven to 375°F. In a large mixing bowl, combine the flour, baking powder, baking soda, 2 tablespoons of the sugar, and the pinch of salt and mix well. Add the butter and cut it into the flour using 2 knives, a fork, or your fingertips. The finished mixture should resemble coarse meal. Alternately, you can use a food processor to cut the butter into the flour mixture. If you do, transfer the mixture to a mixing bowl before proceeding. Using a fork, gently mix in the heavy cream until the mixture comes together to form a dough. (Add a drop more cream or milk if it seems too dry.) Pat the dough into a ball, wrap in plastic wrap, and let rest in the refrigerator for about $^1/_2$ hour.

Divide the dough into 2 equal portions. Pat each half into a circle about 8 inches in diameter and $^3/_4$ inch thick. Cut each circle into 8 equal wedges and set on a cookie sheet. In a small bowl, beat together the egg with the $^1/_4$ cup of milk. Brush this mixture (called an "egg wash") on top of each scone. Sprinkle with some of the remaining sugar. Set the baking sheet in the preheated oven and bake until golden brown and risen, 12 to 18 minutes. If you are not sure if they are done, sacrifice one by splitting it in half. Serve warm.

Variations

Chocolate Chip Scones

Just after you've added the heavy cream and before you shape the dough into a ball to rest, add $^1/_2$ to $^3/_4$ cup chocolate chips to the mixture. Be careful not to overmix. Proceed with the recipe as directed.

Currant Orange Scones

Add the grated zest of 1 orange to the dry ingredients. Then, just after you've added the heavy cream, add $^1/_2$ to $^3/_4$ cup currants to the mixture. For a kick, soak the currants in orange liqueur for a couple of hours in advance. Drain before adding to the scone dough. Be careful not to overmix. Proceed with the recipe as directed.

Links: Buttermilk Biscuits (page 78), Light and Flaky Pie Crust—same technique (page 157).

Kitchen Stuff

Cookie sheets

Food processor or large mixing bowl

Measuring cups

Measuring spoons

Pastry brush

Small bowls

Scrambled Eggs

Makes 2 servings

5 large eggs

2 tablespoons heavy cream (aka whipping cream) or sour cream (optional, but delicious)

Pinch salt

5 grinds black pepper, or to taste

1 tablespoon butter

Kitchen Stuff

Nonstick pan (for optimal results)

Small bowl

Whisk

The simplest dish in the world, you say. Who needs a recipe for scrambled eggs? Well, there are a few secrets to prevent yellow rubber or mush. Use fresh eggs. Beat them well. Season with salt and pepper. Use a hot, clean pan (nonstick if you have it). Stir the eggs constantly while they are cooking to avoid the formation of large, tough curds. Ample amounts of butter and cream always help. Avoid egg in your face.

Required Reading: Cooking Eggs (page 12), Lowering Fat (page 15), Seasoning to Taste (page 19), Selecting Ingredients (page 11).

Into a medium bowl, crack the eggs and beat with a fork to blend well. Add the heavy cream or sour cream, if using, salt, and black pepper, and keep beating until the eggs are frothy, 2 to 3 minutes. Heat the (nonstick) pan over medium-high heat. Add the butter. When the butter has melted and frothed, but not browned, pour in the eggs all at once. With a wooden spoon, rubber spatula, or fork, keep stirring the eggs while they cook, almost as though you are beating them in slow motion. Keep drawing the uncooked egg to the center of the pan, breaking up the curds of egg as they form. The mixture should be almost smooth and creamy. When the eggs reach the desired doneness (about 4 minutes for loose, creamy eggs), remove from the heat and serve immediately. There is no point to making scrambled eggs in advance because they just do not keep well.

Variations

Mushrooms, Onions, and Eggs

Spoon 2 to 3 tablespoons of Mom's Mushroom and Onions (page 166) into the hot butter, add the eggs and proceed as directed.

Onions, Smoked Salmon, and Eggs

To the frothing butter in the hot pan add ¹/₂ small onion, thinly sliced. Sauté until translucent. Add about 2 ounces chopped smoked salmon, pour in the eggs, and continue cooking as directed.

Ratatouille and Eggs

Spoon 2 to 3 tablespoons of Ratatouille (page 193) into the hot butter, add the eggs and proceed as directed.

Pasta and Eggs

One of my favorite uses for leftover pasta is to stir it into scrambled eggs. The result is something like the traditional Austrian breakfast of spaetzle and eggs. Add the pasta to the hot pan (small shapes work best) and proceed with the recipe.

Scrambled Egg Whites

Substitute 8 egg whites and proceed as directed. Not as creamy, but better for you.

Links: Mom's Mushroom and Onions (page 166), Ratatouille (page 193), Real Man's Quiche—really just scrambled eggs in a crust (page 195).

Scrambled Tofu

My sister Leslie has been making this scrambled egg substitute for years. I love it, but I can never remember how to make it. Actually, Leslie makes two different versions, which is why I can't ever remember what to do. This one's actually a combination of both. It's not exactly a substitute for scrambled eggs, but it's delicious, anyway. Try it with toast for breakfast or over rice with Stir-Fried Watercress or Bok Choy (page 228) for a quick, protein-rich vegetarian dinner. Required Reading: Sautéing, Frying, and Stir-Frying (page 19), Seasoning to Taste (page 19), Selecting Ingredients (page 11).

Rinse and drain the tofu. Dice it into ¹/₄-inch cubes. In a large skillet, heat the oil over medium-high heat. Add the onion and fresh ginger, if you are using it, and sauté until the onion is translucent. Add the tofu and pickled ginger, if that's what you are using, and sauté for 3 to 4 minutes more. Add the soy sauce, tamari, or shoyu, and continue sautéing, constantly moving the tofu around, until the tofu crumbles and begins to dry out, a good 10 minutes. Add more oil if the tofu begins to stick. Add the chopped scallions, if using, adjust the seasoning with salt and pepper, and serve immediately.

Links: Stir-Fried Watercress or Bok Choy—great on the side (page 228).

Makes 2 to 4 servings, depending on what else you serve with it

One 1-pound package soft tofu

2 tablespoons peanut oil

1 small onion, diced

4 to 5 pieces pickled ginger, chopped (available in Asian markets or wherever sushi is sold), or 1 tablespoon fresh ginger, minced

3 tablespoons soy sauce, tamari, or shoyu

2 scallions, chopped, white and greens (optional)

Freshly ground black pepper to taste

Kitchen Stuff

Measuring spoons

Wok or cast-iron skillet

Sesame Chicken Fingers

You can make these chicken fingers, my sister Carrie's recipe, in a matter of minutes. They're a great way to use stale bread. And they are delicious dipped in Lemon Tahini Dressing (see page 155). Required Reading: Breading (page 12) Sautéing, Frying, and Stir-Frying (page 19), Selecting Ingredients (page 11), Testing for Doneness (page 20), Using the Food Processor (page 21).

Trim the chicken breasts of any fat and slice into long, thin strips, about ³/₄ inch wide and 2 to 3 inches long. In the bowl of a food processor fitted with the metal chopping blade, place the white bread and process with on/off pulses to produce crumbs. You can also use a blender, if you only do 2 to 3 slices at a time and keep shaking the machine while it's running. Transfer the crumbs to a resealable plastic bag. Add the sesame seeds, salt, and pepper to the bag, close the top, and toss the mixture to evenly distribute the seeds and the spices.

Take 3 or 4 chicken strips and drop them in the bag. Close the top and toss them around so that they are evenly coated with the crumb mixture. Remove them from the bag, set aside on a plate, and repeat until all of the chicken strips are coated.

In a medium-sized frying pan, heat about ¹/₄ inch of oil over medium-high heat. Lay the chicken fingers in a single layer in the hot oil, making sure they do not touch, and fry until they are golden brown on the bottom. Turn them over with tongs or a fork and continue frying until they are golden brown on both sides. Some of the crumbs will fall off, but those that remain will be golden and delicious. Cut one in half to be sure it is cooked through. Remove from the oil and let drain on sheets of paper towel or a clean brown paper bag.

Repeat with the remaining chicken fingers. As you are frying, if any of the bread crumbs that have fallen off the chicken fingers begin to burn, lift them out of the oil with a fork or a slotted spoon and discard. Serve hot with Lemon Tahini Dressing (page 155).

Variation

Spicy Sesame Chicken Fingers
Add 1 teaspoon of cayenne pepper to the crumb mixture and proceed with the recipe as directed.

Links: Lemon Tahini Dressing (page 155).

Makes 8 snack servings or 4 main course servings

4 large (single) skinless and boneless chicken breasts, or about 1 pound of chicken tenders

8 slices stale white bread

¹/₄ cup sesame seeds

1 teaspoon salt

Lots of freshly ground black pepper

Vegetable oil for frying

Kitchen Stuff

Dry measuring cups

Measuring spoons

Large skillet

Paper towel or brown paper bag

Resealable Plastic bag

Slotted spoon

Sesame Noodles

Makes 4 servings

$^1/_2$ pound long pasta
(preferable angel hair, spaghettini,
or Chinese egg noodles)

2 tablespoons toasted sesame oil

1 tablespoon soy sauce

1 tablespoon sesame seeds

1 teaspoon Chinese red chili paste
or other hot sauce (optional)

$^1/_2$ large seedless English
cucumber, peeled and cut into
chunks

4 scallions, thinly sliced including
the green parts

$^1/_2$ cup Lemon Tahini Dressing
(page 155)

Chopped chives for garnish

Kitchen Stuff

Large pot

Measuring cups

Measuring spoons

Medium bowl

Though not completely authentic, this is a great way to use up leftover Lemon Tahini Dressing (see page 155). You can add any vegetables you like, or omit them altogether. For a more authentic dish, prepare the dressing with Asian toasted sesame paste (available in Chinese grocery stores) instead of tahini. A touch of chili paste provides a little fire, if you desire. Required Reading: Resting (page 17), Saucing (page 17), Seasoning to Taste (page 19), Selecting Ingredients (page 11),

Cook the pasta according to the directions on page 177, but don't stop at al dente. The noodles should be cooked through. Drain and rinse with cold water. Drain the noodles very well and toss with 1 tablespoon of the toasted sesame oil. Place in the refrigerator to chill.

In a medium mixing bowl, combine the remaining tablespoon of sesame oil, soy sauce, sesame seeds, optional chili paste, cucumber, and scallions. Add the chilled noodles and the Lemon Tahini Dressing and mix well so that all of the noodles are well coated. The noodles are best if left in the refrigerator overnight before serving. Serve garnished with a sprinkling of sesame seeds and chopped chives.

Links: Lemon Tahini Dressing (page 155), Pasta Primer (page 177).

Shortcake

I make shortcake using **Buttermilk Biscuits (page 78)** or **Scones (page 219)** **as the base. My friends Joan and Edwin brought Joan's mother's biscuit** **shortcake, with fresh strawberries and cream, to my prebook party. You** **can use any fresh fruit as long as it's sweet and ripe.** Required Reading: Increasing or Decreasing Recipes (page 24), Selecting Ingredients (page 11).

Preheat the oven to 425°F. In a small bowl, combine the strawberries with the $^1/_4$ cup sugar and the orange-flavored liqueur and let stand until the strawberries give off some of their liquid, about $^1/_2$ hour.

Divide the biscuit or scone dough into 6 equal pieces and pat each piece into a small disk, about 2 inches in diameter. Set on a baking sheet. Brush each shortcake with heavy cream and sprinkle generously with the remaining sugar. Bake for 20 to 25 minutes, until the shortcakes have risen and turned golden brown. Remove from the oven and split in half like an English muffin.

Spoon some of the strawberry juice on the bottom half of the shortcake and top with some of the sliced fruit. Spoon a dollop of whipped cream on top, and crown with the top half of the shortcake.

Links: Buttermilk Biscuits (page 78), Scones (page 219), Whipped Cream (page 239).

Makes 6 shortcakes

$^1/_2$ recipe Buttermilk Biscuits (page 78) or Scones (page 219)

1 pint fresh strawberries, hulled and sliced

$^1/_4$ cup plus 3 tablespoons sugar

2 tablespoons orange-flavored liqueur (such as Grand Marnier)

2 tablespoons heavy cream (aka whipping cream)

1 cup Whipped Cream (page 239)

Kitchen Stuff

Cookie sheet

Measuring spoons

Pastry brush

Small bowl

Simple Pie Crust

Makes two 9-inch pie crusts

2¼ cups unbleached all-purpose flour

Pinch salt

½ pound (2 sticks) unsalted butter, chilled and cut into cubes

3 to 4 tablespoons cold water

Kitchen Stuff

Food processor (optional)

Large mixing bowl

2 knives or a fork

Easier than the Light and Flaky Pie Crust (page 157), this recipe is every bit as good, just a little less flaky. The only technique to master is cutting in the butter (see page 24), which you will also use to make Buttermilk Biscuits (page 78) or Scones (page 219). If the dough breaks while you are rolling it out, moisten it at the break with a few drops of water and pinch it together in the pie plate. No one will ever know. Required Reading: Cutting in Butter (page 24), Resting (page 17), Shortening (page 27), Using the Food Processor (page 21), Working with Pastry (page 27).

In a large mixing bowl, combine the flour and salt. Add the butter and break it up with your hands to coat the chunks with flour. Using the tines of a fork or two butter knives, or your fingertips if you work quickly and your hands aren't so warm that they melt the butter, break the butter up into small pieces. Keep moving the butter around in the flour. Continue until the mixture resembles coarse crumbs. This may take some time until you get the hang of it. If you come across some stubborn large pieces of butter, break them up with your fingertips into smaller pieces. Don't worry if some of the butter pieces are slightly bigger than others. When the crust bakes, the butter will melt and leave large, lazy flakes. Alternately, you can cut the butter into the flour in a food processor using quick on/off pulses. Transfer to a large mixing bowl and proceed with the recipe.

Add 3 tablespoons of cold water and push the mixture together with a fork until it begins to form a dough. If the mixture is too dry for all of the flour to be incorporated into the dough, add more water, a couple of drops at a time, until you can pinch the dough together and it holds its shape. Try to work the dough as little as possible so that it doesn't toughen. If it is crumbly or there is flour on the bottom of the bowl, but the mixture seems moist, don't worry. Turn the whole mess out onto a lightly floured surface and work with your fingertips until the dough forms a ball.

Divide in half and shape each half into a circle. Wrap in plastic and refrigerate for 1 to 2 hours before using. The dough can be kept for up to 4 days in the refrigerator or frozen for 2 to 3 months.

Links: All pies, tarts, quiches, in fact, anything that has a crust; Light and Flaky Pie Crust (page 157).

Spaghetti Sauce

If you can't find fresh ripe tomatoes for the Fresh Tomato Sauce (page 127) and/or you have a little time on your hands, why not prepare a large batch of Spaghetti Sauce that you can keep on hand for pasta (page 177), pizza (page 187), Eggplant Parmesan (page 116), and other Italian treats? Admittedly more American than Italian, Spaghetti Sauce (sometimes referred to as marinara) is still a delicious sauce. I think it's best if you add some sausage and/or ground meat, but if you want to make a vegetarian sauce, just leave it plain. Required Reading: Patience (page 16), Saucing (page 17), Seasoning to Taste (page 19), Selecting Ingredients (page 11), Simmering versus Boiling (page 19), Smashing Garlic (page 19), Working with Meat (page 21).

If using meat, you have to fry it first to render the fat. Slit open the casing of the sausage and separate the meat. Heat a large heavy-bottomed saucepan or stock pot over a medium-high flame. Add the ground beef and/or sausage meat and cook until browned and the fat has been rendered out, about 10 minutes. Keep breaking the meat up with a wooden spoon as it browns. Pour off the fat (not down the sink, but into an empty can).

Return to the flame and add the olive oil. Add the onions and sauté until translucent, but not colored, about 8 minutes. Add the garlic and peppers, if using, and continue cooking for another 2 to 3 minutes. Pour in the different canned tomato products. Rinse each can out with a couple of tablespoons of cold water and pour the water into the pot.

Add the remaining ingredients and bring to a boil. Set the cover on the pan slightly ajar, turn down the heat, and simmer the sauce for anywhere from 1 to 2 hours, depending on how much time you have, until it has a rich, strong flavor. (I generally think the longer it cooks, the better.)

Variation

The Sauce Doctor

If you just don't have the time or inclination to make your own sauce, you can doctor up a store-bought sauce by adding onions and garlic sautéed in olive oil, browned sausage, and seasonings. Start with a top-quality sauce and simmer it with whatever you add for 15 to 20 minutes before using.

Links: Eggplant Parmesan (page 116), Fresh Tomato Sauce (page 127), Pasta Primer (page 177), Pizzabilities (page 187).

Makes about 4 quarts

1 1/2 pounds sweet or hot Italian sausage, or 1 pound lean ground beef, or a combination (optional)

1/2 cup extra-virgin olive oil

3 onions, chopped

4 to 5 cloves garlic, minced

1 jalapeño pepper, seeded and chopped (optional)

Two 28-ounce cans crushed Italian-style plum tomatoes (if you can't find crushed, use whole, but chop them very finely)

One 6-ounce can tomato paste

One 16-ounce can tomato sauce (like Hunt's, not Italian)

2 tablespoons sugar (optional)

2 tablespoons dried oregano

2 bay leaves

Salt and freshly ground black pepper to taste

Kitchen Stuff

Can opener

Large, heavy-bottomed saucepan or stock pot with a lid

Stir-Fried Watercress or Bok Choy

Makes 2 side dish servings

2 bunches fresh watercress,
or 1 large bunch fresh bok choy
or other vegetables

1 tablespoon peanut oil

2 cloves garlic, minced

1 tablespoon minced fresh ginger
(about a 1-inch piece)

$1/4$ cup soy sauce, tamari,
or shoyu

1 teaspoon toasted sesame oil
(optional)

Kitchen Stuff

Wok or cast-iron skillet

Wooden spoon or metal spatula

When I taught my friend Lonni how to make this simple Asian dish, she told me it changed her life. There have been periods in my life when I've lived on stir-fried watercress. Stir-frying with ginger, garlic, and soy sauce is a technique you can use with almost any vegetable. If you do not have a gas stove, you might find the wok doesn't get very hot. A large cast-iron frying pan works well because it gets hot enough to impart the slight smoky flavor characteristic of good Chinese food (notice I didn't say burned). After you stir-fry once or twice, it may change your life, too.
Required Reading: Sautéing, Frying, and Stir-Frying (page 19), Selecting Ingredients (page 11).

If using watercress, just rinse the watercress thoroughly. No further preparation is needed. For the bok choy, you must remove the tough base of the stems and the hard core. Rinse the leaves well to remove any residual sand, and chop into 1-inch pieces.

Heat a wok or cast-iron pan over medium-high heat until very hot. Add the peanut oil and move it around with a large wooden spoon or metal spatula to coat the pan. Add the garlic and ginger and move around for 1 to 2 minutes to flavor the oil. Don't let them burn. Add the watercress or bok choy and toss to coat with the hot oil. Add the soy sauce, tamari, or shoyu. In a matter of minutes, the greens will deflate to about $1/4$ their volume. Cook for an additional minute or two, until the stems of the greens are tender. Add the sesame oil, if using, toss once or twice, and serve immediately. Spoon the cooking liquid over rice.

Links: Sauteéd Greens (page 214), Scrambled Tofu—goes great (page 221).

Strawberry Soup

Served chilled, this is a great summer dessert soup that was given to me by my friend Christie. It tastes kind of like melted strawberry ice cream, which is okay by everyone I've ever served it to. Required Reading: Resting (page 17), Selecting Ingredients (page 11), Using the Food Processor (page 21).

In a small saucepan, place the gelatin and add the water. Let it sit for about 5 minutes to soften. Set the saucepan over low heat and warm just until the gelatin is dissolved. In a medium mixing bowl, combine the orange juice, lemon juice, and sugar. Stir in the dissolved gelatin, cover with plastic wrap, and chill in the refrigerator for about 1 hour. Once chilled, transfer the mixture to a blender or food processor. Add the strawberries and puree until smooth. Stir in the heavy cream, and chill until ready to serve.

Links: Shortcake—Why not? It has strawberries in it, too (page 225).

Makes 6 to 8 servings

1 envelope unflavored gelatin (available in the baking section of the grocery store)

$^1/_4$ cup cold water

4 cups orange juice

Juice of 1 lemon

$^1/_4$ cup sugar

1 pint strawberries, hulled

1 cup heavy cream (aka whipping cream)

Kitchen Stuff

Blender or food processor

Measuring cups

Small saucepan

Tabbouleh

Makes 2 to 4 servings

1/2 cup medium (no. 2) bulgur

1 cup boiling water

1/2 teaspoon salt

1 cup (about 1 large bunch) finely chopped flat-leaf parsley

2 tablespoons (about 4 sprigs) finely chopped fresh mint

3 scallions, minced

Freshly ground black pepper

1/4 teaspoon ground cumin

2 large, ripe tomatoes, diced

Juice of 1 to 2 lemons, to taste

3 tablespoons extra-virgin olive oil

Kitchen Stuff

Measuring cups

Measuring spoons

Medium bowl

This Middle-Eastern salad is very flavorful and very easy. Serve it as a side dish to Falafel Vegetable Burgers (page 119) or Avocado Sandwiches (page 59). Required Reading: Cutting Up Things (page 13), Resting (page 17), Seasoning to Taste (page 19), Selecting Ingredients (page 11), Squeezing Lemons (page 20).

In a medium-sized mixing bowl, place the bulgur and pour over the boiling water. Add the salt, cover with plastic wrap and let sit until all of the water is absorbed and the bulgur has puffed up, about 30 minutes. Fluff with a fork. Add the parsley, mint, scallions, black pepper, cumin, diced tomato, lemon juice, and olive oil. Chill for at least 1 hour before serving to allow the flavors to blend. Adjust the seasoning and serve chilled or at room temperature.

Links: Avocado Sandwich (page 59), Falafel Vegetable Burgers (page 119), Waves of Grain (page 236).

Thrifty Lemon Pound Cake

This is a recipe from my friend Evelynne, who also happens to be one of the best cooks I know. Evelynne knows that I love lemon desserts so every time I go to her house for a meal, she always serves another one she's dug up from her extensive cookbook collection. This is a recipe of her mother's.

The origin is unclear, but Evelyn explained that it was very popular in the 1940s and 1950s and that every household had a different version. She notes that it is thrifty not only because it uses fewer eggs and less butter than the traditional pound cake, but also because it requires much less effort (which is why I've included it here). The cake is delicious with ice cream or canned fruit or the chocolate sauce on page 98. Required Reading: Bringing to Room Temperature (page 12), Buttering and Flouring (page 23), Cooling (page 24), Measuring (page 15), Mixing versus Overmixing (page 25), Preheating (page 16), Testing for Doneness (page 20).

Preheat the oven to 350°F. Butter and flour a 9-inch tube pan or two 8$^1/_2$-inch loaf pans. In a large mixing bowl, place all the dry ingredients (if you have an electric mixer, use it) and stir briefly to mix. Add all of the other ingredients except for the lemon juice and the powdered sugar and beat together until smooth. If using an electric mixer, beat on moderately high speed for 2$^1/_2$ minutes. If making the cake by hand, beat with a wooden spoon and/or whisk for 5 to 10 minutes to produce a smooth batter.

Turn the batter into the prepared pan(s) and bake about 1 hour and 10 minutes, until a bamboo skewer or butter knife inserted in the center comes out clean. Allow to cool in the pan for 10 minutes, then turn out on a wire rack to cool to room temperature. If using the glaze, stir together the lemon juice and confectioner's sugar until smooth and spoon over the warm cake.

Variation

Lemon Poppy Seed Cake
Add 2 tablespoons of poppy seeds to the recipe and proceed as described.

Links: Chocolate Sauce (page 98), Crunchy Poppy Seed Biscotti (page 111).

Serves 12 or more

3 cups unbleached all-purpose flour

$^1/_2$ teaspoon baking soda

$^1/_2$ teaspoon baking powder

$^3/_4$ teaspoon salt

2 cups sugar

1 cup unsalted butter, at room temperature

4 large eggs

1 teaspoon pure vanilla extract

1 teaspoon lemon extract (optional)

Grated zest of 1 lemon

1 cup buttermilk

Juice of 1 to 2 lemons to make $^1/_4$ cup (optional)

$^1/_2$ cup confectioner's sugar (optional)

Kitchen Stuff

Electric mixer (helps)

Large mixing bowl

9-inch tube pan or two 8$^1/_2$-inch loaf pans

Tomato Salad with Mozzarella and Basil

Insalata caprese, as this salad is called in its homeland of Italy, goes into the category of dishes that everybody loves and that are really easy to prepare. As with most simple dishes, the important thing is to use the freshest ingredients. (Read: don't make this dish in the winter, when tomatoes taste more like cardboard! And don't use that rubbery mozzarella they sell to put on pizza.) Required Reading: Selecting Ingredients (page 11).

Slice the mozzarella into rounds, about 1/8 inch thick. Core the tomatoes and slice them into rounds, about 1/4 inch thick. Arrange the rounds of tomato alternately with the cheese on a serving plate. Scatter leaves of basil around the dish in an attractive way.

Drizzle the whole thing with olive oil and sprinkle with salt and freshly ground black pepper.

Links: Marinated Mozzarella alla Anna Teresa (page 159).

Makes 2 servings

1/2 pound fresh mozzarella (buffalo's milk mozzarella is worth the extra money if you can find it)

2 large ripe tomatoes

5 sprigs fresh basil

Extra-virgin olive oil

Salt and freshly ground black pepper to taste

Kitchen Stuff

Cutting board

Sharp knife

Victoria Sandwich Cake

Makes 6 to 8 servings

Butter and flour for pans

1 cup (2 sticks) unsalted butter, at room temperature

1^1/$_2$ cups sugar

4 large eggs

1 teaspoon vanilla extract

3 cups unbleached all-purpose flour

4 teaspoons baking powder

^{1}/$_2$ teaspoon salt

1 cup milk

Lemon Curd (see page 153)

Confectioner's sugar

Kitchen Stuff

Bowls

Electric mixer (if you have one, but it's not necessary)

Measuring cups

Measuring spoons

Two 9-inch round cake pans

Though named after the queen, it was in fact my friend Victoria who gave me this recipe. It is a classic British butter cake that Victoria, who hails from England, spent many years trying to adapt to American ingredients. The result is, well, fit for a queen. Required Reading: Bringing to Room Temperature (page 12), Buttering and Flouring (page 23), Cooling (page 24), Creaming (page 24), Measuring (page 15), Mixing versus Overmixing (page 25), Preheating (page 16), Testing for Doneness (page 20).

Preheat the oven to 350°F. Butter two 9-inch sandwich tins (that's round cake pans to we Americans) and lightly dust with flour. In a large mixing bowl, cream the butter and sugar using a wooden spoon and a lot of elbow grease or an electric mixer until the mixture is light and fluffy. Add the eggs and vanilla and beat until incorporated.

In a separate bowl, mix together the flour, baking powder, and salt. Alternately add the flour and milk to the creamed butter mixture in thirds, starting with the flour and mixing well after each addition. Divide the batter between the cake pans and bake about 25 minutes, until golden brown and a cake tester or toothpick inserted in the center comes out clean. Cool the cakes for 15 minutes in the pan, then run a knife around the circumference and invert onto wire racks to finish cooling. When cool, trim one layer so it is flat. Spread the lemon curd on, top with the second cake, and sift confectioner's sugar over the top. In my friend's words, Queen Victoria would be happy to have a slice.

Links: Lemon Curd (page 153).

Warm Potato Salad

This is a great alternative to regular potato salad. It's especially good with meats such as Leg of Lamb (page 152) or Roasted Chicken (page 203). Obviously, it's not appropriate for picnics, but then what would a picnic be without regular potato salad? Required Reading: Cutting Up Things (page 13), Seasoning to Taste (page 19), Selecting Ingredients (page 11), Testing for Doneness (page 20).

Roast the potatoes according to the directions for Roasted Vegetables ("Cut-Up") on page 209. The potatoes should be nice and crispy. While the potatoes are roasting, heat a large skillet over medium-high heat to fry the bacon. Place the slices in the hot pan and fry until crisp on both sides. Lift the cooked bacon out of the pan, drain on paper towels, and crumble into small pieces.

In the hot pan with the bacon fat, sauté the red onion until browned, 8 to 10 minutes. Lift the onion out of the pan with a fork and let drain on paper towels.

When the potatoes are finished roasting, remove them from the oven. While still hot, toss with the bacon, onion, and vinaigrette. Garnish with chopped scallions and serve warm.

Links: French Vinaigrette (page 125), Potato Salad—only in name (page 191), Roasted Vegetables (page 209).

Makes 4 to 6 side dish servings

2 pounds red-skinned potatoes, cut up into 1-inch chunks

5 slices bacon

1 red onion, sliced

1 recipe French Vinaigrette (see page 125)

2 scallions, chopped, white and green parts

Kitchen Stuff

Large skillet

Mixing bowls

Roasting pan

Waves of Grain

Makes 4 servings

1 cup grain
(see discussion in method)

3 to 4 cups water

1 teaspoon salt

Kitchen Stuff

Medium saucepan

A few recipes in this book use grains. But there are so many grains and they are so versatile, that once you know how to cook them, you open a world of culinary possibilities. When I say grains I mean those starchy cereals such as amaranth, barley, buckwheat, corn, oats, quinoa, rice, rye, and wheat. They come in a variety of forms—whole, rolled, sliced, cut into pieces called grits, or ground into meal. Depending on the type of grain and the form it is in, there are really only four different ways to cook it: boiling, simmering in a measured amount of liquid, cooking like a pudding, or steeping. In each case, the liquid used can be varied, from water, to stock, to milk, although water is most common. When in doubt about how to cook a particular grain, check the package that it came in.
Required Reading: Salting Water (page 17), Selecting Ingredients (page 11), Testing for Doneness (page 20).

Boiling

The same boiling technique used to cook pasta (see page 177) is the most straightforward way to cook a grain. It works best for whole grains such as rice (for which most people use the simmering method) or wheat berries (which need to be soaked in water overnight before they are boiled). The liquid to grain volume ratio should be 5 to 1.

Bring liquid to a rolling boil. (Do not add salt if boiling wheat berries or brown rice.) Slowly add the grain, stirring once to ensure that no kernels are stuck together. Boil, uncovered, as fast as possible so that the movement of the water keeps the grains separate.

The cooking times vary from grain to grain (white rice takes about 20 minutes, wheat berries about 60 minutes). Whole grains generally absorb more water and take longer to cook than processed grains. When cooked, all grains should have a perceptible al dente texture. They should be drained and rinsed with hot water to remove any residual starch. Allow the grain to sit for several minutes after rinsing, then fluff with a fork.

Simmering in a Measured Amount of Liquid

Sometimes referred to as the "pilaf" method, this technique requires that you simmer the grain in a covered pan with a measured amount of liquid and seasoning, without stirring, until all of the liquid is absorbed and the grain is al dente. For better flavor, you can sauté the grain in butter or oil with aromatics such as onions and garlic before adding the liquid. Rice-a-Roni is a perfect example of this method of cooking, but it certainly isn't the best.

Measurements are determined by the type of grain and form in which it was

Tracing the history of grain is not unlike following an adventure story filled with tales of the hunt, survival under the most trying of conditions by small family groups, the changing weather patterns that determined what might be grown and just which cereal grasses might survive until the harvest... We remember when our own mothers placed the morning hot cereal in front of us and said, with no opportunity for childish rebuttal, "Eat your oatmeal! It's good for you!" Did the mothers of 9000 B.C. also say the very same thing to their young ones?

—SHERYL AND MEL LONDON, *THE VERSATILE GRAIN AND THE ELEGANT BEAN* (SIMON & SCHUSTER, 1992)

purchased. For example, 1 cup of amaranth takes 3 cups of liquid (don't add any salt until the amaranth is cooked); 1 cup whole-grain barley takes 3½ cups liquid; 1 cup toasted buckwheat groats (kasha), quinoa, or white rice takes 2 cups liquid; 1 cup brown rice takes 2½ cups liquid. Check the package.

Cooking Like a Pudding

This is the technique used for cracked grains or meals such as oatmeal, Italian polenta, or southern grits. For this method, the liquid to grain ratio is 3½ to 1. Bring liquid to a rolling boil. Slowly whisk in the grain to ensure that no lumps form. Boil the resulting mush until it is thick and creamy, anywhere from 10 minutes for quick-cooking grits or oatmeal, to 20 minutes for semolina, to 45 minutes for an authentic polenta. Puddings can be finished with all sorts of things like butter, cheese, egg yolks, sugar, what have you. Puddings are also good chilled, sliced, and fried in butter (what isn't?).

Steeping

Some processed grains such as couscous and bulgur simply need to be steeped in hot liquid to cook them. (Note that authentic Moroccan and Tunisian couscous recipes require you to steam the steeped couscous several times before serving.) See Moroccan-Style Couscous Salad (page 167) or Tabbouleh (page 230) for examples.

Links: Mister Bean (page 164), Moroccan-Style Couscous Salad (page 167), Mushroom Barley Soup (page 169), Tabbouleh (page 230).

Whipped Cream

I'm including a "recipe" for whipped cream because it's one of those things that makes an ordinary dessert, like a piece of Aunt Josephine's Chocolate Cake (page 58), Bread Pudding (page 75), or Rhubarb or Nectarine Tart (page 199) a real treat. **You can just whip the cream plain, but adding a little vanilla and sugar, or other flavoring, actually helps bring out the flavor of the cream.**

If you are ever fortunate to have dinner at Peter Luger's steak house in Williamsburg, Brooklyn, you will know what joy a bowl of whipped cream can bring. After you have eaten more steak and home fries, and creamed spinach than you care to remember, and you've broken down and ordered a piece of cheesecake or pecan pie, the waiters always bring a large bowl of <u>schlog</u> (that's "whipped cream" in German) to help wash everything down. Warning: don't try this at home. Required Reading: Beating Egg Whites and Whipping Cream (page 23), Selecting Ingredients (page 11).

Set a clean mixing bowl and whisk in the freezer for about $1/2$ hour until well chilled. Make sure your whipping cream is very cold. Pour the cream into the cold bowl and beat in the sugar and vanilla with the whisk. Continue beating with the whisk until the cream becomes stiff, about 5 to 10 minutes, depending on the strength of your forearms. Serve immediately.

Don't overwhip the cream or it will turn into butter—you'll know when it happens, but, unfortunately, there's nothing to do to save it. Start over and pretend you intended it. You can make the whipped cream a few hours in advance if you transfer it to a fine mesh strainer, set it over a bowl (to catch any liquid that the cream releases), and keep it covered with a damp cloth in the refrigerator.

Variations

Liqueur-Flavored Whipped Cream
You can add just about any liqueur to whipped cream to flavor it. Use about a tablespoon of a strongly flavored libation such as Kahlúa, bourbon, Galiano, Canton Ginger Liqueur, what have you.

Links: Aunt Josephine's Chocolate Cake (page 58), Bread Pudding (page 75), Cream Puffs (page 108), Rhubarb or Nectarine Tart (page 199), Shortcake (page 225).

Makes $1^1/2$ cups

1 cup heavy cream
(aka whipping cream)

1 tablespoon confectioner's sugar

1 teaspoon vanilla

Kitchen Stuff

Sieve (to store it for a few hours)

Stainless Steel or glass bowl, chilled

Whisk

Yogurt Curried Chicken

Makes 2 to 4 servings

2 tablespoons mild curry paste (Patak's works best), or 1 tablespoon Thai red curry paste (see page 104), or 2 tablespoons curry powder mixed with 1 tablespoon vegetable oil or curry oil (see page 121)

²/₃ cup yogurt

Juice of ¹/₂ lemon

4 skinless and boneless chicken breasts

Kitchen Stuff

Baking sheet

Measuring spoons

Measuring cups

Small bowl

This recipe is a favorite of my friend Lonni's (see also Stir-Fried Watercress or Bok Choy, page 228). It's so good that she'll make it for company, and so easy that she even makes it for herself. It's also low fat, fast, and you can use the leftovers to make a great curried chicken salad (see page 113). If you have the time, the chicken is better after it has marinated overnight. Required Reading: Marinating (page 15), Preheating (page 16), Roasting, Braising, and Steaming (page 17), Selecting Ingredients (page 11), Testing for Doneness (page 20).

In a small bowl, combine the curry paste, yogurt, and lemon juice. If you are using the curry powder and oil, mix them together in the small bowl before adding the yogurt and lemon juice. Place the chicken breasts on a plate and coat with the yogurt mixture on both sides by spooning the mixture into the chicken. If you are preparing the chicken in advance, cover the breasts with plastic wrap and let marinate in the refrigerator overnight.

Transfer the breasts to a baking sheet lined with aluminum foil and set under a preheated broiler until slightly browned, 12 to 15 minutes. Turn over and continue broiling until the chicken is cooked through, an additional 10 minutes, depending on how hot your broiler is. Serve hot.

Links: Curried Chicken Salad (page 113), Curry Oil (page 121), Curried Carrot Spread (page 112).

You Gotta Try These Blondies

This recipe comes from my colleague Phyllis. She wanted me to try these blondies so badly that she actually had a little party for me and my friends to sample them. Almost more like a nut cake than a brownie, these blondies are delicious with milk or coffee. This recipe makes enough for a crowd. Required Reading: Bringing to Room Temperature (page 12), Buttering and Flouring (page 23), Cooling (page 24), Measuring (page 15), Mixing versus Overmixing (page 25), Preheating (page 16), Testing for Doneness (page 20).

Preheat the oven to 350°F. In a small mixing bowl, mix together the flour, baking powder, and baking soda, and set aside. In a large mixing bowl, lightly beat the eggs with a whisk. Add the vanilla and the sugar. Alternate adding the melted butter with the flour mixture until both are incorporated into the batter. Switch to a wooden spoon and stir in the chopped nuts and chocolate chips.

Pour the batter into an ungreased cookie sheet with sides (a jelly roll pan) that measures 15 x 10 x 1 inches. Bake for 20 to 25 minutes, until the blondies are firm to the touch. Better they should be slightly underbaked than overbaked so they are not dry. Remove from the oven and cool before cutting into rectangles or squares.

Links: Cheesecake Brownies (page 85), Chocolate Chip Cookies (page 95), One-Pot Brownies (page 171).

Makes about 48 blondies, depending on how you cut them

2¹/₄ cups unbleached all-purpose flour

1 teaspoon baking powder

¹/₄ teaspoon baking soda

6 large eggs

2 teaspoons vanilla

2 cups (one 14-ounce box) "Brownulated" (available in the baking section) sugar or 2 cups brown sugar

1 cup (2 sticks) unsalted butter, melted and cooled

1 cup finely chopped walnuts or pecans

2 cups (12-ounce package) chocolate chips

Kitchen Stuff

Jelly roll pan

Measuring cups

Measuring spoons

Mixing bowl

Epilogue—The Party

Everybody loves a party, right? Well, not my sister Leslie, but she's a self-diagnosed introvert who prefers a more intimate setting than most parties afford. When I first sat down with my editor to discuss the idea for a book geared to a younger, hipper audience than most cookbooks ever attract, I immediately thought we needed to throw a party. After all, most of my friends who fall into the demographic category of the book's target audience are always going to parties. It seemed like the thing to do.

Because the book was supposed to be filled with food that was easy to prepare and that people like my friends would like to eat, the idea came to me to throw a potluck party to see what we would get. The potluck would serve two purposes: it would tell me what kind of food my friends would make to share with other people, and it would tell me where they were at in their cooking abilities (and where they needed help).

My friend Evelynne Patterson agreed to let me use her huge Greenwich Village apartment, and I quickly had my graphic-designer friend Edwin and his partner Julia create a fab invitation based on a fake recipe idea suggested by another good friend, Jennifer. I mailed out two hundred invitations and waited to see what would happen.

Although it hadn't really occurred to me at the time, the joy of throwing a potluck party is that you don't have to cook. Of course, you never really know what you are going to get. But besides collecting the alcohol, flowers, ice, and paper products, there is very little to do.

The party was called for 6:30 P.M. on June 25, 1996. By 7:30 about 130 people had entered Evelynne's apartment, newcomers looking hopelessly for a ledge on which to balance their casseroles and serving trays. People piled their paper plates with tastings of the offerings, some hundred dishes in all. There were salads, dips, spreads, soups, fish dishes, meat dishes, vegetarian dishes, cakes, brownies, cookies, you name it. Linda, whose husband, Scott, is a chef in New York, brought chocolate palm trees on flourless chocolate cake islands that she dusted with confectioner's sugar to resemble falling snow. Evelynne herself had a little culinary fun with a canapé cake that was featured in *Vogue* magazine (November 1996). The cake was composed of brioche layers filled with foie gras, caviar, and smoked chicken, frosted with cream cheese and garnished with flowers to look like a wedding cake.

Not everything was as complicated as the chocolate islands and the canapé cake, however. I was surprised by the variety of the food. I hadn't told anyone what to bring and yet almost every area of food was covered. I was also surprised by the diverse cultures that were represented on the potluck table—Argentina, Guatemala, Korea, China, England, France, Italy, Portugal, Mexico, and others.

After everyone left and we finished cleaning, I stopped to contemplate what I had learned. First, and this may be the most important lesson for the aspiring cook, I realized that if you want to have a party with great food, you don't have to make it all yourself. Ask your friends to share in the work by bringing a dish or two. You end up with tons of food and everyone seems to have a lot of fun. If you get the recipes, you'll also broaden your culinary repertoire. (I'd say about 40 or so of the recipes in this book came from my potluck experiment.)

I also learned that even among people who don't consider themselves good cooks or who aren't particularly interested in food, food serves as an important facilitator, with roots that run deep to the soul. The dishes that people brought told everyone at the party a lot about themselves: their background, their culture, and the way they are in the world. In this particular instance, the food served as an introduction to a room full of strangers, alleviating that otherwise awkward moment at a cocktail party when you have finished learning what everyone else in the room does and you have nothing else to say. People talked about what they made. They shared recipes from their mothers or fathers who did the cooking. They told stories.

Food is magic. Cook something and you'll be surprised what's in store.

Index

Recipes are also classified by category, event, cooking time, and main ingredient in *The Recipe Guide*, 33–48. Recipes in the book are organized alphabetically by title.